BUILDING INCLUSIVE
COLLABORATIVE ORGANIZATIONS:
A CAREER ON FOUR CONTINENTS

BUILDING INCLUSIVE COLLABORATIVE ORGANIZATIONS: A CAREER ON FOUR CONTINENTS

Rolf P. Lynton
with
David H. Kiel
Nandani Lynton

First published in 2022 by NTL Institute
NTL Institute is an imprint of Libri Publishing

Copyright © Rolf P. Lynton

The right of Rolf P. Lynton to be identified as the author of this work, and Nandani Lynton and David Kiel as the editors of this work, has been asserted in accordance with the Copyright, Designs and Patents Act, 1988.

The author is a member or affiliate of NTL Institute for Applied Behavioral Science. Views expressed are those of the author alone.

ISBN 978-1-911450-48-1

All rights reserved. No part of this publication may be reproduced, stored in any retrieval system or transmitted in any form or by any means, electronic, mechanical, photocopying, recording or otherwise, without the prior written permission of the copyright holder for which application should be addressed in the first instance to the publishers. No liability shall be attached to the author, the copyright holder or the publishers for loss or damage of any nature suffered as a result of reliance on the reproduction of any of the contents of this publication or any errors or omissions in its contents.

A CIP catalogue record for this book is available from The British Library

Design by Carnegie Publishing

Libri Publishing
Brunel House
Volunteer Way
Faringdon
Oxfordshire
SN7 7YR

Tel: +44 (0)845 873 3837

www.libripublishing.co.uk

Contents

DEDICATIONS ix

PERSONAL PROLOGUE xi

INTRODUCTION 1

Summary of the major themes of the book; outline of the six "cases" and the transcendent challenges faced; definition of terms, frameworks, and theories, including my "string of worry beads" framework for approaching organizational development.

CH 1: Western Scotland: Engaging a Community in Transformative Change 23

Scotland, 1949–50. To introduce employment for women outside the home. Detailing and anchoring the development locally, finding and developing local leadership, ensuring HQ and nation-wide support for effective practices.

CH 2: Sri Lanka and South India: Young Leaders Learn Through Building Community 47

Ceylon, 1956–57, and Mysore, India, 1959–61. To start and direct a world-wide training center, "Aloka," for young public servants in post-World War Two newly independent countries. Building community among ten-plus cultures; familiar setting(s)/new demands; "best professional practice" seen through a multicultural lens; using inclusion and equity to create a place of empathy and compassion, of promoting new routines, mapping and benchmarking, amplification through reaching beyond the individuals back to their institutions; ensuring the funders' long-term interest.

CH 3: Developing Small-industry Employment Across India   77

Hyderabad, India, 1961–66. To work as a consultant in Extension Education and then as team leader for the newly created Small Factory and Extension Training Institute (SFET). Transferring earlier career experience in training for collaboration while facing the challenges of trying to "lead from below." Learning from crises and taking risks as a consultant, delaying until conditions favor success then securing fresh assistance; my Indian "alter ego."

CH 4: The American South: Re-tooling the Academy for Updated Public Service   107

Southeast USA and Latin America, 1966–77. From sabbatical to tenure-track appointment, to founding deanship, and project director. The academic world, politics and culture, racial issues; state funding; making headway and facing headwinds. The pros and cons of being an "outsider" in a conservative system; creating an enduring institution in spite of it all.

CH 5: Indonesia: Creating a Health System That Serves the Whole Country   135

Indonesia, 1978–84. Team leader in project to "decentralize" Indonesia's health services. Go/no-go test for institutional support; instituting collaboration through inclusive tri-party structuring with local consulting; taking account of local strengths to ensure equity and sustainability; major amplification and permanent restructuring; onward recommendation.

CH 6: North and Central India: Up-scaling Rural Programs to Help the Poorest of the Poor   157

Part time from 2007. To help large rural NGO with local consultants for vast expansion. Joining local consultants; mapping expansion and forward demands; grappling with growth that threatens to change a successful organizational culture; the importance of flexibility in a consultant, creating special self-directed programs for the hardest-pressed middle management.

CH 7: Sustaining Life and Learning in Collaborative Development   187

Strategies for maintaining a career as an international consultant: choosing projects, joining communities, nurturing the family, saying good-bye.

CH 8: Building Collaborative Institutions: Frameworks, Mindsets, and Approaches   213

Lessons learned from each setting; using the "string of worry beads" and other frameworks to approach and carry out the work, organizational development theory, building relationships, sustaining change.

CONCLUSION: The Work Continues   233

Centering oneself in turbulent times, putting the focus on working together, an encouraging farewell, and a gallery and acknowledgements.

LIST OF WORKS CITED   239

ALSO BY ROLF LYNTON   241

AUTHOR AND CO-AUTHOR PROFILES   243

Dedications

First of all for RONNIE LYNTON, of course, researcher-writer-teacher in her own right, my life-partner and collaborator-in-residence – for life, everywhere.

Then FRITZ SCHUMACHER, whom I met first as chief economist for the National Coal Board in 1950 London, in the newly nationalized industry then employing a million men, and I a field research officer for the equally new British Institute of Management. We next met 15 years later in India; he came as an internationally recognized expert in intermediate technologies and area development to advise the new SFET Institute. From then on we met yearly in London. I have his deeply felt books and stay in touch with the international society in his name.

BILL COUSINS we first met in Kolkata on a last-minute stop in summer 1956 to start Aloka. Solid, in a dhoti, he looked like the Bengali farmers he was advising. Outgoing, fluent in Bengali, walking with a heavy limp from early polio, he was directly, enthusiastically (and practically) invested in Aloka. He took us to meet his wife Gouri and their two little sons; to our children he became "Uncle Bill". First African-American professor at Wellesley College, Bill went on to help plan the US Peace Corps and head it in Iran, led the first Federal University, and finished his career as director of UNICEF urban programs.

VIKRAM SARABHAI, scion of one of India's most prominent families, astrophysicist of world standing, forever calmly creating innovative institutions of whatever kind needed: an interactive science museum for the young, basic health services, textile research,

India's first and leading management institute; he headed several industrial enterprises and also the Atomic Energy Commission of India. He housed us for Aloka's first urban program when Ronnie was pregnant with our first-born, and we became a "joint family" over the generations.

TOM KESSINGER, we first heard about in Hyderabad as "the Peace Corps worker in the Punjab who raised chickens," and then he and his wife Varyam were our neighbors in Indonesia, where he headed the Ford Foundation and chaired the International School. We became close friends and often stayed with them in Delhi and then in Haverford College when he was president. He ended his career as head of the architectural wing of the Aga Khan Foundation.

DEEP JOSHI spun PRADAN out of the India Ford office, received a Magsaysay award and highest India recognitions for its development of self-help women's groups in India's poorest villages to create new livelihoods for their families and make their villages more self-reliant. With 80,000 new livelihoods created in the first thirty years and 300 "executives" in the field, it was Deep who asked me to help PRADAN "go to scale." Three determinations of his attract me most strongly: that even after carefully structured selection, all recruits have a year-long apprenticeship in the field; that the only grounds for "letting one go" is a failure in relationship (not for technical error); and that Deep himself continues his finely nuanced involvement in Pradan even as his other responsibilities and positions have multiplied.

Personal Prologue

> "Often it's while I'm in the middle of doing all these other things, that I take a few breaths to find the centre in myself."
>
> Mirga Grazinyyte, Lithuanian conductor of the Birmingham Symphony, quoted in the *Financial Times*, 29th July 2017

This book is about building a career in international development, but it is also an account of *finding meaning in a life*. I do not just mean finding it as I went along, although I did, but I mean taking the meaning as life presented itself, from the very beginning. Growing up and responding better and better to what is "actually to hand" – my own professional practice, increasingly well recorded and built on. Of crucial importance in each new opportunity and setting is what my life has taught me by way of sense of Self and sensitivities, connections, blind spots, competencies, hopes, and values. They circumscribe what essentially I can offer a client. So this prologue traces that "centre in myself," starting with my very beginning.

I am the middle son of three, and so grew into extra awareness and solid experiences of "managing" upward and downward, from the very beginning. Born in Berlin, my part-Jewish ancestry made escaping Hitler's Germany imperative – even in the middle of upper-school years, with no English, and parents most reluctantly heading into "no cultural life," no income, and no work permit in depression-time England. Making that emigration decision was itself totally uncharacteristic for our aesthetic, intellectual, and "wholly impractical"

Vati: one noon in the early 1930s, he simply declared that Hitler's Germany "is no place to bring up children" and so, he declared, he would head out to England and the rest of us would follow; and, even more improbably, our "all-practical-decision-making" Mutti, steeped in post-World War One Berlin's rich cultural life, *did* follow with us children – I was eleven.

So we became "refugees" – and there is really nothing better for a consulting career in which one is always the outsider, eager for inclusion but having the ability to see the whole in a way that insiders (locals) do not always master. The school to which we were assigned (on scholarship) was blessedly small, so we "did everything," learnt English fast and passed exams well, and I made squash and choral singing into life-long habits – a way to join into local life, wherever one may be. Essentially, I was abandoned by one country and embraced by another, and in this way learned the benefits of being included, especially when the possibility of exclusion loomed so close and present.

World War Two interrupted my plans. I turned sixteen (becoming officially "adult") just at Dunkirk time, and so, not yet judged "safe," I became the only one in my family to be collected from boarding school as an enemy alien and interned behind barbed wire on the Isle of Man with no outside contact, books, or writing materials, among thousands of men of all ages. Only by a lucky break did I avoid getting shipped across the Atlantic at the height of U-boat sinkings and so, after four months, resumed my schooling. Also of lasting importance was that the prominent "old-boy" network of families at school had invited us to stay with them for school holidays; some stayed in touch after school was over and later connected me to suitable work.

But first, on finishing school in the middle of the War, I was immediately conscripted for war work in an aircraft factory. Fast-trained to be a press-tool fitter, I actually spent my nearly four years of 63-hour-per-week night shifts as a final grinder of cylinder sleeves for fighter-plane engines – I must have made 25,000 of them. Along with the factory work I studied for a basic degree (by mail), passed my BSc Econ., and then used my free time for systematic reading and keeping fuller notes about the strange, ineffective management I witnessed in my factory. Specifically, the leadership believed that positioning machinery far apart so that workers could not talk made for better production value, and that hiding supervisors and inspectors behind screens or walking silently around the floor made for better management outcomes. Even then I knew that collaboration, camaraderie, and a sense of connection with the organization as a whole would actually improve morale and output, especially as bombs fell all night around us and workers worried about their families. My reading and notes became a published book (*Incentives and Management in British Industry*). This writing and a school connection landed me a position in the new British Institute of Management (BIM), as a field research officer set to study the repeated, hugely damaging strikes in the London docks and to guide the new Labour government in what to do. While driving through bombed-out dockland, clueless about how to set about "studying" it, I noticed a sign for the Young Christian Workers HQ, went in, and indeed found them interested, well-connected, and eager to join my enquiry. I stayed connected with the top team, and only weeks later they asked me to join the UK delegation to the first World Assembly of Youth (WAY) meeting in the US. I became the UK representative on the board of the European Youth Campaign headquartered in Paris, and headed into my life-long international career.

In the US that first time, I had visited my BIM partner's erstwhile colleagues on the Human Relations faculty at the Harvard Business School and returned to a fellowship there two years later. On the faculty there I met Ms Ronken, my wife-to-be and closest partner and full-time "alter ego" ever after. The rest of this book describes the journey we took together.

I write in this book about keeping eyes and mind open for the next opportunity, connecting with people, and being open to the possibilities of serendipitous meetings. My life had many of these opportunities. But you do not have to have lived through war, exile, and internment to have a meaningful life in which you address important challenges; you merely have to "find the centre" in yourself and be open to what comes your way.

Introduction

"[T]here is no seeing without looking… [and] no perception without action."

Oliver Sacks, *The Mind's Eye* (2010), p.236

A Guide for Addressing Global Challenges

People around the globe face "transcendent challenges" – urgent issues that represent grave trials to humankind – to our health systems, political institutions, environmental conditions, and the more equal sharing of economic and social development. We four – Rolf the primary author, David and Nandani the supporting cast, along with Anne Menkens our organizing editor – have written this book to help those working to meet this high order of challenges.

Despite the alarming rise of authoritarian, corrupt, and reactionary regimes, people of conscience are nevertheless struggling the world over to eliminate the persistent and widespread conditions of poverty, illness, violence, and environmental degradation. Often these conditions are closely tied to discrimination and exploitation on the basis of caste, creed, color, gender, and economic status. Thousands of well-meaning individuals are working on a daily basis to correct these conditions via community coalitions, innovative non-profit organizations, entrepreneurial social ventures, and in government agencies that are willing to try a creative approach. This book speaks to those thousands who would make a difference.

Through detailed narratives and reflections on six major engagements that Rolf undertook to affect social change in Scotland, Sri Lanka, India, Indonesia, and the US, we identify attitudes, perspectives, tools, tactics, and strategies that can assist others who also want to work with, rather than just *for*, those who might benefit from a more compassionate and humane social order. At a time when technical or hierarchical solutions exclude or disenfranchise many actual stakeholders, helpers need the perspectives and the tools to build collaboration and inclusion for lessening and solving real and pressing problems.

This book is meant to aid change agents who are now, or soon will be, engaged in such significant efforts. There, on the spot, problem-solving, program and policy choices must often be made quickly and in rapid sequence. Unless practitioners have a strong sense of the value of collaboration and inclusion, and a firm grasp on what equity may mean in a given situation, the opportunity for transformative development may be lost. "Solutions" without this commitment to engagement, participation, collaboration, and empowerment may give rise to new problems of exclusion and inequality. Most common – and most understandable but important to overcome – is the tendency to halt a significant development after the first step or two, creating one or two quasi oases of significant innovation. Instead, with some extra effort and courage, significant developments can spread more widely.

This book provides a way forward. It tells a true story that describes a human-values- and behavioral-science-driven approach to social change and collaborative development, and provides tested guidelines, principles, and practices for equity and inclusion.

A Model for Practice

The book is primarily for reflective practitioners, the change agents who consciously and intuitively grow in skill and competence through their work; and it is especially for those who choose to work on major "transcendent" challenges. To these practitioners, such as our fellow workers in the field of international organizational development, this book also offers a model of advancing knowledge. When we speak and write about our work, we contribute to developing the practices that enlarge and diversify the capacities that we need, collectively, to address these pressing problems.

The story starts with a "personal prologue" about life events through which Rolf Lynton, our primary author and protagonist throughout, formed basic values and perspectives in a Europe riven by authoritarian ideologies and large-scale persecutions. He, like thousands of others, needed to start anew, build new friends, new homes, new livelihoods, and new communities. Rolf's experience "came of age" in the immediate post-war period, and his story and the tide of his (and our) learning rolls on in six chapters covering the following settings, which spread across four continents:

- To help introduce paid women's employment in a coal-mining town in Scotland
- To start and direct a training center in then-Ceylon and in South India for young public leaders from newly independent countries, women and men together
- To be one of several instructors in a US-foundation-funded interdisciplinary team for the Indian government's new institute to train small-industry consultants and multiply entrepreneurialism across that vast country
- To help develop an interdisciplinary population center and then be the founding dean of a field-based school of public health in the US South
- To help the Indonesian government decentralize and spread its health services "to the outer islands"
- To join with local consultants to help a large NGO scale up to develop family livelihoods in the poorest villages all over North India.

Work in each setting after the first extended to six years, and the last continues part time. We present these "cases" in life-order, with all their complications, successes, and implications for professional and personal development, so readers can see this career in the making and thereby see one fully developed model for a life built around addressing transcendent challenges. Helping communities and institutions develop this way is very different from testing particular hypotheses drawn from academic research and yet has its own discipline, based on recording, reflection, and learning from experiences of fostering inclusive change. Determined social-change practitioners proceed with a view for the long term and work to develop reliable principles and practices to guide these efforts. This approach involves drawing on promising and tested social-change practices and models, but also comes from a wellspring of examined personal life experiences.

As we shall see exemplified in the following chapters, practitioners in this style map the stakeholders involved in the development, position themselves closest to the decision-making and action, record fully what takes place, and monitor stakeholders' continuing engagement. This kind of practitioner takes substantial time for reflection and sense-making on the way, along with "sabbaticals" between projects, to draw maximum learning for the just-then experience and to publish and otherwise share learnings to advance the profession.

During a lifetime of professional practice, this type of practitioner learns to become part of new communities, cultivating lifetime colleagueship and close friendship across decades and continents. Through dialogue and mentoring, and through training and development, by founding supportive organizations and, above all, by providing an inspiring example, this kind of practitioner develops erstwhile clients to become colleagues and then practitioners in their own right, carrying on the efforts for constructive change.

Each chapter explores both the day-to-day and the context-specific learnings offered by a significant engagement of wide consequence. Lessons from all the settings are collected and explored further in two chapters at the end: in Chapter 7, learnings for building a career, nurturing the family and collegial relationships, and generally thriving in a lifetime of such engagements; and in Chapter 8, lessons for working effectively with clients, understanding client needs, and engaging with internal and external stakeholders to develop programs that promise the best success. Each chapter builds on those preceding, as a career builds upon past experiences, but they can be read out of order to great effect as well.

Why, one may ask, are there co-authors for a book about one man's career? The experiences and stories are Rolf's, of course, told from here on out in his first-person voice. But the focus on inclusion amidst change, the identification of applicable learnings, and parts of the structure all developed through over a decade of regular exchanges between the three of us. Over long lunches, we shared our several and changing current challenges in all our not-for-profit, academic, and corporate settings, asking questions, sharing related experiences, and discussing how to move our profession forward. The first public result of these exchanges was the series Rolf and David wrote for the NTL Practitioner's Journal *Practising Social Change* that appeared in three separate articles 2011–2014. Nandani, David, and Rolf kept returning to the overall themes such as inclusion, intrapreneurship, innovation, and the importance of naming things for clarity, throughout these discussions. These talks and the exchanges of the many drafts now shape and inform the book. Even so, it is hard to imagine that we could have told this story so well if Anne Menkens – professional editor and author in her own right – had not woven it all together for us at the end. She was the D'Artagnan of our previously triadic collaboration.

With this brief preface ended, Rolf begins his story in the first person, and we will join him hereafter in the telling as "silent partners."

A Life in the Work

Chosen or unchosen, the personal encounters of my life became the treasure of actual lived-with and lived-through experiences that I can offer to clients. Actual experience with encompassing transcendent challenges came quickly and multiplied: social–religious discrimination in Hitler's Berlin, followed by immigration to the UK, where I became an "enemy alien" and was interned when I turned sixteen. Then, at work on sixty-three-hour nightshifts in a war factory during World War Two and the London Blitz, I first started keeping notes about the strange ways management kept us workers from talking "instead of working:" machines far apart, foremen "too busy to talk," and inspectors hidden behind walls. I also saw London's docklands go up in smoke and then, just a few years later as field research officer of the new British Institute of Management (BIM), "chanced" on colleagues to help understand why dockers were "always" going on horrendously costly strikes. Within a week those new colleagues provoked my first journey to the United States and meeting my future wife, then the second woman member of faculty at the Harvard Business School (which had at that time no women students). The BIM also connected me with the Tavistock Institute of Human Relations, and so with a Tavi-trained engineer I researched the setting up of a new branch of a hosiery mill in Scotland, which is the first of the six settings on which I report in this book.

The reader will notice that my career began long ago (before, I dare say, most of you were born!), but the issues dealt with here transcend time and place and individuals. Gender, racial, and economic disparities; poverty; health inequities; hunger; the impacts of war; the need for meaningful and remunerative work – these are not particular to India, Indonesia, or the other settings of my career, and the methods and mindsets for addressing them, as well as the career lessons they offer, transcend these places and times as well. The work was urgent in my day, and this type of work is unfortunately still urgent today, when authoritarians around the globe rail against diversity and social change, and re-emphasize traditional hierarchies. All six interventions presented here show ways to break down hierarchies of caste, gender, creed, position, and rank, as well as hierarchies across objective "tasks" – to find new work and raise women and all kinds of degraded others, increase production, strengthen health care, develop better training, and develop livelihoods and self-respect among the poor – and across all kinds of locations.

So this timeliness (or rather "time*less*ness") and the wide range of examples should speak particularly well to the many people I keep meeting who declare themselves "eager to work on things that really matter" but are perplexed about how to do it along with managing their daily lives. Just as I wondered why my World War Two factory management seemed so fixated on a physical set-up and management style that squelched teamwork when more talking and working collaboratively would have been so much more productive, while bombs were crashing outside and we worried about our families and homes.

The world is not lacking proof that collaboration "works better" – that has been proven over and over – but acting on this understanding often gets sidetracked into abstraction and academic respectability. In the path-setting Hawthorne experiment in the 1930s to test the theory that workers' output would "obviously" vary directly with changes in lighting or other technical manipulations in the environment, it was actually revealed that production rose and kept rising as bench workers felt attended to – or just "seen and heard" in today's parlance – regardless of technical changes, individually and even more so as a group (Roethlisberger and Dickson, 1939). Elton Mayo's *Social Problems of an Industrial Civilization* (1945) built on that, but new accounts suggest these lessons are still unlearned in the vast warehouses from which our online orders reach us today, and in enterprises across the globe. It took Dunkirk and other early disasters of World War Two before the British Army changed from selecting officers for trim and precise marching on parade to selecting those actually capable of leading in battle. So, with its humanistic, experiential, and pragmatic approach to social change and social justice, this book may help wear away at our long-standing and self-destructive resistance to better ways of doing things – together.

What truly helps real shifts to occur is what practitioner–helpers bring to the work by way of personal lived and lived-into experiences: we see the setting for potential change and the opportunities it offers, pay attention to stakeholders and engage them in change, comprehend the client's organization and environment as an unfolding whole and in process, and we try to stay in closest awareness of all that and use it in each new setting.

For me, this fullest use of Self gives high priority to the fullest recording of my practice and accurate learnings from it. Since memories from way back fade and also tend to be self-serving, only comprehensive recording on the spot followed by times for enough regular reflection is good enough. So recording and reflecting have become my main way to improve my practice – not only on what happened "out there" but also what I learnt about myself doing and not doing on that spot and at that moment: how all-round, reliably, truly I learned to understand the others there, under these conditions, with these aims of theirs, in x, y, z particular moments and instances. What, on reflection, did I assess well (as evidenced by later events)? What had I missed that later turned out to be important, and why? How might I notice better and act differently next time? And so also, what competencies can I truly offer enquirers in future? What types of projects am I best able to help successfully? And what better not?

What I bring to my work – that personal compound – is thus distilled from what life has actually offered me and what I have made of it. Since the six cases here are in chronological order, they also show me learning over time. Newcomers to the work may find all this especially reassuring and concretely helpful – and perhaps all the more because the experiences that have mattered most include many unplanned and even hazardous events. Reading such an account may actually turn out to be good preparation for working on truly transcendent challenges in our ever more turbulent conditions and to "being the change you want to see in the world," advice long attributed to Gandhi.

Having started in the middle of World War Two, my career also pretty well spans the evolution of organizational development as a profession. In addition to being a hands-on change leader (or, I prefer to say, "helper") in the various major global engagements detailed in the book, I have contributed to the fields of organizational behavior, institutional development, and social-change studies, both through publishing several previous books and taking an active part in the development of the field:

- With the Tavistock Institute in the UK[1]

---

[1] Formerly the psychoanalytic Tavistock Clinic, which, following the disastrous retreat of the army at Dunkirk, was engaged by the UK government to recast the focus of selection and training of army officers from marching skills to effective commanding in actual battle conditions. Engagement in social issues

- With the NTL Institute for Applied Behavioral Science in the US and then globally[2]
- With the Indian Society for Applied Behavioural Science, that I helped launch and with which I still engage,[3]
- And in dialogue with leading practitioners who formed this field, including the early practitioners of the socio-technical approach, of the Tavistock and NTL-style training groups, of the Future Search and the Appreciative Inquiry model, and of Dialogic approaches to Organizational Development (OD).[4]

The same seven decades have also seen the birth of the Internet and ever faster communication and round-the-clock workdays, and so made turbulence and personal exhaustion the increasingly normal conditions for visualizing tasks, reaching decisions, acting on and revising them, and providing leadership. Working "with what's to hand" – the maxim to draw from my life overall – suits these conditions just right. And to encourage any still-hesitant reader, each major account of mine – every last one – also begot fresh developments beyond the original intent: new collaborations and programs, fresh teaching, training, and developments, and professional networks and associations that continue.

Innovative Institutions – Midwives of Transformation

Inventors can create new technologies, revolutionaries can shift power from one group to another, social movements and the media can change ideas about what is right and wrong, but it takes entrepreneurs and "intrapreneurs," and ultimately the organizations they create, to implement complex changes in the ways communities

---

became its flag, advising the reorganization of industry, including newly nationalized coal mining, its early fields, and *Human Relations* its journal (www.tavinstitute.org).

2 Also founded right after World War Two, as the National Training Laboratory for Group Development (www.ntl.org).
3 Founded in 1972 with Udai Pareek, my long-time "alter ego," colleague, and co-author (www.isabs.org).
4 Methods that came to define my approach of asking open-ended questions to engage stakeholders and generate ideas for change from within. Formally defined by Gervase Bushe and Robert Marshak.

get organized, educated, and cared for, goods are produced, and services are delivered. In my discussion I argue that these organizations must not be in the bureaucratic mold, carrying out prescribed societal functions with a neutral competence, but instead, *they must be institutions that are self-consciously focused on the processes of social change.*

Enduring and continuing social change requires that these new institutions be innovative, that they change things but also do them in more inclusive, collaborative, and equalitarian ways – no minor challenge, since organizations of all kinds tend towards hierarchy and bureaucracy. My own studies and others' writings about the special characteristics of institutions that promote social change suggest that organizations of this type have some common characteristics:

- Social-change institutions are focused on changing the relationship of society as a whole to a given problem (for example, civil rights, rural poverty, health-care access, and so on) not just on delivering services, though this may be an important component of what they do.
- Social-change institutions are likely to be innovatively working out methods of advocacy and education service delivery, as well as their business models, as they go. They may have models and theories, but the "facts on the ground" are always challenging plans and assumptions. (In this, they are like entrepreneurial and innovative organizations in the private sector but their social goals constrain and direct them in different ways than those of for-profit organizations.)
- They have to pay intense attention to the broader environment, and particularly the social and information environment, because they are in the "norm-changing" business.
- They often demand that individuals both within and outside the organization behave in new and unaccustomed ways (for example, live among the poor, adopt different environmental practices, attitudes toward gender, and the like).

Social-change organizations have open-ended goals like alleviating policy, extending health care, or resolving long-standing conflicts. While it is important to evaluate "concrete" outcomes along the way, like increases of production (for example, of wheat) and "people served" (health-care encounters), it is even more important to document and assess the progress made in social change. This might be done, for example, by expanding the groups of stakeholders involved actively and increasing collaboration, such as by helping participants to iron out traditional differences, clearing the path for long-haul relationships, and building active partnerships. The social dimension of social change involves increasing capacity for collective action beyond ordinary measures of goods and services, incomes and infrastructure. Social-change institutions, rightly understood, deliver all these, but only if they operate with integrity, long term. The role of the social-change consultant then, as this professional biography will show, is key to getting these crucial organizations off "on the right foot" in these ways and then helping them stay "on track."

Concepts for Understanding and Helping Innovative Institutions

Organizational Development theory, until recently, has been dominated by the perspective that an organizational problem can be investigated by consultants, objectively defined, and solved by clearly delineated sequentially implemented plans. OD theory has begun to come around to viewing the process of furthering change more as I have experienced it: a back-and-forth between clients and consultants, seeking organic, emergent change opportunities, negotiating initial steps and field experiments, and holding tight to the necessary connections between social purpose and values. These values include especially collaboration, equity, and inclusion of those often excluded from decision-making and institution-building. Through this lens of emergent, collaborative, equitable change, I think always about various interconnected elements when considering, planning, and implementing projects. I have found three frameworks especially useful for "awakening" clients to the complex processes and sequences in the development they have embarked on and helping them to commit themselves to approaches that are actually open to them.

One is for locating the institution clearly in the particular stage of development it is in now, identifying the part(s) that call for early attention, and mapping the likely developments ahead and preparing realistically for them. Institutions going through change seem to have regularities analogous to Erik Erikson's "life-cycle" for individuals: institutions also "develop" through managing a succession of "crises" – birth, crafting a particular identity, becoming mature, developing further, and seeking renewal (Erikson, 1950).[5] Each crisis poses a characteristic dilemma, the resolution of which comes with pausing for reflection, a "moratorium," and only as that crisis is resolved can development go further. In my practice, as we shall see, I am constantly assessing and asking clients to locate themselves on the table below and consider the possible implications, their own and other stakeholders' responses, and useful action.

Crisis	Characteristic Features	Dilemma	Resolution
1. Birth	A few individuals full of ideas and zest. Frenzied activity. Attention oriented outward – PowerPoints, sister institutions, customers.	When should the institution be born and how large should it be? Planning for every contingency or have a crash program?	Strong continuing leadership.
2. Identity (a) Seeking identity	Search for main focus or foci. Conflict and uncertainty. Internal competition for attention.	Perfection of one thing or value all possibilities?	Clearly explicit long-range objectives as a priority system for decision making.
(b) Seeking acceptance	Search for relationships with existing systems. Inter-organizational jealousies. Attention outward.	Stress likeness and conformity or stress novelty and differences?	Moratorium to establish standards, largely in isolation.

5 Published in Erikson's landmark *Childhood and Society*.

Crisis	Characteristic Features	Dilemma	Resolution
(c) Seeking balance	One or two activities have made a quick start, but now threaten to dwarf or belittle others. Jealousies within.	Curb fast starters or let them run loose?	Focus on lagging functions to encourage their momentum.
3. Growth	Great demands for services, mostly short-term. Temptation to take on too much load. Meeting demands increases demands.	Consolidate and develop slowly or expand in all promising directions?	Moratorium to re-examine objectives and priorities. Publicize long-range plans.
4. Maturity	Success revives inter-organizational jealousies, even threatening sponsors. Attacks on autonomy and independence.	Forego identity and submit or revolt and break away?	Develop interdependent relationships focused on tasks.
5. Further Development	Self-satisfaction. Temptation to rest on laurels. Reluctance to work out new ideas.	Fossilize or break up into progressive and conservative, young and old?	Check objectives against changing situation. Rejuvenate institution. Build in indices of relevance.

Table 1.1: Crises in the Life of an Institution[6]

As we go through the six cases to follow, we will see many examples of how I have used this chart to locate organizations in their current stage and plan an overall perspective on the complex challenges an institution has to negotiate if it is to fulfill its innovative mission. Where they fell determined much about the project. Some were at their very beginnings, like Aloka – "at birth," with my wife Ronnie and me as "midwives," as it were – which meant we were able to have great influence in its creation but also that as time went on, it became more important to understand its emerging identity and to understand and engage the stakeholders who would sustain it. Each

---

6 From Lynton and Pareek, *Training for Development* (third revised edition, 2011), p.289.

institution we encountered was on its own life-cycle path; for example, PRADAN (Professional Assistance for Development Action) was in a stage of growth, and the US universities were mature organizations with a charge to further develop, while in the throes of conserving tradition and forging ahead in new ways.

The Institution-Building (IB) Model (Figure 1.1, below) also helps clients gauge the current strengths and weaknesses of their system, this time by helping them think about *internal components* and *external linkages* that all institutions need at all stages of development.

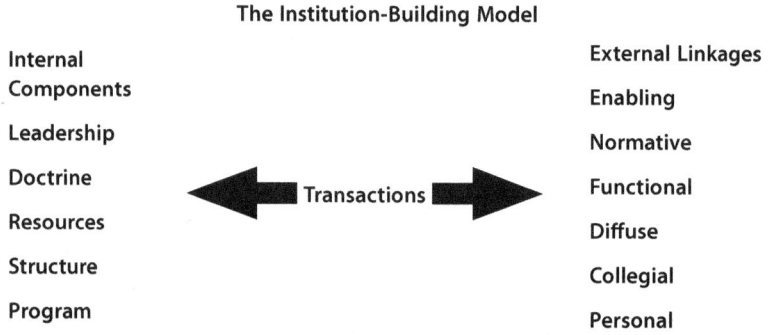

Figure 1.1: The Institution-Building Model

The internal components – leadership, doctrine, resources, and so on – provide a guide and checklist for which parts of the organization need attention to address the issues implicated in the current "crisis." Discussion may start with practical matters of structure, resources, and leadership needed, followed by an exploration of institutional doctrines (core values, policy choices, and practice guidelines and the like), which are often unspoken. As we shall see in many of the following examples, until they are acknowledged and formalized, these core principles may be at risk of being weakened or even obliterated by change. Often it is the outsider who can best articulate those things that organizational insiders may ignore, take for granted, or under-value.

On the other side of the ledger, we shall see in every case the work of identifying external linkages that are necessary to the project – modes of connecting with political or business stakeholders who may enable the work, colleagues doing comparable work who may become partners and thus spread the project's impact, and so on. These stakeholders will not only strengthen the work but also amplify it and sustain it going forward.

The innovative institution is the means by which practitioners marshal resources and mobilize the efforts of many to address the transcendent challenge. Yet to proceed strategically, the institution and its leaders must have a roadmap of sorts to address the key issues in the chosen field of development. In my experience it is counterproductive to come into a situation with a detailed plan of action. Rather, it is best to set some starting common-sense parameters and then jointly explore the situation to arrive at a course of action. Even then, this course of action is not a five-year plan or even a five-month plan but a series of joint experiments in service of the common vision, which are then amplified after due reflection, to increase impact.

So the final chart – and for me the most important – is the one that most guides *my* work, reflection, and decision-making, as well as the help I provide to clients. It is a modified version of one I developed years ago to visualize the essential elements I must keep in mind (and help the client to consider) while the development is planned, launched, and under way. This chart puts the elements graphically into what I've come to think of as a "string of worry beads," with the "beads" representing essential elements of the development. Another metaphor may be a radar constantly rotating to track planes landing and taking off at airports: keeping attention on all key components of institution development as the work goes forward, some continuously vital and others in and out of focus depending on circumstances. This chart helps me to keep all parts in view and to think about how to strengthen the development as a whole.

All of these elements arise multiple times throughout this book, illustrated in much more detail, but the basic definitions will now be given here.

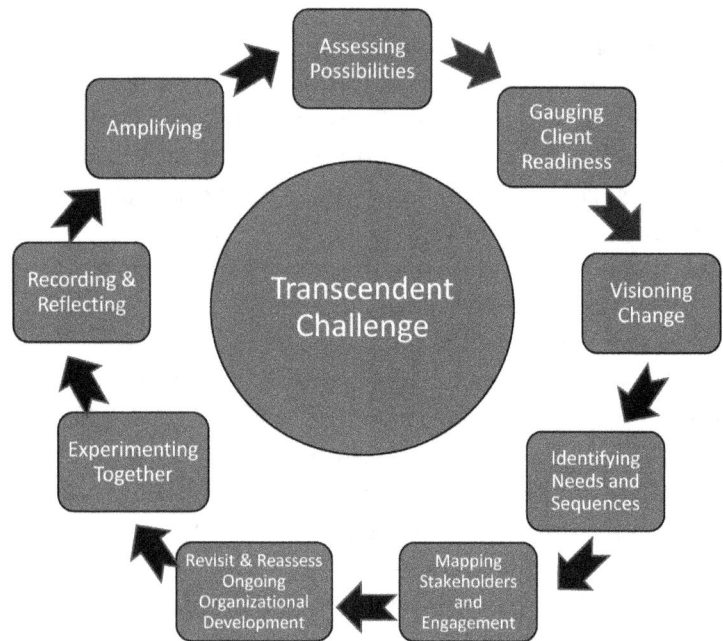

Figure 1.2: Transcendent Challenge Worry Beads

The first few beads are used before even taking an assignment and then revisited later at major turning points. *Assessing Possibilities* means to understand and use what is already available to the organization. It could be the people, organizational culture, interested supporters, and the like – assessed at the very beginning and kept in mind as the development goes along. *Gauging* (or understanding) *Client Readiness* means to examine what the client has already done to prepare for this work. Have they tried to do the intervention already (and are thus more than ready for your help)? Have they dealt with legal requirements? Have they brought their staff (and others) on board? Have they planned enough time for the project to be successful? There are many different ways for clients to prepare – and understanding their preparation goes into deciding whether to work with them at all *and* what needs to be done with your help. *Visioning Change* means imagining in as much detail as is reasonable the kind of change you want to see on the ground.

Identifying Needs and Sequences is done using all the tools at one's disposal – for understanding what the client needs (as opposed, sometimes, to what they think they need or what they *want*) and also the potential outcomes of the intervention. It is important to address these needs up front and throughout a project.

Mapping Stakeholders and Engagement is one of the most important elements of doing meaningful and important development work. Keeping stakeholders involved is equally or even more important. The range of stakeholders always includes the board, staff, and those served by the new institutions, but also funders, regulatory and facilitating agencies of government, sources for specialized technical resources, and the general public and media to support the development.

Revisit and Reassess the Ongoing Organizational Development: even before taking on an assignment, I assess the client's openness to transformative and inclusive change, present my ideas for moving forward and gauge their reaction to my ideas. If I choose to go forward with the development, I then go back to my worry beads as the development unfolds so we can together reassess and revise the map. Particularly at a turning point after significant goals have been met and new challenges arise (or at the point of an unforeseen impasse), it is important to go back and revisit the questions with the new circumstances in mind. What are the possibilities for *further* change? Is the client ready to go that *next* step? What would those *new steps* look like? What are the *updated needs and sequences*? Who might be some *new stakeholders* to help carry it forward? The answers to these questions help us decide whether and how to continue the development, and may be revisited multiple times over the course of a long-term engagement.

Experimenting Together (that is, piloting) when at all possible is key to the earliest and quickest success. Working collaboratively can take more time up front, yet it helps ensure that processes are best suited to those who truly need them and helps institute continuous learning in the organization itself, thus sustaining the project beyond the implementation. *Recording and Reflecting* is my way of making sense of action – who did what, and why, and to what end? – allowing for reflection and learning for current and future projects. The importance of reflection on the details of everyday actions, people, and outcomes cannot be overstated and is a central part of my practice. And finally, *Amplifying* is using what is learned to expand the project's impact beyond the immediate effects, or even the original institution.

Keeping this chart in mind helps me to keep all parts in view and think about how to strengthen the development as a whole, as well as my own future endeavors. The aim is to consider the big picture strategically before planning the details, then to continue to keep the "radar" running as the intervention unfolds. These tools and their utility will become clearer and clearer throughout this book, as we take them out of the realm of theory to show the concrete, meaningful improvements they have brought throughout my career.

The Six Global Settings

Six "settings" spread across four continents provide the structure for this book. In some cases, names have been changed, but in all cases they are true stories told in as much detail and with as much frank reflection as possible. The first setting is a coal-mining town on the west coast of Scotland, "Minetown,"[7] just after World War Two in Fall, 1947. I was a field research officer of the new British Institute of Management, and joined the Tavistock-trained engineer-in-charge in fostering community involvement and ultimately a sense of ownership in establishing a branch hosiery mill for women to do skilled work in a traditional male-dominated coal-mining town. There I first explored and appreciated the power of collaboration, inclusion, even co-creation to bring about positive social change.

A few years later it was off to then-Ceylon for a project of potentially global significance, our second setting. In the intervening years, as I summarized above, I had worked for BIM to study the strikes in the London docks, served on the board of the European Youth Campaign, headquartered in Paris, and participated in the

---

7 In some cases in this book, the names of organizations or locations have been changed.

Harvard Business School's internship program in Human Relations, where I met my life partner in work and family, Harriet Ronken Lynton. "Ronnie" was a fine case researcher, writer and teacher, and together we created Aloka and operated it for six years. Aloka offered twelve-week residential programs of training for emerging leaders from newly independent countries in Africa and Asia. Immersive learning and living in an egalitarian community produced transformative impact on the young leaders and their organizations, reverberating to this day.

 I took what I learned at Aloka to a new project, helping to build a new training institution, the Small Factories Extension Training Institute (SFET), viewed as critical to helping India lessen its dependence on agriculture. This is the third setting for social change explored in the book. With eager support from the Indian leadership of SFET, we were able to deploy quickly a model of training that engaged consultants and business owners directly in problem solving. Then, using a politically daring and somewhat radical plan, this training spread across India and inspired this kind of work world-wide, also providing a base for founding the Indian Association for Applied Behavioural Science.

 By way of a sabbatical following SFET, I accepted a faculty position at a prominent university in the Southeast US, completed master's and doctoral degrees, and became founding Dean of a new School of Public Health in the next state south. This period of my career taught me much about the limitations of change agentry in some settings, although along the way I was able to create a consortium of eleven international universities to promote curricula related to population studies, support the development of neighborhood health centers in North Carolina, and aid in the development of a new graduate school in Colombia, South America. Even though this fourth setting ends with my effort to pilot a new interdisciplinary model of public health training in South Carolina, where the headwinds against racial integration blew strongly, this work resulted in institutions and programs for diverse professional health and environmental workers, teachers, and researchers.

 While still in my faculty position, I was invited to help the Health

Ministry of Indonesia develop a plan to decentralize health services to the outer islands of that geographically sprawling and culturally varied country. An initial one-year engagement became six, and with Ronnie once again on the team, we set up a system that included working from both Jakarta and far-flung provinces simultaneously and recruited a team of Organizational Development consultants committed to collaborative practices. As a result, health-care services better reflect local needs and the approach led to the creation of new networks and organizations to support professional development.

And finally to setting six. Now in "retirement," I accepted a long-term engagement with PRADAN, one of India's premier anti-poverty programs anchored in women's micro-enterprise development, that is, self-help groups with technical assistance. I assist PRADAN's top team, middle leadership, and long-time consultant team as they expand support of rural livelihoods from 100,000 people served to over a million across all of North and Central India.

As previously mentioned, I end the book with two summary "lessons learned" chapters. From Aloka onwards, our family grew and came with us, and our circle of friends and the four I refer to as "alter egos" grew more salient in our lives – professional and personal. Each chapter includes a look at the effect of all of this on our children and ourselves, and we dedicate a summary Chapter 7 to lessons learned on how to keep Self, soul, and family together through a life filled with such challenging work that necessitated such diverse adventures in living. In this chapter we also address how to construct such a career that additionally takes on the responsibility to contribute to the field of knowledge about how to bring about truly constructive change in a world that surely and sorely needs this guidance.

Chapter 8 summarizes the more technical learnings about how to be successful with clients who want to address transcendent challenges in a spirit that is collaborative and inclusive. Using each of the nine "worry beads" from Figure 1.2 above, we review the way actions at each stage brought positive results in the six settings. This chapter provides a guiding compass for practitioners who dare to address the big problems of this time, just as we tried to work for change over these past decades.

The Personal Roots and Reach of it All

Throughout this book I reflect on what is most personal, including my life experiences that led to the career that followed. For readers who have their own careers, this is also my way of saying, "look at what is most personal for you and from this build your own authentic career." Having been a refugee in some ways set me up for a career in which one is always the outsider, but with the ability to see the whole in a way that insiders (locals) do not always master. What is also key for me is my penchant for going with whatever is to hand. This is still the best metaphor for my almost century of life and work: no "grand theme" or "strategy" planned in advance. It has helped me tune in, in a rich variety of ways, paces, and manners while engaged in the work of social transformation and fully inhabiting the empty spaces in between. Engaging in this manner will lead to lasting developments again and again.

My life and early experiences sound major themes of how a career working on transcendent challenges comes about through openness to the unknown, holding on to a sense of what is important, and with a penchant for constant reflection. Potential clients ask and you test whether that is what they really mean to do, and also whether they have the wherewithal to do it – as against getting some technical help to improve current methods. If they "pass" the test, you listen and proceed with whatever the client and you, as consultant–helper, can plan and do *together*. The togetherness of all stakeholders – the present ones and potentially also those still in the wings for when the development unfolds – is the essence of help, *real help*. The consultant–helper stays current with the emerging science of organizational development and also reports new experiences and understandings to colleagues in the profession.

Looking back in this fashion makes my life and career look "whole," and "good" in the long run, but certainly, as these pages show, the successive happenings were not always encouraging or even inviting at first or even at second sight. So an attitude of faith, trust, and fortitude pervade the experiences that unfold in these six settings and the life they framed.

Looking Forward

This book is being written at a time (2021–22) when democracy is imperiled everywhere, it seems. Inequality is on the rise, conflict engulfs many countries, natural disasters borne of climate change threaten whole regions, and novel diseases (such as Ebola) and pandemics (Covid-19) appear to be more frequent and virulent. It is not unlike the time at the end of World War One, shortly before I was born (in 1924), or the period shortly after the end of World War Two, when I started to practice organizational change work (in 1947, the very same year that Kurt Levin started the journal *Human Relations* under the auspices of the Tavistock Institute). If anything, the need for practitioners to pitch in and help solve major human problems is as great now as it ever has been. From the very beginnings, my life and career took off through a series of quite unpredictable coincidences and connections, and have continued in this unforeseeable and often quite improbable way, life-long, with home(s) and work mostly "overseas" and with one, two, and then three children – it has been long, active, and satisfying. Beyond advice about working with clients, implementing interventions, and adding to the profession, then, my advice is to *notice* these coincidences and connections, take hold of them as they race by, and find your own way to a meaningful career.

CHAPTER 1

Western Scotland: Engaging a Community in Transformative Change

"It is *not* a journey up a ladder but a spiral of expanding consciousness that has no limits…"

Matthew Fox, *Breakthrough: Meister Eckhart's Creation Spirituality in New Translation*
(Garden City, NY: Image Books, 1980), p.9

Background: A New Consultant Sets to Work in Post-war British Industry

World War Two is over, the Labour government is in and has nationalized the coal and public service industries, and joined with private employers to create the British Institute of Management (BIM). Looking to recruit staff, they noticed a letter of mine in *The Times* about working hours in the cotton industry – I had reported that shortening working hours had actually raised output – and they asked me to join the Field Research unit.

For this assignment the BIM had joined with the Tavistock Institute for Human Relations, a British not-for-profit organization which engages social science in contemporary issues. Tavistock had begun as an international center for psychoanalytic practice and research, then also increasingly with groups, and, following the disaster of Dunkirk, had vaulted into prominence when it refocused the training of army officers on "decision-making in action." After the War, Tavistock also became the leading institute it now is for improving management practices and organizational development, and understanding and helping upgrade technologies and management around the globe.

My first assignment was in the coal industry, where the local father-to-son tradition for management succession had faded away, but no process for training new managers had replaced it. My task was to observe the workings in Scottish coal mines, describing the mostly dark and dangerous settings and issues, sketching professional programs to help train newcomers, and exploring the implications for organizing and managing the industry. The research was anthropology-like, from a distance and minimally involved: seeing and recording how the workers and supervisors worked, their ever longer walks lit only by headlamps shining into the dark and their backs bent over to the coal face, in the deafening noise of coal cutters and assembly belts and carts rattling past, work breaks spent huddling in the dark. Very little talking.

Every railway station on the line between Carlisle in the north of England and Ayrshire in western Scotland had a coal mine nearby, and I had already researched three of these when the BIM sent me to document the establishment of a hosiery factory – and so the first formal institution of women's employment outside the home – in the next mining town up the line.

Specifically, I was to observe and record how a Tavistock-trained engineer would help the "Acorn Hosiery Company"[8] set up a branch factory in Scotland for finishing operations. No doubt, and quite in line with the generally current views of "research," the BIM expected similar anthropology-like recording-from-a-distance from this next study too: uninvolved, maximally "pure," academic. Rather as I had made notes looking over the top of my grinding machine during the War, watching the foremen in white coats strolling silently among the hundreds of machines, which were spaced far apart to discourage "too much talking." My observations there, plus extensive reading in the British Library and professional societies, became my first book, *Incentives and Management in British Industry* (1949), which, along

---

8 The names of the company and town are changed.

with the *Times* letter mentioned above, led BMI to recruit me to the Field Research unit and these current projects.

Modernizing and improving industrial output in both mining and the textile industries were urgent in post-World War Two Britain. The newly nationalized coal industry faced a severe shortage of managers, and the traditional way of promoting from within was not working. And fine hosiery was a star candidate for poverty-struck Britain's Export Drive, but the assumption was that women had to be "born into it" – that is, born and raised in England's traditional textile areas like Lancashire – to be any good. Acorn Hosiery had its long-established and well-regarded headquarters mill in Lancashire, and by long tradition also assumed that the finishing work "could not be trained;" it had thus, of course, failed miserably to set up new mills elsewhere, although it had tried. Complicating it all was that finishing work on the finest and most desired silk hosiery, called "linking," was "women's work," but most Scottish communities, focused as they were on mining, were not accustomed to having women in the workplace. The hypothesis going in – and confirmed by these earlier failures – was that, indeed, the Lancashire women may have actually been "born to the trade," and so we would not really be able to replicate their success elsewhere. But with the Tavistock Institute's help, the Acorn Hosiery directors were determined to try again, with the BIM to document it.

Establishing this branch factory for linkers in "Minetown" is the first of six major settings for my institution-building career. Although the immediate case was establishing the hosiery factory, the overarching goal was to introduce the full-time employment of women outside of the home in a community that had traditionally only employed men. For a reader today, this may seem irrelevant to a career in modern-day international development. I expect young practitioners will not have occasion to do anything like this, not in a Western nation. However, the conditions in this Scottish post-war town exist in many parts of the world today: old industries or traditional livelihoods are vying with a new world order, new technologies, and new markets to survive; and in many cases new workers are needed and women may need to become breadwinners for their families, which traditional gender norms may make difficult or complicated. In Britain after the War, women who had been working during the fighting were expected to leave their jobs when the men returned from the front. There was still a bar on married women working outside of the home and women who became pregnant would leave or be immediately fired. In essence, women's wages were not considered central to family income, so they were paid less, had fewer benefits, and were strictly segregated in the types of jobs they could hold. In a place like Minetown, these mores were taken for granted, by men and women, a cultural reality important to take into account, even as we aimed to help the community choose and embrace change.

The Frame: Women's Work in a Mining Town

Minetown was a small one-occupation town of working men and home-bound women. John L. and I arrived in Minetown already disposed to understand the town and its people. John was the Tavistock consultant engineer who had come to start the new factory and I was there to take notes. Our goal was to connect with town voices, make ourselves part of their community, and tap into their understanding of their fellow citizens, history, and potential future. We started by meeting with the town council and the area labour officer. "No applicants likely," the area labour officer promptly warned when we asked him about "housewives" going to work. The town council was more open, favored our exploring possibilities, and suggested a couple of possible sites for starting the factory, as well as a boarding house in which we could stay for the duration of the project. Staying "right here" was important to us – most practical for discussion and planning and also the right signal about our roles as collaborative consultant and observer, rather than top-down experts.

As one of the leaders of the industry, Acorn Hosiery was well positioned to establish a new factory and add to production. It had the funds and, as mentioned above, had already tried starting two new branches on its own, along the familiar lines of central planning and sending an experienced top-down manager, instructors, and supervisors out to the branch. The results had been discouraging: even by the third year, the new linkers turned out finished hose at only half to, at best, two-thirds the rate of the old timers back home. Acorn's directors were ready for change. Although they themselves had worked their way up in the mill "family-style," without formal introduction to modern concepts of leading and managing, they had been in the War and witnessed first-hand the disastrous shortfalls of officers born and groomed in traditional ways. They had also witnessed the radical reorientation of military leadership by the Tavistock Institute, to learning in action and in groups, and other new psychological and social-science applications to training.

The Acorn directors had turned to Tavistock first to reorganize the layout and operations in the main mill, finding that this redesign greatly raised production and lowered costs. They then involved the Institute in union negotiations for nation-wide systematic training for skills traditionally "passed down" in hosiery families. Now, they contracted with the Tavistock Institute for member–engineer John L. to start the Minetown branch, and with the new BIM to have me "record" the experience for wider dissemination. By the time we arrived in Minetown, Acorn had cleared the formalities there and the national agreements on working conditions and training schemes were in place.

The Starting Point: The Community

Minetown was an ideal community in which to introduce new employment for women. It was small – just 6,500 inhabitants – and entirely focused on one industry, coal mining, all men's work. For the upwards of a thousand women of working age there were hardly eighty jobs in local shops, pit canteens, and one little garment factory an hour's bus-ride away. Wage standards and working conditions were low and protesting them rare. Factory work would represent a major development. Finally, many of the women of Minetown had experienced war-time call-ups, travel, and new experiences, which along with the change of government and the nationalization of the mines had readied them and the whole community for a fresh start.

All this is not to diminish the transformative change that would be represented by this community's departure from generations of men-only employment, but it indicates the types of "readiness" signs I learned to look for in development projects.

My charge was to observe and record, not to interfere with, John's work for Tavistock on behalf of Acorn to effect change from the bottom up, not top down. John aimed to "tune into" Minetown, its people and their ideas about how to set up the factory and how best to reach, select, and motivate new employees. The goal was to do things differently: more practically, more outcome-oriented, more collaboratively, and more inclusively than had been done in the past.

My early notes highlight two things: first, how easy-going John was with people of all kinds and in all types of situations (which was less common then and there than it is now); and second, that he wanted me to be *practically involved*, to be present and to take part fully. Essentially, I became "John's assistant," present where the action was, and in the conversations, recording discussions, decisions, and outcomes right where they took place. This was an important shift in the helper's and the recorder's roles, and very different from the "diagnostic" OD mindset that assumes an organizational problem can be objectively defined (using methods based on empirical social science), based on third-party assessments and solved by clearly delineated sequentially implemented plans for solution. Development was then and still is for me more of a flexible search for solutions to concrete, on-the-ground problems as the communities and organizations directly affected perceive them.

Although the community was open to our presence, they had been "burned" before by absentee owners of the mines, bitter labor strikes, and the few out-of-town administrations and enterprises imposing top-down policies. They "tested" us with many questions. Understandably, the most urgent first question was "where?" – where should the factory be built and where would the employees come from? Where would they be trained? Would the company bring in a manager from headquarters? This was a small, tight-knit community used to working in one place for generations. Even more than most communities, a mining community is used to staying put for work, and working where you and your ancestors have always lived. So, their expectation was that we had come with solutions in mind – based on education and experience, social-science theories, engineering and manufacturing principles, and the company's plans. But for us, it was most important to start with dialogue about the community's needs and ideas. To this end, we met with town councilors individually and in small groups, the vicar, the solicitor, and the local reporter. We visited the recommended factory site with the local craftsmen to assess its suitability and what would have to happen to make it workable. They advised on where training could take place, before the actual factory would be built. We met with the leader of the active girls' club and also several school teachers about where to find potential trainees, what would be the appropriate target for recruitment, how we should limit recruitment by age or marital status, or full- or part-time hours.

Some asked, anxiously, whether workers would be sent away for training, "like at the other new factory, four miles away." No, all training would be done here, we said – and we also announced that we would find instructors right here and help them develop as needed. Also, if at all feasible, from the community would come the supervisors and the manager – a local manager would take over as soon as we could find a suitable candidate for the job.

Everything local was the main theme, but it required a calculated risk. We were walking a thin line: the solution had both to suit familiar ways and to fit into the longer-term future of the community. It is a line between old and new that should be familiar even today: a line between traditional ways and modern innovations; evolving relations between industry and government; changes in gender relations and roles; a diversifying workforce; top-down versus grassroots efforts to manage change; dying industries and new industries with new technologies and new markets, inevitably leaving some workers behind but also requiring new workers. Although outside experts can provide much technical information, such as, in our case, on the need for extra-strong lighting for such detailed work, and work spaces that would be ergonomically comfortable and conducive to the best work, only the community knows how they will walk the line between past and future. This may go against the current push for embracing (or "leaning in" to) disruption of the status quo to effect change, but it speaks to my experience of the realities on the ground when the goal is for the people affected by change to truly adopt it.

From the beginning, the community took a keen interest in our work, keeping up with our activities through the gossip mill. On the third day, the local paper had an article about it all and about us. The article broadcast our recruitment principles – that the training would be done in town and that management would be local. The article opined about how welcome all that should be to the populace and contrasted it to the factory a few miles away, which had sent its recruits away for training down South and also "imported" managers, strangers who wanted to do things "just like at the parent company."

With help from local property owners, we settled on a former firemen's recreation hut for training space, a narrow wooden building with good natural light and large enough to accommodate thirty trainees. Many villagers thought it unsuitable, too run down even for temporary use, but then they also guided us to local craftsmen to clean it and put it in good-enough repair, fix the lighting, and install the tables and the machines on them.

Finding and Selecting Workers: Building Rapport

No doubt, we had to prove that we would do what we said we would do. At the same time, the community was generally open to the need for change. The positive response from the town council, the newspaper article, the girls' club, and the teachers' identification and convening of young women preparing to leave school, all meant that we did not do any traditional advertising for this opportunity. The first applicant came the day of the newspaper article, and a group of seven the very next. This began a regular stream of applicants – sisters and friends of those who had already stopped by the workshop or been updated by the craftsmen or by the life-insurance agent selling door-to-door, or who had picked it up at street corners as they went about their everyday lives.

Our goal was for thirty employees; sixty-three applied during the first month, still more for part-time work. After that, the flow reduced but never ceased, not even when there were no more vacancies and little prospect for more employment until the permanent factory would open. Twenty prospective school-leavers that summer asked to be interviewed for that eventuality. In fact, of the young women about to leave school, only four did not apply, either because they did not wish to seek paid work or they had already obtained other employment.

So, without public meeting or special publicity, we simply engaged with enquirers and relied on the grapevine and local stakeholders to make and keep our activities public. That we stayed locally – John's wife even came and joined us in our downtown lodgings – multiplied our personal contacts and connection with the town. That all training would be local stood out as most important of all – that only one first instructor (a woman) would come "from the centre, just to start us off," and, clearly most telling, that the manager too would be local and take over from John and me as soon as possible.

Choosing from among the applicants would involve assessing both technical factors, determined by the needs of the task, and psychological or personality factors, determined by the close-working conditions, employment laws, and mores of the community. Technically, we needed women with good eyesight and dexterous fingers without calluses or rough nails that would catch on fine fibers. The women's fingers should also be relatively thin, able to link sixty threads per inch onto very fine needles. We would have to see their hands and test their eyesight using the most up-to-date eye tests and also teach them to use mostly touch in order for them to avoid eyestrain while gaining speed and accuracy.

The modern reader may need to be reminded that in Britain at that time there were clear geographical traditions for what work was "properly" of a place. As mentioned above, the idea ran deep that Minetown men were "naturally" miners and the women naturally homemakers, while only Lancashire women were born to work fine textiles. Minetown women wanted this job, but even they had great anxiety about their ability to perform it. Even the most basic things about hosiery linking caused tension. For example, the first applicants came as a group and, knowing that smooth fingers and good nails were important for linking, came holding their hands behind their backs or wearing gloves – in summer! The first few applicants became extremely flustered with our process, and informed their families and friends of what went on, which threatened to render our tests meaningless for subsequent waves of interviewees. Several, whose eyesight tested perfectly good, insisted initially that they could see nothing at all or gave up on a board dexterity test which they had earlier found "really very simple."

So, we changed our method and discarded formal interviewing altogether. Instead, we encouraged each woman to talk about herself and so learnt about her family, interests, and friendships, if she had had any previous employment and why she wished to work here, and whom amongst her women friends we had already interviewed or accepted. For assessment, we administered the eye test first and followed it with the dexterity test, which ensured that everybody would have some success. Then, while some continued testing, we encouraged others to "look around the factory," for example, at the photographs up on the walls of linkers at work at HQ, and look at and finger test samples, while John or I answered their questions, encouraging their questions and comments. All of this ran counter to more formal interview processes, and reflected Tavistock theories about what would come to be called "unstructured" and "semi-structured" interviews. It all drove home to me how important flexibility is when it comes to managing change.

Beyond mechanical expertise or potential, we relied on local laws and mores to determine who would make the best employees in terms of their personalities and other non-technical aspects of work. Although married women were allowed by law to work in such professions, we had assumed that older, married women would not want to work outside the home, as was customary then and there. It was also still the law and custom that pregnant women could not work outside of the home. For these reasons, we had decided early on to target recruitment toward young, unmarried women. However, because we were determined to hire locally and to hire women for most positions, it turned out we needed some older workers too, to become instructors, inspectors, or supervisors. Thus, we accepted a widow of forty-two (who tested rather low for finger dexterity and skills) and a married woman of twenty-two, both patently good candidates for supervisors. The third was a woman of twenty-three with capacity enough to sort stockings coming off the machines at different stages into separate piles, a function for which one with greater capacity would be wasted. Two transferred from other jobs, one because this opportunity was "too good to miss," as she put it, the other out of degrading domestic employment.

The informal interviewing process made the assessment of their personalities and what today would be called "soft skills" or "fit" more reliable. In this area we had to rely on community-based limits, even those that, looked at now, seem to "date" us and place our work in Minetown firmly in a world that emphasizes gender-based judgment of character. Specifically, the applicant must be known as "a good type." With factory and community so close, we deemed it important not to employ anyone regarded as someone who could not get along with others, or whom the others would not respect. An example was one young woman who scored quite high on the tests but was deemed inappropriate as a colleague. Strikingly well dressed, her hands fine and well-tended, she was clearly used to "getting her way," and had a reputation for "going with the boys." Although today such prying into an employee's personal life and proclivities is considered intrusive, at that time and in that place, as in some places even today, such a notion as reputation affects whether others respect and will work with a person.

My data show a striking lack of diversity in the women chosen for the first positions. About half the applicants turned out to be suitable. Plotting their homes on a simple map showed that they came almost exclusively from the newer housing areas and so from families paying higher rents for more space and cleanliness and for more pleasant surroundings. None came from a farm; the only such applicant had been sent by her mother and stated bluntly that she herself liked farm work and wanted to continue with that. Six of the first ten recruits were members of the girls' club; seven of the first twenty-nine lived in one short street and six in another. One linker, two "menders," and the woman engaged to sweep up and make tea were all relatives. There were also two pairs of sisters. On our initial four tables, close friends worked next to one another and all partnering was with others of similar age and capacity.

All of this demonstrates that although adding women to the workforce was a significant step toward diversity, the prevailing social structure extended into the factory. It was a lesson that would give my work perspective going forward: to take the cultural and social realities into account and not always aim to "change the world" with each project.

Training for Expertise and to Build a Culture for Success

By coincidence the instructor sent from the parent factory to start the training had served in the War alongside the sister of one of the women at Minetown, and quickly became part of the community. She came to the role with a detailed program to guide her and photographs, diagrams, demonstrations, and exercises to use at each stage for teaching proficiency in linking. At the same time, she varied the pacing and details of the training program to suit individual needs and even momentary preferences. She planned activities and targets with each trainee at the start of each day according to the trainee's own progress and problems, and then modified even these plans during the day in the light of actual experience.

We sat the trainees in pairs. The goal with the organizational structure was to inculcate a sense of group responsibility and investment in the success of the new factory. This was in line with the Tavistock Institute's "socio-technical" approach based on observations that groups provide incentives, assistance, and social support better than individualized performance evaluation and close top-down supervision. Pairing the workers facilitated expressing and sharing work strain, along with helping and pacing one another. If one asked to do what the other was doing, the instructor encouraged it. In many instances, this worked out well, and if it did not or proved premature, the women recognized and accepted it. At set times in the daily programs, partners timed each other off a large clock hung at the end of the hall.

Partnering continued to be important. From the time a trainee started work on a regular linking machine, her best performances were recorded daily on her personal graph on the wall next to her partner's. When one was absent, the other's performance always dropped, and her partner's absence was blamed for it.

More widely, we encouraged contact among trainees who had started at about the same time and worked with these cohorts together on current issues and next steps. Close to their work areas we regularly posted group outputs and individuals' averages. Those postings begot lively and sometimes heated discussions, particularly when a member had failed repeatedly to keep up with the others. As length of training ceased to distinguish individual outputs significantly, we also charted the whole group's output, using earlier performance as chief guide and the group's own estimates to push forward.

Each group divided the target among its members according to their previous performances; any other way, like averaging out the total, no one ever even considered. So, even quite large differences between individual targets continued. The greatest we ever recorded had the most advanced member urged to contribute fifty percent more than her slowest mate.

Output differences occurred and were dealt with in many different ways. The most extreme response was a group's proposal that a member be dismissed: she had fallen out with her partner, failed to keep up with the others, repeatedly come late, and altogether alienated the goodwill of all. Instead of sacking her, we shifted her to the end of the table to work beside a woman who was very much better than she was and took no notice of her, and, on the other side, women of another group with whom she, from then on, tried to keep up.

Group performance was made the basis for special bonus payments on passing traditional milestones in output. Where different capacities continued and threatened conflict, we encouraged regrouping according to capability. It became the norm to check and confirm any changes with the linker(s) directly involved – for revised pairing and grouping, for setting and displaying individual and group targets, or for settling any special question or difficulty about a training device. Eventually, the group would also be consulted about allocating extra-difficult work, for choosing and changing over to local instructors, and for accounting and paying them for the time they spent instructing instead of increasing their own outputs and pay. Assigning output targets on the basis of demonstrated skill reflected the Tavistock theory that workers work best for the team rather than either their own (competitive) advantage or for the distant "bosses" or other external motivations. It worked to boost total output, to maximize the performance of the group and thus their individual incomes.

Four weeks into training, the trainees urged us to have a "Parents' Day." We invited their family members as well as many others, who milled about and engaged the budding linkers in explaining the eye tests, training aides, and other features of their work and their factory. The new employees' pride in their work was obvious.

Changing to Local Leadership: Now They Own It

Six weeks after starting her own training, one linker also became a part-time instructor. It cannot be overstated how important this step was. It showed that we were committed to the parameters of local leadership we had set out at the beginning. It also showed that our process was nurturing a sense of leadership potential in the women; they were rising to the occasion. At the time of her promotion, we also instituted more formal and regular factory-wide consultations. The linkers-in-training were given regular opportunities to propose best candidates for instructors by secret ballot and selected three colleagues to sit with John and me for weekly consultations. The five of us met every Friday, and these meetings were very practical, about the allocation of work, the uneven quality of supplies and the need to alert the parent mill about that, the persistent lag of output on Fridays, and a visit to the parent factory in the city down South. We met early enough in the day to discuss relevant outcomes that same afternoon in our end-of-the-week chats with each working group.

Another sign of worker investment was that the work groups were consistently curious about each other's rates of progress. As employment increased, we added a large graph of output rates near the factory door and, on the individual graphs of later trainees, marked the average outputs of all previous women at the same stage. The most common reaction to falling behind was to come to work early and stay late, and this continued no matter how we tried to limit it.

With no further action on our part, by week three from starting we had received five applications for manager. All were men, which represented societal norms and the realities of the working world at that time. We chose one of the two applicants from Minetown, a man who had become a motor mechanic in the army during the War and returned to Minetown to look after the Cooperative Society's vans and to deliver meat. He was well known and liked in the community. Two weeks on, he, together with the two local instructors and an additional "linkers' representative," went on a weekend visit to the parent company in the Midlands. They came back encouraged, sure that in only a little while they would match the output levels of old timers there. They proudly reported that working conditions in Minetown, though "less fancy," were at least "as good;" and that the "large, noisy" town in the South had really more disadvantages than attractions. They added current headquarters' production levels to their own graphs and set about exceeding them.

By any standards and on all scores, this development rates very high. The new linkers in Minetown surpassed the old timers' usual output by twenty percent within the first year. Absenteeism was less than one percent, and even that was more than offset by continuing readiness to work overtime. Only one linker had left. When the factory had twenty-one linkers and eight menders, further recruitment had to be held back not to outrun the production program of the parent factory. Soon, supplies of unfinished hose from the head mill did not keep up with Minetown's linkers' output. This became a sensitive topic with the parent mill, but the Minetown manager asked for (and received) more reliable alerts about supplies-on-the-way, using which he could then guide further recruitment for the Minetown branch.

John and I worked full time in Minetown for just eight weeks. By the time we left, production, further recruitment and training, finding the permanent site, and plans for erecting the factory were all well in hand, and the local manager's relations with the parent mill were proceeding to all parties' satisfaction. I remained "on call" while working at the coal mines nearby, and John and I promised to return for one or two weeks if needed. However, the only time the manager called us back was immediately after the move to the permanent site, and that turned out to be mostly for affirmation and celebration.

Transcendent Challenges: The Elements of Success

In the Introduction, I presented my "worry beads" diagram (Figure 1.2) which is both for deciding whether the conditions are ripe for success with any particular intervention, and for planning first steps. Three elements most relevant at Minetown were *Assessing Possibilities*, *Gauging Client Readiness*, and the opportunities for *Recording and Reflecting*. The Minetown project is an example of enabling and applying inclusive emergent change in an organization that has tried and failed to institute top-down planned change. The possibilities for emergent change were there: the organization (Acorn Hosiery) and the community were primed to undertake the establishment of women in the workforce, and I was empowered to record the process to allow for greatest application at Minetown and amplification beyond.

Possibilities in the Community: Inclusion and Collaboration

The company was the obvious first stakeholder, but the community immediately became equal partners in the effort. Looking back, it was really Minetown's own town council, local people, and the local journalist who took the initiatives that launched this effort. Of lasting interest is that, after having welcomed the prospect of the factory's coming in general, the town council and local people had held back, as if waiting to see how we newcomers would actually behave. And after our formal calls on the council and the Labour Exchange, we initiated no public events. Instead, we kept asking for guidance about how best to do what had been agreed upon, and relied on our numerous and widespread workaday contacts to answer practical questions. This method showed our openness to engaging with whomever and whatever arose. With that assurance, the community's grapevine then served to do the rest.

But this level of community engagement carries risks. Our openness and responsiveness also involved us in Minetown's conflicts. About unionizing the factory, for instance: that we allowed the opportunity pleased Labour but offended the company's lawyer and local Conservatives. Shop owners and the garment factory feared having to raise wages and improve working conditions. However, it turned out that with unionization and a growing sense of investment among workers, sales increased and the new linkers quickly opened savings accounts in the local bank. Although the cause and effect of this phenomenon are not clear, it may be that raising wages and providing good working conditions for these women resulted in measurable benefits to the community that convinced everyone, even those opposed to unionization, that the net result was positive for the local economy.

That both workers and managers were determined to be highly productive by traditional measures is a logical outcome of the emphasis on local ownership, teamwork, and pride. This is perhaps the same aspect of culture that leads to identification with local sports teams and, in Minetown, had always been associated with the local mining culture. It points to a broader challenge within organizational development, of how to maintain the identity of locals while being part of a broader modernizing and universalizing economic scheme. Large-scale change often reflects and must work for many different sites, and many different "change agents" with their own inevitable influences. For our part, even though we connected so eagerly and enjoyed widespread interactions from the very beginning, John and I stayed *personally* distant. The community truly needed to own this effort; it could not in any way be seen as "our" project or responsibility. We avoided social contact outside working hours and the factory itself. We had come for the least possible time and would leave as soon as Minetown with its new factory could manage on its own.

Recording and Reflecting: The Key to Learning and Amplification

The opportunity for close recording became increasingly important for me in my career; it started before my career really began, in the factory where I had kept notes and written up my ideas for more efficient design and management. Minetown was the first time I used it as a researcher become consultant–helper. If Dialogic OD is about amplifying positive changes generated by successive experiments, then one way to help that happen is to keep accurate records of what has been done and the results, and to make those records available to others. In Minetown, what I was originally tasked with doing – providing an academically distanced, objective record of events – was not what I ended up doing. As described above, my role became the provision of on-site learning from close to the action. If, in the classic academic mode, I had observed this development from afar in order to avoid influencing the outcome, then my recording would have been limited to unimportant details. This recording was instead for all to put to immediate use. Such close engagement may not be appropriate in every situation but it is certainly preferable when the goals and engagement are as clear as they were here. So it differed from my ongoing research down coal mines and also in dockland. In the coal mines I had been tasked with observing what habitually went on and could be built into degree programs for mine management. The "anthropologist's" role was appropriate there because the change needed had to start with the situation as it existed. Also, incidentally, it was helped there by the surrounding dark and deafeningly high machine noise in the mine and of the cranes on the docks.

In projects with fewer possibilities and organizations less prepared for change, such close, collaborative recording as I undertook in Minetown might also not be possible. In the docks, for instance, all I had for recording were fortnightly meetings of a few handfuls of employers and workers, who had volunteered to talk with each other on neutral ground while their organizations were fighting it out on the picket lines. There the record could only be for identifying and beginning to explore what practical issues might make a promising agenda for formal discussion and negotiation, not for identifying a process for immediate implementation.

The recording and reflecting at Minetown helped firmly establish a set of five habits and conditions in my career:
1) Always undertake detailed recording from the very start, my antennae out against losing or fudging details (obsessively so, some valued colleagues have commented);
2) Describe and document fully and in an unbiased manner, and only then analyze and incorporate ideas into action;
3) Have a senior colleague constantly accessible to discuss the findings and for planning and revising next steps (in Minetown, an added benefit was that John was an engineer who valued precision);
4) Don't spend time trying to anticipate what local office holders, local people in general, or trainees might or might not do or recommend, but instead go with whatever comes up and as it comes up; and
5) Consciously and openly *own* my part in a development, in order to assess and learn the most from experiences, whatever they are, and also to gain a perspective of the whole as it unfolds and for wider sharing later. I have also grown to value this owning as my best way to put particular experiences "behind me" and so clear the decks for my part in the next development.

More Thoughts about Why it Worked

What best explains Acorn's readiness to pioneer this development, quite contrary to what was then established practice? Executives elsewhere, after all, had lived through the same war-time disasters and changes, and shared the same general conditions and promises for the future. Our collaborative ways were not that strange to understand:

of course local people know their own situation in practical detail and naturally incline to collaborative ways, from living and working continuously with the same others – they would not get very far in any other way. But still, most companies like Acorn were not applying this common sense to their own industrial development.

Minetowners' own experience with outsiders had not encouraged openness at all. Being individually and communally utterly dependent on absentee owners of the coal mine, a memorably bitter strike and then the long Depression aroused their suspicion of outsiders, and the recent nationalization of the mines had made no practical difference to that. So, it is no surprise that Minetowners held back until John and I showed how we would actually proceed and keep going, and also that these latest absentee owners were supportive of our methods.

Transcendent, against-the-grain change is best started where its promoters a) have little to no choice and b) are already involved in change that shows promise. So, when selecting new developments, I often look for places that have already tried and failed with standard ways of doing things. This distant parent company, Acorn Hosiery, backed our methods of putting people and relationships with the community first because standard ways clearly had not worked for them. The directors had tried the headquarters-outwards version and failed, just like the others in the trade. Unlike others, though, Acorn did not settle for the "linkers are born" explanation but, instead, identified a professional resource with success in reimagining management best practices. Acorn had already worked with Tavistock to test their methods *on home ground*, at their own mill. So, their wide-open backing of us was rooted in the Acorn executives' own experience with reorganizing the parent plant along collaborative lines so successfully. As the pressure to expand output and exports persisted and intensified, they were ready to apply these fresh ways of thinking to Minetown's development and prepared for it well, by securing trade-union agreement for systematic training for the new linkers and the Tavistock Institute's recommended candidate to start up the new branch factory.

Especially difficult to assess because it warms fellow feeling so subtly is the effect of the long experience of Acorn's decision-makers. These owner–directors had worked their way up and knew the hosiery mill operations thoroughly. The Minetowners understood that although the executives were "outsiders," they were clearly experts through hands-on experience in textile work. John was a practicing engineer whom Minetowners also saw arranging the workshop and fixing problems as they occurred; and I was clearly familiar with operations on the factory floor and also with coal mines like their own. Outsiders we were, yes, but also reassuringly familiar and knowledgeable.

Learning for Action: What Minetown Taught Me

A major learning-for-action from Minetown was mentioned above in regard to the social–cultural structure of the Minetown community: to take the realities into account and not aim to "change the world" from the very beginning. Practitioners who aim to lessen the world's problems have been classified as "Planners" or "Searchers" (Easterly, 2006: 5). "Planners" are those who aim to *solve* the world's problems by identifying them and applying technical solutions, while "Searchers" ask those most closely affected what they need, and work to apply homegrown solutions. The plans of Searchers may not be as big – we were not going to change everything about gender relations, industrial productivity, or small-town life – but our project was feasible and, it turns out, successful at what it – and we – set out to do. I like to think of the Minetown experience as an early step toward the broad realization that a breadth of perspectives is necessary for lasting change and growth.

The Planners versus Searchers dichotomy is another way of illuminating the role of the Dialogic Mindset and Practice in understanding organizational development. When I began my career, there was a dominant "scientism" of OD that implied that development was a laboratory experiment where a specific outcome was foreseen. Minetown was the first formal setting in which I came to see development projects as "field experiments" where practitioners (and "owners") must be willing to let things develop and see what happens, to allow an innovation to "find its best form" rather than steer in a predetermined direction. I developed an emphasis on learning from experience and a reluctance to smooth over conflicts where the risk was to backtrack on innovation. We will see more of this latter emphasis in the subsequent settings, but it became clear for me here.

In more recent years, Dialogic OD Theory has begun to provide a framework with which to understand both what seems to be "out of step" and, simultaneously, what is intuitively creative and common-sensical (and iconoclastic) about this way of working. In Minetown, I experienced the ethic of what would later come to be called, in dialogic terms, "co-creation:" the concept of using dialogue with all stakeholders involved to create "supportive" decisions and choices at all stages of the development. The transformative vision for this project was opening up the employment to women workers outside the home, and helping the community support that departure from generations of men-only employment. The theme of partnering and co-creation continued, and proved to be the critical success factor in this engagement.

Thus, certain themes of Dialogic OD, consistent with the socio-technical systems/group oriented approach pioneered by Tavistock, surfaced even in this very early experience: engage with a sense of direction, count on the emergent to produce the hoped-for results, allow information in from all parts of the system, if not via a large group meeting, then interactively from many small conversations and discussions ("talk a new reality into being"), make progress visible so the whole community can see what is happening (via public meetings and the public production charts in the plant), create trust by fulfilling promises to hire local people and include locals in the management, operate with respect by taking into account whom the community thought deserved to be hired, and use that data along with objective tests for technical skills – and then leave as soon as the capacity to operate with internal resources is demonstrated.

As outsiders, we must often walk the line between professional authority and openness to local ideas. A final learning-for-action from the Minetown experience is to look for decision-makers who already have some experience in community building and have lifted it into personal awareness. An outsider brings fresh views, new assessments and skills, confirmation, and appreciation to a new development in a functioning community. We may challenge what has long seemed obvious, assumptions that have gone unquestioned. The famous Hawthorne "experiment" of the 1930s is a reminder of the outsider/other's contribution. Though chair of a department then titled "Human Relations," Fritz Roethlisberger's professional degree was in engineering and he went to the Hawthorne plant of Western Electric (the manufacturing arm of AT&T), tasked with recording production increases improved by best lighting. Instead, he found – and recorded – that output went up and up no matter what was done to the lighting, that operators experienced all changes in lighting as increased attention to themselves and their needs and produced more in response to *that*. As a result, the company instituted greatly enlarged human-relations programs for first-line supervisors. Back at the Harvard Business School, the Human Relations Department came to be retitled "Organizational Behavior."

Back in Minetown, then, as central as the town's openness to change or Acorn's unorthodox backing may have been, it was the continuous attention to the women's opinions about everything from siting the factory to having their parents come to admire their work and making them partners in setting work goals that mattered equally in bringing out the best in them, and offers lessons for organizational development more broadly.

CHAPTER 2

Sri Lanka and South India: Young Leaders from Different Countries Learn Through Building Community

> "[W]e sat down in a circle under the shade of pine boughs. By chance I was sitting on the highest fruit crate… Saying jokingly that it was uncomfortable to be elevated like a preacher, I turned the box so that it would be lower. But it was weaker in this position and I had to turn it back again. Jim then silently turned his seat so that he was sitting as high as I was. I remember this as but one incident of a quiet tact which Indians are apt to show."
>
> Erik H. Erikson, *Childhood and Society*
> (New York: Norton, 1950), pp.121–2

Background: Learning to Start from Scratch

The next setting was utterly different from Minetown, where we helped a prominent corporation establish a branch factory in the long-established coal-mining town. Here there was *nothing coherent* overall but only scattered bases for support and other resources – not even an appropriate site at which to establish this international training center. There was only me, as director (on what the team leader in the next setting would call a "missionary's salary"), newly wed to my already pregnant Ronnie, and an annual budget for three years that would fund the participants' international travel and a world-class auditing firm with a local office, and board meetings of the World Assembly of Youth in Paris, to which I would report twice yearly.

In the five years since Minetown, a string of improbable events had propelled me across the Atlantic and then into this wider world. A call from London's docklands had come first: could I be a last-minute additional UK delegate to the World Assembly of Youth (WAY) inaugural meeting in the US? Although I was not a member of any youth organization, and they needed me there "next Monday" (!), I decided to go. At the WAY meeting I became highly visible, even notorious, by loudly singing "O Ye Lost Sheep" with a Canadian trade-union leader to jolt the Assembly into decisions for action. Then, back home in England, I was asked to be the UK member on the board for the European Youth Campaign, just starting in Paris, and continued full time to ensure that we seven youth-organization representatives did not get outmaneuvered by the seven foreign ministers on the adult side of the board.

I spent 1952–53 based in Paris, travelling the twelve countries then heading into the European Union. In 1954 I began a training fellowship at the Harvard Business School Human Relations department. It was there that I worked with and married faculty member Ronnie. Which brings us to Ceylon (now Sri Lanka), and Aloka.

I received a foundation's request that we plan a residential training center for young public leaders from newly independent countries in Asia and Africa; I would be voted its director at the next WAY meeting in Singapore. The WAY national committee in Ceylon had chosen the site, they said, and the name, too: "Aloka," Sanskrit for "light of the world." The WAY secretary general had visited and approved all.

Marriage to Ronnie helped make me a plausible candidate to direct Aloka. We were a good team – she from the American mid-West, *cum laude* Radcliffe graduate, and Harvard Business School faculty member (even ahead of women students there). I German-born British with recent experience in European unification and governments at high level; both of us Christian but of different denominations. I would be the director with a salary, and Ronnie – woman, wife, mother-to-be – would work "for free."

Aloka made an obviously timely and personally attractive idea for starting our life together. But it was just an idea, even so: was it at all feasible to train young leaders far away from their countries, the fifty-plus newly independent nations with their different conditions and different traditions? Would it be more feasible if we limited it to English-speaking applicants, or tried it out first in one or two Asian ex-colonial territories? And what were the true goals of the project's champions at higher levels? Politics and the Cold War were in the background: there was Western interest in supporting anti-Communist development in emerging countries, so programs to promote democratic values and ways of working were more likely to receive international support. What might happen when that political urgency was over?

Notwithstanding these uncertainties, the sense of opportunity – the chance to take advantage of the optimism and new-found freedoms – was palpable, and irresistible. Uppermost in our minds while visualizing Aloka and its programs was to offer an alternative to the male-dominated and top-down cultures of the ex-colonial countries. That was all these young leader candidates had experienced in their families, religions, and communities, and the erstwhile colonial powers had also supported this structure politically. Including others and leading collaboratively would challenge their most deeply embedded habits and beliefs. Only with well-focused experiences to the contrary, in a straightforward and consistent program of sufficient length, could we hope to make *collaboration* become the new normal and survive the participants' return home. As leaders, even especially as leaders, they also would need others' support, which had implications for building cohorts and integrating ongoing assistance after the program was completed.

CHAPTER 2

Aloka in Theory

When taking on a consulting project, I always strive to get a sense that my ideas for approaching the program's goals are reasonable. Ideally, we would have used advanced knowledge of the organizations, political actors, and other constituents involved, as well as field testing, to assess our assumptions about what Aloka should entail. However, with newly minted countries scattered over three continents, even minimal field testing of these ideas was ruled out, and the players were too new to have a history we could study. So, in lieu of "best practices," we took a calculated risk and proposed eight conditions essential to us for accepting the directorship, and presented them at the Singapore meeting:

1. Each program to be for twelve weeks and residential, focused solidly on experiential learning
2. Participants to be chosen in pairs, up to fifteen pairs per program
3. Participants to be selected into programs for their usual setting – rural or urban or formal education – and one program for each setting per year
4. Women as well as men to be included in all programs
5. Simple cooperative living conditions to maximize opportunities for participants to make decisions and act cooperatively and also to keep costs low
6. Participants to come from new, post-independence organizations as well as organizations that had existed in colonial times
7. All organizations to contribute to the costs
8. The director to have final say for admission.

The inclusion of women and the last three conditions raised serious objections in Singapore. Young women and men together flew against traditional hierarchies and gender norms in most (if not all) participating countries. However, women had played prominent parts in the freedom struggles and could not now be kept out. The other objections were more practical than "traditional" and were more easily answered: I pushed back against the objections of established organizations eager to keep newer organizations from sharing in the opportunity, and a provision for in-kind contribution resolved the issue of cost contributions from organizations without access to foreign exchange and/or prohibited from spending on "political" endeavors. Aloka was a bare-bones operation: our mini-bus, deepfreeze, and professional camera came by way of in-kind "tuition" over the years, among other things that were highly appreciated. I got no push-back about the length of the proposed program, although twelve weeks is a long time for a residential program of this sort, asking a huge commitment of the individuals, their sending organizations, and their families. As to my having final say about admission, a reference to well-known corruption dissipated any objections.

With that, "they knew what they were getting," as it were, and I was voted into the directorship. That Christmas and New Year, I took an around-Asia trip to meet WAY's national committees in East Asia. We had operational plans and the budget ready for board approval at its next meeting in March. Including international travel, the annual budget totaled $200,000 (equivalent of almost $2 million today). And the first program, for leaders in rural areas, would start on 19th September "so participants could return home by Christmas."

That April, Ronnie and I were married.

Planning and Preliminaries

An international program can easily feel overwhelming. I did all this before the Internet, of course, but the sense of having too many contacts to make and keep up, too many variables to plan for, was intimidating, even then. It helped us to use the "journey out" to Ceylon to make connections, both formal and informal, that would solidify the program and help assure broad buy-in and deepen support. Our trip had seven planned stops, starting with WAY's headquarters in Paris, meetings with national committees and UN agencies to follow. This was much trouble, indeed, and we were newly married and Ronnie pregnant. But even with time-consuming courtesies and formalities all properly done, our practical agenda advanced at every stop.

In Beirut and Karachi, we selected three women for the first program and identified organizations with likely candidates for later programs.

We were determined to find local faculty members for the program from the beginning. Delhi officials contacted the development commissioner for Bengal, who proposed the retiring head of a major community development training center, and we settled his coming.

Also in Bengal, we first met Bill Cousins, a Bengali-looking-and-speaking American consultant, who quickly became an avid supporter of Aloka. Bill came himself to experience the program and then had us add extra programs for Indian rural development officers.

In Ahmedabad, India, the last stop before Ceylon, we made a connection that led to a strategic change in our plan for Aloka: Vikram Sarabhai, the scion of one of India's most prominent families and a world-class scientist and institution-builder himself, proposed that Aloka hold its first urban program there, in collaboration with the Ahmedabad Textile Industry's Research Association (ATIRA) meeting. A large city like Ahmedabad would surely be a better site than anywhere in Ceylon for training young leaders from urban areas, and here half the participants could be young managers and city officials. A large family mansion with staff could house the international participants and us at no extra cost, and ATIRA's director – already a friend of Ronnie's from Harvard – could join our faculty for the program. Starting with our first urban program we located all urban programs in major cities across Asia – Tokyo, Jakarta, Dhakka, Karachi – which also would free up Aloka's home site for additional programs.

The importance of taking the time to make these kinds of connections when setting out cannot be overstated. Moreover, I believe the act of physically traveling around and seeing people in person is important, even in today's world of LinkedIn business networks and Zoom conferences (barring a global pandemic, of course). Even activities seemingly unconnected with professional goals have value when working in an unfamiliar international context. Aloka was determinedly local – local faculty members, local sites, and local participants too. As an outsider, it was important to me to know where these individuals came from, to adjust myself to their reality, rather than imposing my own upon them. And insofar as I was imposing my own agenda, as in our goal to address traditional gender roles, it helped that they trusted that we had stopped off to connect with their leaders and cultures and shown our respect for them even as we wanted them to adopt new values. We found out later, when participants explained to Ronnie why they had disliked a particular facilitator, that the reason they allowed us to make some of the same *faux pas* that person had made was that, simply put, they *liked* us. Beyond personalities, they liked us, perhaps, because we did not hold ourselves apart, as this particular person had done; moreover, the idea that Aloka was addressing a "felt need" by educated and concerned people, plus our openness to meeting and embracing people of all backgrounds, was a contrast to the negative stereotypes of the colonial powers who had so recently left these countries.

And, traveling is fun! At every stop on the sub-continent, we ate no end of mangoes (and properly praised each kind as the absolutely best of all), clearly endearing ourselves to our hosts. All over South India, the sweet dessert rasgulla "was just as good as that made in Bengal;" sweets that filled shop windows in Calcutta like tennis balls of various sizes made particular villages into mandatory stops. And the decision to take Vikram Sarabhai's generous offer to house us for the first urban program had great ramifications for our family: Ronnie was due to give birth to our first-born. He assured us she would get the same family care as their own, with their doctor and his nursing staff and all extra help. This was a great relief at the time, and we have been "family" ever since, a fact also true of Bill Cousins, our champion in Bengal, who has been "Uncle Bill" to our children since we met him and his family on our journey.

Launching the Program: Where and How

The round-about trip to Ceylon did more than build the program: it honed my own vision for Aloka and established our support from allies far and wide, creating the sense that we could be leaders rather than merely manage the endeavor. In fact, the need to lead by taking an unpopular decision happened immediately: the site the Ceylon National Committee proudly showed us on that first day, "immediately and all ready to sign," was entirely unsuitable. It was a four-storey stone mansion amid tea estates in the rainy and often-cool up-country, miles of winding roads away from useful field sites for our participants. I accompanied the officers for the meeting with the owner and vetoed it, upsetting her and causing (most of) the Committee to resign.

The Committee vice-chair, a leader in Ceylon's cooperative movement, stepped in and, over the next three weeks, sent us driving 2,000 miles to inspect possible low-country sites. With just four weeks before the start of the first program we settled on a six-acre pineapple plantation by a little river twenty miles inland, south of Colombo. For three years' rent in advance, the owner undertook to build the six additional cottages we needed. Meanwhile we lived and worked in "the big house," and women would stay in "the boat house" – which, happily, had a bathroom.

The program design, requiring the grouping of participants in sessions with others like themselves (rural/urban/academic), was an important first step, and having each group in its own particular setting was a major step better. Participants would have new experiences away from their regular workplace, which forced them to deal with and attend to these experiences, but the sights, activities all around, noises, and smells too would be "just like at home." So, Ceylon's low country would serve well for the rural programs: tropically warm, among villages but away from the rush. And big, industrial Ahmedabad or another city would serve best for urban participants. Participants from formal education would be hosted in the quiet rural site in Ceylon.

Now, logistics. With new chair Sembu's help, we recruited a cook, a driver, and a manager, and bought and installed a generator in a shed amidst the coconut palms on the upper ground to run from morning to night. Saj, the cook, was lord and master of kitchen and meals. Beds – individually made to our design to accommodate luggage and drawers under the frames – arrived one by one and barely ahead of the program start because the workshop had closed for the week in honor of its founder, who had just then died.

September 19th came. The following summary of that first session illustrates how our conditions, set so optimistically and self-assuredly, played out in reality.

The first session included twelve participants, all new leaders in rural settings: one each from Ceylon and Lebanon, and pairs from India, Pakistan, Indonesia, Singapore, and Tanganyika. The eight men sorted themselves into the remaining rooms in the "big house" where Ronnie and I and the Indian faculty-family also stayed, and the four women members and faculty stayed in the boat house. As they arrived, participants were asked to take charge of their living quarters and plan their turns for setting the (ping-pong) table for meals and washing up the dishes.

"But men don't do that!" was the first challenge; then, "Well, if you insist – but don't tell people at home!"

The site was a perfect setting for beginning this work of encouraging and promoting drastically new ways of approaching work and colleagues. In this secluded setting and simple living quarters, and working closely together, these strangers from wide-ranging participant countries and organizations got to know each other quite quickly across all differences of beliefs, country, status, and gender.

The Program Unfolding: Experiential Learning

Experiential learning means different things to different people, and the participants of Aloka, although sorted into groups based on their settings, had different "experiences" to deal with back home. In order to put everyone on equal footing, we planned significant daily time devoted to experiences that none of them would have to do at their home organizations, tasks to plan and undertake that were removed from normal political activities and goals. At Aloka, we began every day with fieldwork. By fieldwork we meant, literally, *work in the field* – identifying things that need doing in the grounds, in the gardens, and so on, and planning when and how to do them. For example, from the first walkaround: the main gate "obviously needs painting," there are banana trees to replace and plant, the lime tree to prune, the main path needs straightening and raking. When should we do this? What will we need by way of supplies, tools, expertise? How much, and how best to get them? Who knows how to do that, and wants to try? And will they do this alone, or with someone else?

To be clear, this was not just "busy work:" the tasks were of real importance to the community and setting. And in *none* of them was I or any other staff member an expert: although we staff had ideas about what should be done, it was the participants who planned and completed the projects, down to the smallest details. For example, repainting the gate: should this be in the same color? How much paint is required? How many brushes and of what size? New banana plants need holes measuring 2 x 2 x 2 feet. In this stony soil it may be best to plant just one per morning. The discussion and plans quickly became concrete and practical, and so also the choices about partners to team up with.

Incidentally, participants did not necessarily pair with the partner who had come from the same sending organization. Coming in pairs was more about guaranteeing all participants a modicum of support (here, and back home), and ensuring fuller and truer reporting of conditions and opportunities back home. In a practical vein, partnering also allowed participants to drop into the home language with the partner when English became too burdensome. But in the context of this fieldwork (as, ideally, in the real world), teams and partnerships were built based on what needed to get done and how best to do it.

After an hour and a half of assessing needs in the field and accomplishing the tasks set for that day's work, the "inside" Aloka program began. After clean-up and breakfast came an hour and a half discussing how the fieldwork actually went, compared with the plans and "theories" shared about how it should go. Sitting in a room arranged for high participation, with a fifteen-foot wall covered with green plastic sheet for any and all to use chalk on (and easy to wipe out), we asked, "What did you see, hear, notice, what struck a bell for you?" The questions were concrete, specific, and based on their senses. They were meant not to imply a judgement by the facilitators, yet required the participants to judge themselves and relate to one another.

Reflecting for themselves on what actually happened in this first round, in an environment free from external judgment, was important. In their "real jobs," leaders spend much time and energy theorizing about the work that needs to get done, planning how it will get done (sometimes by themselves, more often by others), and then moving on to the next problem or crisis that arises. With these types of concrete tasks and specific questions, we were working to get them used to reflecting on their work, from questioning the theories that underlay what they decided to do and reflecting on how they actually worked to solve the problem that was identified. (How many coats of paint did the gate actually need? What kind of pruning shears worked best?) Putting it all in the context of yard work ideally took away some of the ego and many of the assumptions they may already have held about how things should be done. It exposed potential biases, weaknesses, and strengths they may have had in an unthreatening, essentially inconsequential setting unlike the one in which they worked. And at the end, they had accomplished something real and measurable in which they could take pride.

We also emphasized reflecting on the whole fieldwork process: the walkaround, the physical work, and the outcomes. Late in each morning session, we asked, "Who took the lead, came in later, proposed a resolution, stayed silent?" "Did patterns emerge, even the hint of one, that may be worth watching for in the next activity?" "So, for tomorrow's fieldwork, how will we organize ourselves?" This all served to exemplify and prefigure the "What? So What? Now What?" model of reflection that is accepted generally as good practice today.

A tea break followed and then the daily session to track the developing relationships in and of the group: a "lab" like the NTL runs in the USA, and even more like a "training group" at the

Tavistock Institute in London. After lunch was an hour and a half discussing a written case that had been distributed the previous day for preparation in advance. After a day or two, participants offered experiences of their own to discuss, and Ronnie helped to develop them into "draft cases" for the group. The day's final session was a review of the whole day, to identify new relationships and insights and the pressing agenda, and to fine-tune plans for the next day and beyond.

This daily pattern held through week eight, and then we all left for a three-week community project planned jointly with a local organization. That put the new experiences to use, put the participants to the test as a group, and gave them practice solving real-world civic challenges. The final week was for planning and preparing for the return home, for generating ideas to try to initiate there, and for discussing how best to muster personal and organizational support for these ideas.

Participants asked for a certificate to show at home, and we did provide one for attendance but without "grades" or faculty members' or directors' comments. This fostered a sense of accomplishment without giving in to the desire to measure oneself against others competitively.

Awareness and Inclusion of Self and Others

At Aloka, experiencing and reflecting upon how relations actually develop *right here and now* took precedence over all else. In and out of sessions, any happening was subject for recalling, discussion, and recording. In this intimate setting, fresh questions and interactions arose constantly, with a widening sense of why this was important beyond the immediate context or "trigger." For example, after several days of outdoor work, the following arose:

- Who took the lead in deciding the next task? Who responded and how? Did it get done?
- Particular pairings seem to have become regular. Why? Is it easier, more comfortable to pair with the same person repeatedly? What risks might that have?

- There are never enough "best tools" – how did you sort that out?
- What are the reactions when some members regularly take more breaks than others? Or when some profess prior experience and start "instructing"?
- Women so often opt for weeding – why? And, why do the men let them do that?

Awareness of Self with Others and experimenting with this awareness became virtually continuous. All was open to questioning, recording, and review, in or out of session, and to facilitate this we encouraged journaling – "of anything you see, think about, dream" – and the sharing of it whenever, with whomever, in and outside of sessions.

Politics were never far away. For example, for Aloka's formal grand opening (five weeks into the first program) the Ceylonese participant took undisputed lead, insisting that the Prime Minister do the honors in a traditional opening ceremony. So, the fieldwork became building the Sanchi gate with its lowest crossbar high enough to let "the six tallest elephants" process through it to the traditional drumming and trumpeting, with the Prime Minister followed by diplomats, ministers, high officials, and prominent elders. Unsure how the other participants would take all this political show, I took close notes of the event, at which all participants took turns garlanding the PM. How they had decided to garland him not just with one for their own country but for all hundred countries in WAY I never knew, but three times he virtually disappeared under the piles, laughing. I asked in the session the next day: "How did you know it was your turn?" – trying to get at what it felt like for the non-Ceylonese to be part of that show of respect. The local ferryman had anchored his raft on the Colombo side of the waterway for the whole day, so awed was he by the PM coming. I asked, "What does this tell you? Would *you* do that – like, for me?" "What are the implications of that for the ferryman's understanding of leadership or power?" "Do you share that sense of awe?"

An event that raised political tensions was when the World Health Organization representative came for an evening session, who, as it happened, was a Dutch man. The Indonesian participants were present but got up and left as a group as he entered. Asked to explain themselves the next day, they recounted how the Dutch had fought Indonesia's independence. Some responses included: "You could have just stayed away." "It would have been better than insulting him... and all of us." "You could have checked with him how *he* feels about Indonesian independence." These interactions showed not only how some of them were internalizing the need to notice and question everything but also a sense that some of them, at least, wished to move on from colonial era reactions and assumptions, while others found it difficult to do so.

In another example, Haq, a Sikh long-time Gandhian worker for non-violence, got into an increasingly angry confrontation with Ahmed from East Pakistan (now Bangladesh). Haq's "BIG hands," several who were there told later, "loomed extra huge against the open window as he clenched and unclenched them on the table before him." Then he suddenly fainted, slumped down, and collapsed under the table. Some participants froze, others rushed over, some counseled each other. Haq recovered in minutes. I halted the session for a much-needed break, asking all as they left to recall and record their experience of the event for discussion next day.

The main take-home for me was how valuable it is, first, to notice what is happening, then to reflect on how one feels about it, then to have a safe space in which to articulate and talk with one another about the event, even if that conversation raises complicated issues. I was also open to discussing things with individuals, such as more personal challenges inappropriate or not ready for larger discussion. For example, in the urban program at Karachi three years later, I sat all night with an Indian participant as he relived fleeing with his family at the of time partition and seeing his parents and younger sister killed in a railway compartment.

Sometimes the real world away from politics intruded – a bit too close to home! – to give us what would today be called a "teachable moment." A shout was heard outside: "The director's cottage is on fire!" The session emptied. Some participants rushed up the hill, helped Ruben pull the burning stove into the open, clear out loose furniture, and sweep and beat out the smoldering cinders. Others watched from below. Ahmed stood apart, stiff, unmoving, and murmuring over and over, "Must be put out, must be put out…" Yet, it turns out, he was the one participant who was a trained and certified firefighter. The next day's discussion clustered around two themes: the wide variety of immediate reactions that seem to repeat life histories, and the limitations of formal and even certified training.

At mid-morning on the second day of the very first program, an Indonesian member said, "I thought English was the language of this program."

"Well, yes," we replied.

"Then what are all these others speaking?" (They were speaking English.)

"What is most difficult for you?"

"Mrs Lynton's [American] accent!"

Not all experiments pan out, though, and some boundaries are too critical to the mission to allow blurring. This "bias for action and learning from experience" did not really work with our participants from academia. After finding that the first two programs for educators became bogged down in competitive "getting a word in edgewise" and the like, we merged those participants into rural and urban programs according to their location at home.

The Aloka Concept of Leadership

One of the most important elements at Aloka is the role we – the director pair – played in the day-to-day program, in this continuous togetherness and learning. By rights Ronnie and I were the "leaders," even stand-in parents; however, even more potentially problematic, we were the senior/Western man–woman couple, "the authority" on all things Aloka. Putting collaboration and egalitarianism front and center, even or especially when it came to ourselves, mattered crucially for settling these young leaders into active collaboration. We would not only enforce anti-hierarchicalism, but also model it consistently. Put simplest, we lived with and just like the participants.

In the big house we had a room off the hall and shared the bathroom with them; even behind the closed door, participants could easily hear Ronnie and me talk, laugh, arrange things together. Ronnie continued to take an active part in everything as much as her advancing pregnancy allowed – she joined in the morning fieldwork, and had her meals and shared many casual encounters during the day with all. Later, when the cottages were built, ours was just like theirs (only differently arranged inside for the baby). We participated in all scheduled activities – I bare-chested like the other men at the mornings' fieldwork and again at volleyball at sunset. We had no special, honorary seating at the meals around the ping-pong table or in the singsongs after hours.

Such continuous intermingling runs counter to classical psychoanalytic work, and only a little less severely so for facilitating the daily training groups (or T-Groups).[9] Both of those call for confining contact with other participants strictly to session times. Such distancing would have been awkward and virtually impossible in Aloka's close living arrangements. We were taking a risk that we – and thus what we were trying to impart – would not be respected or accepted by the participants; however, more determining for us was that staying distant would have come far too close to reproducing the traditional up-down relations that we were determined to counter. Our behavior was as matter-of-factly, steadily open to discussion as everyone else's there, modelling as much as possible dramatically different inclusive and collaborative relationships for the future. As for a slighted attention to issues of developing as authority figures, I continued to see that as a minor loss compared to the evident great gains from our mixing with them so closely. Such decisions were important in the post-colonial setting and later in other arenas, such as the American Civil Rights movement, where white volunteers worked in Black organizations, sometimes without attention to the

---

9 "Sensitivity Training Groups," or "Encounter Groups," pioneered by Kurt Lewin in the 1940s at the NTL Institute to allow participants to move toward change by sharing emotions and reflecting on attitudes and behavior. Traditionally, the group facilitator minimizes his or her own leadership role in the group meetings (which we did), but also outside of them (which obviously we did not).

implications of their interactions. And most recently, white participants in the Black Lives Matter movement, for example, are ideally acutely aware that they are not the leaders, speakers, or "movers and shakers."

Setting ourselves up as equals opened us up for questions, of course. From the first week participants started asking why I did things so differently. Several asked about a staff meeting they heard I had held, at which I had asked all to sit down. When Zeb, the cook and also the eldest, responded with thanks but explained that they were quite used to standing and happy to do it, I had simply said I preferred seeing them eye to eye, all at the same level. The participants were astonished at this lapse of protocol: "What, with you the director – the cook, the driver and Ranji too [the teenaged "lady" secretary]!?" Later, in India, participants asked about our decision to do without a manager, to let "the office" – that is, the (female) secretaries – take on managerial functions and, when they needed help, to consult with Ronnie or me. And lo and behold, these secretaries, after coming timidly for their interviews, each accompanied by a parent who spoke for her, rose strikingly well to the challenge, becoming lively, outgoing young women as they lived and worked as equals among the participants and us.

What the participants each learnt from the close contact with "any and all others" – participants, staff, and surrounding neighbors – we can only surmise, but I closely noted how they responded to Ronnie and my talking and doings things together so very differently from what they were used to. They saw and appropriated our behaviors – and recorded that in their diaries. Then with our first baby (a girl!) and our second daughter, and also with the Indian baby boy we adopted and the nursery school we started with them and children from the city, our interactions with participants and as a family had an impact. The participants' comments and questions showed clearly how this all challenged their past experiences and opened them to trying new ways.

We also welcomed participants into our family space. At the end of the first program, when two participants' flights home were delayed, they joined us for our first Christmas dinner together as husband and wife. Later, as our babies arrived, hardly an off-session time passed without one or two participants in our home singing and playing with them and talking about missing their own children. I drew the line at being endowed with the title "grandfather" to a Zambian as old and taller than I was – and when our growing family took more of our time, and Ronnie and I needed more rest and time for just ourselves, we raised a Japanese fish mobile on a pole by our cottage to signal that we were unavailable just then.

So, participants heard and saw us work, play, laugh, sing, fool around, and deal with our babies and with staff so much more freely than was normal back home, and in that freer atmosphere many raised this difference for discussion. The participants themselves made this free interacting much easier as they showed themselves well able – program after program – to respect our different roles at Aloka, with staff and outsiders as well as with themselves in different parts of the program. When in the first few days of a program a participant raised a personal issue or made comments on the group's working outside a session, we simply referred them to raise it in the group, and this quickly became the response all soon expected. In fact, it is only when facilitating T-group sessions that we maintained the orthodox distance. There we sat in the same place each time, spoke rarely and then only about developments we saw in the whole group, including ourselves.

But "going with all that is to hand" also had its cost. Such a way of approaching leadership was alien not only to our participants but, in a few cases, to our faculty. For example, we had not checked this personal openness, departure from professional rules, and general intent with two colleagues in Boston whom we had asked to join us, one of whom was similarly trained as Ronnie, and who came in the first year. Andy led some sessions but otherwise stayed apart as best she could. At the end of the first program Andy had just driven off to the airport for home and some participants stood around with Ronnie after seeing her off. Ronnie asked them why they had stayed so distant from Andy. They readily listed *faux pas* she had made.

"But," said Ronnie, "we made the same mistakes, and you helped us!"

"Yes, but *you like us!*" was the answer.

So, staying distant had come to mean not being friendly. The culture did not always fit for everyone, and otherwise competent and likeable faculty members held back. But without a commitment to diversity and inclusion, the vision of Aloka would have been threatened.

Many participants raised this different way of "leading" in the discussions and planning for returning to their home organizations. For my own ongoing practice, I am now even surer than at the time that "staying more distant" would have harmed our best and most lasting work at Aloka. As I found at Minetown, keeping apart would have severely restricted my surest and truest understanding of the participants and the situations. And although Minetown was a relatively homogenous community, Aloka participants came from so many different and distant cultures, so keeping distance between us would have restricted the many spontaneous opportunities to understand, influence, and support them. I would not have got to know how authority issues actually came up for them and theirs and what could most effectively encourage behavior in fresh directions. Most important, the effect of this program would have stayed behind when they went home – if I wanted to truly amplify its effects, I needed to help spread a new definition of what it meant to lead.

Discussing, Understanding, Developing

Most of this would not have been possible without close attention to details, so carrying notebooks and pencils quickly became the norm at Aloka. Notes on paper – today it might be computers or voice memos – helped in raising questions and sharing observations and insights, even overnight dreams, the next day. The daily case sessions were the most useful for adding lasting understanding to the new experiences and building on them to develop new futures.

We shall see many examples in this book of the use of writing, reading, and discussing cases from actual, relevant practice to aid learning. At Aloka, to begin, we used cases already proven useful elsewhere, then added participants' draft cases about their own experiences at home and also now here. Outside the sessions we worked with individuals or small groups on the detailing and precise writing that cases demand. As we "test-taught" some of their own cases, they came to understand the setting, involvements, and actions even more clearly. How did that decision *actually* get taken? What did X's silence turn out to mean? How could Y have responded more effectively? What opportunities and problems does *that* organizational arrangement make more likely, and how could it be assured or lessened? Or, how important was it to get X or Y stakeholder on board on that issue, and how was this best done and by whom? The discussions of their own increasingly well-recorded experiences fostered hard-headed understanding of common development situations and problems elsewhere.

Aloka Going Forward

By the end of the first year, some home support for returning Alokans had already surfaced: eight organizations in seven countries proposed clearly suitable candidates for next year's programs and also inquired about additional short programs for senior officers. On our round-about stop-offs in Singapore, Rangoon, and Dhaka to the program in Ahmedabad, we confirmed that these "seniors" were quite ready to pay travel and extra program costs. We realized that including the senior officers was a way to amplify the effect of the program, something that would become a central goal of any program I undertook.

We continued to use our travels to the sites of the urban programs to reconnect with alumni and their home organizations, support their development efforts, and participate in selecting future participants. On the way to the urban program in Tokyo in Year 2, we added an Indonesian alumnus of the first program to the faculty and settled on Jakarta for the following year's program in collaboration with the Moslem Youth and Student Organization and the Cooperative Movement. And in the Philippines, we recruited forestry officers for the rural and education programs and two officers for the first senior program at Aloka itself.

Aloka's third year was momentous: first, for running that first program for senior officers. Then, national elections in Ceylon turned the government inward and inhospitable to world-wide Aloka, so Indian alumni, led by the Young Farmers, got the Mysore state government and the all-India government to invite Aloka to resettle there at no extra cost. From there, in Year 3, I held the first additional program in Tanzania for a growing group of new East African leaders, while Ronnie stayed home with the children and also ran Aloka's first program for Indian community development officers. Year 3 became also the time of our first dissemination effort: we published *The Asican Cases*, "teaching-cases" written by seventeen participants from ten countries and edited by Ronnie, including instructors' notes about major concepts and likely points and processes to use when discussing them.

We were also asked that year by UNESCO for a full report of our work. This writing project had major lasting consequences for my future work and writing by initiating the tape-recording of the whole next program. Audiotaping proved so much more accurate than memory that I developed my use of the fullest possible recording into a regular practice for all meetings and thoughts throughout my working days. The book, titled *The Tide of Learning: The Aloka Experience*, was published the following year.

All along, participants proposed colleagues for programs, and clusters of alumni began to form in particular organizations, including the Young Farmers in India, the Ministry of Social Welfare in Singapore, the Moslem Youth and Student Organization in Indonesia, the Forestry Department in the Philippines, two women's organizations in Pakistan, the youth wing of the Tanzanian government, two organizations in Kenya, and departments in the university in Ghana.

Oh, and in Year 3 we also procured three more years of funding.

Why Aloka Ended

How to broaden and diversify Aloka's influence became the strategic question during our second three-year stint. By the end, we had decided that doubling Aloka's size would help fulfil this growing need and also enable us to diversify and round out the faculty, and give it a more sustainable permanent core. Unfortunately, the lead funding foundation and the government behind it did not support these goals further, and we resigned the directorship.

As in the Open Space method,[10] which has come to be known as a method associated with Dialogic Organizational Development, when something is over, it is finished and that is OK. My commitment was always to amplifying impact, so at the end of our second three-year contract, when the Aloka board turned down my condition for renewal (doubling Aloka's size) and my continuing directorship and the program ended, its further impact would be carried by its many graduates the world over.

In retrospect, more diligent attention to Aloka's funders (who by the end extended to two government ministries and two UN agencies, with the participation of nine committees of the founding WAY organization) might have prolonged the life of this early experiment in international living. On the other hand, larger political forces, such as a slackening in the post-World War Two emphasis on using such programs to ensure democratic institutions in the developing world — forces well beyond my ability to control — may have been at work.

Aloka by the Numbers

For building and managing a program to develop emerging political leaders in South Asia, this time and these places could hardly have been improved upon. In the late 1950s and early 1960s, the energy and excitement of national independences – at last! – were in the air. The participants had been on the front lines of these struggles, and were energized by the importance of what they and their countrymen had accomplished. Many participants came soon after long years in student armies (Indonesia), in passive resistance (India and Pakistan), and in freedom fights and post-independence

---

10 This is a technique for running meetings where the participants create and manage the agenda themselves.

public services in all countries. Issues from independence were still live and to the fore, such as the murderous partition of the Asian sub-continent and the religious and political antagonisms it heightened, the drawn-out ejection of the Japanese occupiers and then of the Dutch colonizers, and the often-heart-rending personal memories that participants came with and needed to resolve at last.

Over six years, 365 young public servants from twenty-six newly independent countries experienced the twelve-week residential programs of Aloka, and twenty-eight seniors attended the shorter programs for them. The personal and interpersonal development of many continued impressively afterwards, and especially so where clusters of them worked together. For example, when, thirty years later, we worked in Indonesia again, nineteen of Indonesia's twenty-six Alokans were still meeting regularly and doing things together; one had become a member of the Planning Commission, another the head of the trade union federation, a third the head of the Moslem wing of the Ministry of Religious Affairs. Seventeen alumni took turns as faculty members, two became full time from Year 4, and one accompanied us to our next work.

In the six countries that also hosted urban or additional Aloka courses – India, Bangladesh, Japan, Pakistan, Tanzania, and the one planned for Indonesia – organizations and national committees supported the alumni as they involved themselves more and more in development. That also applied to the Philippines, Kenya, and Singapore, which had also sent officers to the programs for seniors.

Some Learnings from Aloka

Aloka occurred early in my career, early in my marriage, and relatively early in the modern post-world-war era. We were open and responsive to unforeseen events, a tendency that ran throughout the program, and Ronnie and I round-the-clock helped participants measurably to do this too. Two general learnings from this openness we still especially prize. The first learning was to refrain from asserting general maxims from elsewhere and previous times, and only use one or two "rules to live by" that were likely to matter in *any* new setting. The other general learning was the importance of building in the support(s) that a development needs to last. A number of things since Aloka's end have become clear about how we might better have assured its survival beyond six years. The specific learnings below are based on my experiences then, as well, in some cases, as my long career and life-long habit of self-reflection that followed.

1. Identify the funders and include them in the active stakeholders.
Allowing the funders to stay hidden behind the Foundation was like staging *Hamlet* without the Prince. We should have made that identification and ongoing inclusion a condition for planning. Aloka was the first opportunity for insisting on it – although, looking back now, doing so in that political atmosphere might have ended my candidacy for director. However, in retrospect, I see four opportunities I may have had for identifying and including these principal stakeholders for longer support:
- At the start, when the Foundation asked us to plan the development at the second international WAY meeting
- At the board meeting at which Aloka's budget was passed
- When, after holding the first urban program in Ahmedabad, we decided to locate *all* urban programs in major towns in Asia and actively involved institutions in several countries on two continents and their governments
- When those *prominent stakeholders* requested that we add programs for their own training at their own cost.

If nothing else, this experience reminded me that each of the "worry beads" must be revisited from time to time in light of changing circumstances, and this may be especially true of the mapping of organizational stakeholders. By the time of this last opportunity, the core list of external stakeholders included two governmental ministries of Ceylon and four in the state government in South India, two UN agencies, nine foreign embassies in Colombo and Delhi, and nine national committees of WAY, six in Asian and three in African countries. With this many stakeholders so heavily engaged and supportive, assured financial support and/or wider sources of funding would have allowed Aloka to continue.

2. Continuously upgrade and enhance what I, the initiator–developer, bring to the table, through developing my own knowledge of Self, and building my own competencies.
I began orderly work on self-improvement in Year 4, when I asked an Indian analyst to come periodically to monitor my facilitating T-group sessions and counsel me after each. In future developments, I would continue to seek this type of support from colleagues or advisors.

3. Build in enough reflection time for the director of a major development, like a sabbatical year in academia.
These six years of Aloka in a position of top responsibility, close and rustic living, and growing a family in a new country, called for substantial time off, in a block. It did not take me long to learn this, and when I accepted my next job, the "extension education" consultancy in the new team for India's Ministry of Industries, I insisted on a six-month break before starting. This does not need to be a "vacation," just a chance to do something different, using a different part of the brain, as it were. So, after family visits in Europe and the US, these months enabled me to continue my personal analysis, and review and relive the Aloka experience while also playing a small part in the creation of the first "therapeutic community" in the USA, set in a large state mental hospital, where for four months I observed community meetings and ended up helping the hospital re-work its occupational therapy offerings through this community.

4. Be flexible about continuity of support and consider succession.
After Aloka, I thought about how long support should be assured for before going ahead with building a new institution or deciding whether to continue. Three years? Six years? How "complete" does the map of external stakeholders have to be to start with? In the half-century's experiences since Aloka, six years has turned out to be a good rule of thumb. On the other hand, a program that had the

striking successes and generated the personal enthusiasms created by Aloka deserved the right to be considered for continued growth after the founders left. So looking back now, in setting conditions we could have begun to develop a (home-grown) board-of-directors-like committee with government and agency ties that would have had among its purposes the continuation of Aloka in some form. And in that vein, we might also have paid attention to the issue of succession – could there have been some others (perhaps among current staff or alumni) who could have led Aloka with a similar spirit, after the founders left? We shall see in the next chapter that the new institution described there took just such a turn and continued on its own after the major engagement ended.

The Best Laid Plans…

Some things we planned did not work out. Keeping educators together (and apart from other leaders) hindered significant learning: they preferred arguing over words to actually working together for some specific practical purpose. It was not clear why. Was this a function of desiring to avoid real personal growth, or related to intellectual, cultural, and political differences that needed to be worked on, or something else? In any event, it is a small example of how plans do not always succeed, and how changing the program mid-stream made it better for that group.

Support for Aloka's alumni back home was clearly another essential, one that remained unclear and only unevenly achievable. This is customary in international work, although keeping in touch and providing continuing education might be easier in today's virtually connected world. Pairing Alokans was a minimal start with this goal. Requiring them to have their organizations' backing was good as well, validating my condition that organizations pay towards the costs. But the wider support most developments would need remained unclear. This lack of clarity was mitigated beginning in Year 2, with the first session for senior officers from eight countries. The addition of these programs both indicated that Aloka was providing something of value to the original participants and also added organizational support to the core values and directions for change that Aloka stood for. In a sense, the program now extended beyond the physically and time-specific sites of the Aloka sessions themselves.

Why Aloka Matters Today

We shall see in the next chapter how Aloka, and specifically our experiential and field-oriented approach, influenced the next endeavor of my career, a major initiative through the Small Factory and Extension Training (SFET) Institute to upgrade small industrial operations and multiply employment across all India. Beyond SFET, and beyond its effect on my own career, however, and into the modern day, several elements of Aloka have survived as critical elements of development training and public health intervention education.

It is now a given, for example, that effective collaboration is best learned through immersive involvement in experiential learning in a supportive environment, a sort of "cultural island" where people can experiment with new behaviors without putting key relationships at risk. That learning environment must include real (enough) tasks and ample time to reflect deeply and personally on them, and this learning is best supported by skilled facilitators who have participated in similar processes themselves.

The understanding of new experiences at Aloka was grounded in concrete events and practices elsewhere, anticipating the Dialogic OD preference for honoring experience, reflection, and action over theory and its application. Some of their own examples became cases to assign in future programs. As noted above, we collected the twenty-one most widely useful cases, from seventeen different case writers who came from eight countries, and published them with instructors' notes in *Asican Cases: Teaching Cases from the Aloka Experience*. The cases in the book are grouped in sets of increasing complexity, addressing understanding a person's feelings, building a picture of a person, rivalry and leadership, authority, and social change and learning. Several of the cases are in regular use in the participants' countries to this day.

It may seem obvious to most current readers, but the learning about the dynamics of race, class, caste, and gender were hard won, and uncovered deep and difficult experiences in all cultures. However, the general principles of Aloka become evident in all group settings. The realizations that authority and hierarchy can be softened and humanized, and that one can befriend – and sometimes confront without negative repercussions – "the Other," are powerful and life-changing, especially if encountered during a time of personal openness and during a key stage of personal development.

Even today, this learning can only occur in a supportive environment with diverse participants and facilitators, and including time for reflection and response. These learnings can be "carried back" to the sponsoring organization if there builds, over time, a body of participants who become a critical mass of alumni of these programs, and leadership is supportive. To this end it is important to train the leaders, and not just mid- and lower-level employees of the organizations that benefit from the training. Essentially, we were developing organizations as much as individuals. By encouraging satisfied alumni to recruit others, the design also favored concentrations of alumni in a few organizations and so helped those institutions develop along inclusive and participative lines. The short programs for their senior leaders and our own travels between programs helped solidify those commitments.

At the time that we were leading Aloka, the world existed in the aftermath of the demise of the colonial social order, a time of re-drawing the boundaries of states and nations, of emerging new nations, of ongoing conflicts, crises of agriculture and industrialization, and the challenging of racial, caste, and social hierarchies. Aloka, of course, did not "solve" these problems, but it pioneered some of the methods of addressing them that still ring true today. Most observers would say the world has come far from the days of international colonialization and post-colonial struggle, but disruption is still a major reality, in terms of the environment, the economic order, gender relations and hierarchies, the technological order, the understanding of public health, the re-evaluation of social and economic policies and recognition of past injustices, and the resurgence of latent grievances. True problem-solving across these divides still requires these cross-culture, cross-hierarchy, cross-gender, cross-race, cross-caste, cross-nationality skills that Aloka taught.

In the Dialogic OD framework, the decisions about structuring the experience in Aloka might be described as "creating the container" in which people can learn about themselves, experiment with new behavior, and transform themselves into more aware and self-confident catalysts for social change. In addition to building a container where new behaviors, attitudes, and values could be shaped and formed, Aloka was designed to disseminate effective values and practices by seeding catalysts in other organizations, then reinforcing their influence with successive generations of alumni, and by working with higher levels in the participating organizations. Ideally, over time, a "tipping point" would be reached and whole organizations would experience transformation that allowed them to be more effective catalysts of needed changes in communities and societies.

The personal connections and organizational supports back home lasted impressively too, which we saw when visiting thirty years later, as mentioned above, where dozens of Alokans were still meeting regularly and doing projects together, developing their own careers, and having lasting impacts across organizations. Change is disseminated through real relationships, strong networks, and by talented people who "go to training" and then become influential in their own right. Beyond the participants from across the target continents, another example is Bill Cousins, the American Friends Service consultant we met in Bengal, who insisted on being a normal participant in the India program. After that he regularly sent Indian extension agents, government employees who worked to "extend" the central government's support for agriculture and other industries, for additional programs. Crippled by polio from birth, the first Black sociology PhD from Yale, the first president of the Federal University, in the initial planning group and then country head of the US Peace Corps, we had first met him wearing a dhoti and looking and talking like the Bengali farmers he advised. To the end of his life – he retired from heading UNICEF's urban programs world-wide – he proclaimed his program at Aloka to have been "the most significant in his life." Such occurrences contribute to the emergent nature of change, and such notions were the generative ideas behind Aloka.

CHAPTER 3

Developing Small-industry Employment Across India

"See – judge – act"

Motto of the Young Christian Workers, Belgium,
founded as the "Young Trade Unionists" just after World War One

Introduction

One overarching goal motivated the establishment of the Small Factory and Extension Training Institute (SFET) in India, my next major development project after I left Aloka: to support and increase industrial capacity and employment across India. Two approaches to this goal were envisioned: first, to retrain existing and new government consultants who advised small factories on management and other administrative functions throughout India; and second, to attract new entrepreneurs in large enough numbers to create massive modern employment through new industries.

Essentially, I was one of a team of international "experts" hired to teach current Indian small-industry consultants as well as new ones as they came, some of whom would join us as instructors. Each of us was knowledgeable in things like marketing, management, and finances; my field was "extension education," which meant extending the work of the Institute beyond the boundaries of the classroom and out into manufacturing workplaces across India. This was all in service of the first approach, improving the existing Indian consulting service to factories. How to implement the second approach – vastly increasing the numbers of *new* entrepreneurs across the country – was not in any sense defined at the outset. Moreover, nothing about the structure of the training program itself had been set when I came on board.

More details follow that illustrate just how complicated this seemingly straightforward goal and these approaches would be to implement in a culture of hierarchy, tradition, and political constraint. I approached my task with my experimental and inclusive bent and overriding disposition toward facilitating transformative change. I found a set of stakeholders, historical contexts, and realities on the ground that would test me with the problem of how to address complicated philosophical and practical differences in a highly charged political context. And unlike at Aloka, I was not the leader at SFET; for the most part, I had to work through others to try to implement change. Significant challenges arose during this project, and in coping with them I took on a level of risk heretofore unprecedented in my career and became "a true change agent."

Historical, political, and personal contexts

India's partition and establishment as an independent nation after World War Two brought with it legislation that abolished princely states, outlawed discrimination, limited land ownership, and created reserved seats in higher education and all government for low-caste and other discriminated-against populations. Under Prime Minister Nehru's leadership, the "Green Revolution" was under way, while massive food imports warded off future famines, and programs had been started to limit population growth. Private foundations stepped in where official funding was too slow or controversial, as for family-planning programs.

Two philosophies of how best to develop the economy prevailed in India at this time: Western-style rapid, technology-forward industrialization versus expanding the tradition of simple non-mechanized work in villages. Simply put, the competing visions for development could be boiled down to "mechanizing industry versus multiplying hand looms." Prime Minister Nehru had clearly declared for the former, over the Gandhian tradition of simple living in villages. In service of this vision, a large Western foundation with a highly influential representative with a large office in Delhi was engaged to help establish the Small Factory and Extension Training Institute (SFET). The Foundation had started by funding an international study group of experts to undertake a world-wide tour of the most promising small-industry developments. This team reported to the Indian government, in order to design the Institute to improve and increase industrial activity.

The current elite consensus was that only *large* schemes and *rapid* development promised to "save" continent-sized India. There was already a governmentally based consultant service for small industries. The SFET was to upgrade and greatly expand this consulting service, and attract large numbers of small business owners in India and help them to build successful enterprises. Along with this initiative, the Foundation and other funders were also helping develop six other institutes of management and technology, as well as multiple institutions for higher education. Locating SFET and the others away from Delhi and incorporating them as autonomous bodies was meant to free them from governmental constraint to develop in new ways. Yet the enterprise was still closely tied to the Ministry of Industries, while the Foundation was also helping develop a new Ministry of Community Development to house the service.

From my first days in Delhi for this new development, this sense of massive rapid change – formally democratic, but also top down and rapid fire – was obvious to me. I noted in my diary the uneasy impression of people *rushing*, their sense of urgency outrunning the thoughtfulness that a complex new development should command. It was an urgency born of a sense that India needed *saving* – from the next famine, for sure, but beyond this, there was an almost evangelical zeal among the Ministry and Foundation officeholders. Each officeholder I met in the first few days spoke fervently of what to do and how to get obstacles and delays out of the way. Especially at the Foundation, there was the sense that we were missionaries delivering a message. I heard little – nothing positive, really – about connecting with others here to ensure effectiveness and success, learning from them how to make new ways fit and persist in their cultural milieu. There was no acknowledgement that we were outsiders who might need some guidance from those with lived experience of their own incredibly diverse and complex, ancient and yet new nation.

In this atmosphere of already knowing the solution and rushing to get things done, what the authorities called for was "maximizing throughput" – a new term at that time, implying the smoothest efficiency and persistence, causing the least trouble. The original international study group's emphasis was on increasing technical competencies and for international experts to pass their competencies on to the local "counterparts" – members of the Indian consultancy with similar technological expertise who would carry on the Institute's work after we were gone – as smoothly as possible. In this climate, any more in-depth understanding of what true development really requires in order to spread and take root was considered extraneous. Such understanding might even be considered a nuisance, for it would get in the way of implementing what "we experts already know."

Also, from my first contacts, I concluded that plans for the new Institute had not in any meaningful way been informed by pilot testing or actual experiences with doing it elsewhere in the country or even in Hyderabad, where it would be located. In fact, the structure of the program – how it would be run on a day-to-day basis, what would be its "logic model" for teaching – had not been decided, so how could it have been piloted? This is not how I would ideally have proceeded, but I was not in charge: I was an expert, hired to teach and develop Indian consultants how to extend, that is, spread their managerial expertise beyond the classroom, and, it was my understanding, to develop the new institute's capacity to do that after my consultancy was completed. I had my own ideas about how the Indian Ministry consultants could best serve these goals – to become more inclusive, hands-on, practical, and engaging, less telling and more interactive and collaborative. This is what would best serve the clients, and also what would allow the consultants to best communicate and work with one another within and across their disciplines. This was the type of program for training Ministry consultants I hoped the Institute's first director would embrace. I did not consider the possibility, or risk, of his taking it on *too* enthusiastically or quickly. I also had not thought yet about the Institute's second goal of recruiting, and programs for, large numbers of new entrepreneurs.

On the personal side, for Ronnie and me and the children, taking on this consultancy meant turning the world upside down a second time in a few months: from our thirty-by-fifteen-foot cottage in Aloka's simple living, we had moved for the four months' sabbatical to a trailer park among migratory workers from Latin America, our trailer furnished with make-do furniture and minimal household items from the Salvation Army shop. I had bicycled to and from the state hospital while Ronnie kept our battered old station wagon for moving about with the children and shopping for whatever cost least. Now, with my salary up fifty percent and on a three-year contract with the international foundation, flying to Delhi *in first class* turned out to be just the start. Treated like foreign diplomats, we were met by Foundation staff right at the plane, expedited through customs, and driven by chauffeured sedan to the Foundation guesthouse overlooking green lawns where, middle of the night though it was, uniformed staff offered us American drinks and snacks and all attention to any wish. For our son Devadas's first birthday two days later, with staff members and their children joining us to celebrate, candles and US-style paper hats were on hand. We were to realize that the Foundation was determined to indulge any request that could help keep a Western consultant here, like wall-to-wall carpeting in the house – on top of the polished stone floors put originally there to stay cool – and king-size beds "like at home!" Anything to keep "the expert expatriates" happy in this so needy third-world country.

Thus it all began.

The Organizational Setting

The Indian industrial consulting service to be served by SFET was anchored with the Governmental Commissioner for small industries, with state-level offices in each of the two dozen or so state capitals. The Indian government had a hierarchical and formal culture inherited from the years of British civil administration, and its industrial "outreach" program was now to be "enriched" with best technical methods observed in the US and other Western countries. The goal would be to develop SFET to very rapidly train existing and then new cadres of industry consultants who, working from central and also state government extension agencies, would help small business owners build successful enterprises.

The existing small-industry consultants were civil servants in that forever top-down culture, who retained the ingrained and superior airs of the civil service from colonial days. With a career in government, each man (and they were all men) had met his parents' highest aspiration – a career in the vaunted Indian administrative services. This position justified his costly top-level education and graduate school, which his success in the highly competitive selection had then confirmed, entitled him to the exclusive residential training in the government's new institution in the foothills of the Himalayas, and assured a pension on retirement. All were of high caste except for the quite recently legislated sprinkling of lower castes into reserved seats. From this exclusive club in which they had "arrived," each came to the Institute aspiring to rise within his particular disciplinary hierarchy. They would attend the SFET training program to become "counterparts," that is, experts to carry what they learned from the Western teachers in the classroom into the field. They came expecting merely to be updating their accustomed practice to teach it to newcomers. These attitudes and behaviors would be reinforced by the arrival of the international team of experts with advanced degrees from major Western universities and corresponding (if misplaced) confidence in their specialized knowledge and superior education.

So, the Foundation and governmental representatives I would be working for saw the development of industrialism in India as a technical problem, one that could be rapidly solved top-down by experts with technical expertise in particular fields, such as financial management, engineering, or marketing. In contrast, I saw it as a complex problem that was variable and fluid, with no one clear solution, which would require the inclusion and input of multiple voices and an ongoing openness to new ideas about process, funding, goals, and the like. In my view and experience, participants should be helped to rethink their roles and relationships to the work entirely. Much later, this type of issue would be called an "adaptive challenge" in the language of leadership theory (Heifetz et al., 2009).

The attitudes and approaches of the Ministry ran counter to everything Ronnie and I had learned about effective working in urban–rural development. They contravened the methods and dispositions that had previously brought us success working with the local community in developing the new factory in Scotland, in addressing leadership in the newly decolonized nation states at Aloka, and in my earlier work with European youth organizations and striking miners after the War. It was different from the principles and practices learned in my engagement with BIM and Tavistock and NTL approaches to training and development.

As we have seen, as directors at Aloka, Ronnie and I had fashioned collaborative living and working into a virtual oasis, an almost literal cultural island, in both rural and urban settings, that successfully trained and empowered community development leaders who went on to work in emerging nations. It had been a risk, contravening the participants' sense of hierarchy, gender norms, and other passed-down values, but it had introduced our inclusive and collaborative ways of working. And it was a risk we could take because we were in charge. Now, my task was to act not from the top position of director but from the position of one of six team leader–consultants paid for by (and also answerable to) a powerful Western foundation, yet housed in a new institute within the Indian central government. At SFET I had none of the isolation and authority that allowed us to create the experiential, collaborative, hands-on conditions of learning and doing that had worked so well over the past six years.

And what support could I expect from the US foundation? Its local head came out of American agricultural extension (the USDA), was friends with the Prime Minister, and strongly backed the creation of the new Ministry of Community Development, thus cementing the whole project into the governmental bureaucracy. Of the many surprises I found at the Foundation office when I arrived, several important ones were not at all in line with how I usually worked. First, I met Dan, our liaison with the Foundation – and, Dan quickly added, "also with the Ministry." So, my connection with two important stakeholders would be indirect and at least two degrees of separation away. I was also to be screened off from other top-level stakeholders I thought I had come to work with: the Foundation had its own "liaison" with them. Also, Foundation policy forbade Ronnie working with me at the Institute, even unpaid, thus effecting the loss for me of my true partner and no integration of work with family life. We were to live off-campus in separate Foundation housing, not close to participants as we did at Aloka, not integrated into the community as at Minetown.

The Small Industries Commissioner, who oversaw the project from the government end, had a particular interest in "spreading industrial estates all across the country" and the rapid expansion of the consulting service that this would demand, from the 500 consultants now to several times that number. But the Commissioner said nothing about what "Extension Education" was to contribute to the SFET program or any particular part he expected it to have in drawing in and helping prepare these hordes of new consultants, much less new entrepreneurs.

The new institute "is autonomous, of course," Dan assured me on the way to the Deputy Secretary of the Ministry's office. The Foundation insisted on that for all of the new institutes it supported. The Deputy Secretary chaired the Institute's board. White-haired and of few words, he wished us well.

All was top-down, with clear marching orders but hands-off beyond those, or so I concluded from the morning tour of VIPs. Delhi had settled all in advance and to specifications that satisfied sponsors, funders, and "international experts" – leaving just "details" to be worked out locally, in practice.

In essence, the situation seemed in my view (to use a current expression) "a perfect storm," with the winds blowing against helpful change. Or to use another colorful turn of phrase, the new institute, poised to deploy the worst of post-colonial domestic approaches combined with likely inappropriate "best practices" plucked from

Western cultures, was headed for a "train wreck." However, although there were storms, SFET did not wreck. Six years later, a new model of training had been adopted, several hundreds of Ministry consultants had been and continued to be re-educated about how extension worked, and they were fanned out to help state governments recruit and train thousands of entrepreneurs across the country. India was making the transition from an agriculture-dependent economy to a more modern industrial nation, and SFET had become an international model of how to enact such change.

How could such a promising result be achieved from such an inauspicious set of initial conditions, where intent and reality were at such cross purposes? The answer to this question comes in examining the calculated risks we took in two decisions at the core of the project: advancing a radical design for the training of new consultants and then for advocating a controversial approach to spreading entrepreneurship across India.

Training the New Consultants: Action and Reaction

I think the previous section amply lays out the ways in which the organizational setting and historical context made me question the chances of success. However, I was excited by the opportunity – the Government truly wanted to build this, and financial support was there for major, meaningful change if only we could design a truly impactful program.

Change agents with an OD mindset have to deal with the likelihood that the models of change and organizational functioning and leadership they believe in are not shared by most of their clients, or at least are not *practiced* by their clients. In fact, what we bring is usually counter-cultural. Moreover, while the more familiar OD planned-change paradigm (diagnosis, action planning, and implementation) is at least comprehensible to most decision-makers, though often viewed as unreasonably participative, the emergent change paradigm (explore, discuss, experiment, amplify) often seems even more strange and threatening. To support and manage an effective emergent change process, then, especially in a traditionally hierarchical and linear-thinking organization, we must attend particularly to those key engaged and influential stakeholders whose decisions and example will set the course of the organization.

When I arrived to begin my work at the Institute, contrary to all I had encountered so far, great good luck was with me in this last regard. The Institute was being established in Hyderabad, the capital of Andhra state (halfway to the south of the continent, 1,000 miles from Delhi), and the state-level director had been chosen and was already in Hyderabad when I arrived. Being the first international consultant to arrive, even ahead of the team leader, Joe, I had the Director's attention to myself first and for several weeks.

An engineer from inside the service, the Director declared himself to be totally agnostic about how to organize training programs. He was open to hearing my thoughts on the matter, so I asked what he'd like the programs to achieve – the *purpose* as he saw it. His answer: "That the Indian Ministry consultants work more practically." He explained that at that time, technical assistance consisted of the Ministry consultants taking turns sitting in the factory office and reciting the problems in their disciplines that the owner–managers could expect. The Director stated that he thought consultants needed to work in teams instead, and on problems the particular organizations faced in fact rather than in theory. I described how we instituted team thinking at Aloka with an on-site program of collaborative living, addressing concrete problems in teams, constantly reflecting on and discussing these problem-solving exercises, and placing learners in the field to apply what they were learning. Intrigued, and with an idea emerging, the Director invited his department heads in for intensive discussions. It was certainly a good sign that the Director was open to having a conversation with key stakeholders in the program to generate questions and brainstorm about goals and methods.

Over the next week the Director held meetings with me and department heads deputed from the Ministry. No higher-ups were there; I did not know enough to advise him on this. Most importantly, I did not know that senior Ministry officers had asked for a seminar to discuss how the program should be designed and started on the way. This would prove to be an important omission in my horizon-scanning, but the immediate result of these conversations was positive.

The Director and department heads and I discussed the current state of consultancy in India and how a more effective program could work. The Indian Ministry consultants who would come for this training were accustomed, as described above, to sit with factory owner–managers in an office in an industrial estate describing their own professional expertise – for example, machinery and layout, marketing, or accounting. I asked, "Do they go onto the factory floor?" No, hardly: "Back in the Ministry office each writes up a report about his own special field to share with the owner–manager only if they're asked." The Director and the other deputies admitted this method did not work, and the consultants needed training in other methods, but "How should a program be developed to change it?" I described my experiences at Aloka and elsewhere, and they raised increasingly detailed questions.

On the fourth day, the Director declared himself satisfied. He would announce similar programs for the whole year ahead: Ministry consultants in cohorts of thirty, resident for twelve weeks, with three weeks of daily sessions in interpersonal relations and working in teams, continued study and teambuilding in interdisciplinary teams, ending with three weeks of fieldwork in teams in a factory, providing practical recommendations to owner–managers.

A reader who has never been in a sensitivity training group, or is unfamiliar with the norms of programs like this, may not understand how extraordinary it is to spend three entire weeks in sessions devoted to building their interpersonal team-working skills. The international expert instructors would provide technological updating of skills, but the program would largely be focused on collaboration, cross-disciplinary communication, reflection on practice, and other "soft skills," as they're known today. I guessed that participants and faculty members alike would be shocked, yet was excited by how it would dramatically transform the understanding of the tasks and the norms of hierarchy and individuality they were used to. The Director approved my bringing an Aloka faculty member and my secretary from there into the Institute's staff. I was thrilled with this result – any consultant would be: he had asked for advice, he had heard and respected my experience and input, and I was able to influence the design of the program, far beyond my formal position in the organization.

The plan that carried the day came out of the dialogue between me and the department heads about their needs and goals for the program. The resulting design matched my own past experience of what works and their understanding of what was needed: training that was simultaneously practical and collaborative instead of traditional (hierarchical and abstract). The training plan was no less rapid than a traditional format would have been; in fact, the approach much better fit the "rush–rush; do–do" climate of the setting because it would result in specific benefits for the factories involved from the very beginning and be based on their real needs. It would also provide immediate successes for the Ministry consultants being trained, building their confidence through real experience as part of interdisciplinary teams directly on the factory floor, rather than isolated specialists merely talking about individual issues. Today this process might be understood as "rapid prototyping." Beyond the overall structure of the program, the ways technical expertise would be shared would make a big difference as well: working with local entrepreneurs and industries as colleagues, minimizing distinctions of rank and hierarchy, and above all working practically to solve real problems. These all furthered my own goal as resident expert in extension education, which was meant, after all, to spread the methods and collaborative mindset most broadly, and also fulfilled the Director's core objective: solutions to challenges actually faced by manufacturers.

Identifying and choosing small factories for field placements was relatively simple. As so often happens when one approaches each opportunity with an inclusive mindset, it came about through Ronnie's and my personally engaging with the local community. On our very first evening in Hyderabad, Ronnie and I had been invited to a social event where we talked with a couple of entrepreneurs who had recently started manufacturing a small engine for powering farm machinery. These two said they would be happy to have consultants come and help work out the issues they were facing, in investment choices, factory layout, and other technical decisions, as well as in accounting and marketing and overall administration. In fact, they could use several teams, the sooner the better. The same couple of manufacturers then also connected the Institute with other owners and to Rotary lunches and professional societies in town. In fact, by the end of the first year's programs, owners competed for participant-teams to do their fieldwork at their factories, and finding local units for field practice never became an issue.

Having such a positive start may not seem like a challenge. However, it had unforeseen repercussions for the program, most of which were not my responsibility to solve, but which affected me and risked the program's survival. The whole design process felt like a coup for me because it was all decided even before the other international experts arrived. However, those Western instructors were only the tip of the iceberg of others who had an interest in how the program was run. My early and intense connection with the Director may have blinded me to my responsibility as an advisor to query him about the potential interest and reactions of other stakeholders, especially those above *him*.

Working with a Team that Will Not Gel

A potential roadblock to the new Institute was that the international team was resistant to working together toward the goals the Director had set in place. I describe this challenge *not* because I was ultimately responsible for it – I was not the team leader of this effort and was not in a position to solve this problem. However, I felt great ownership of the program's design and some responsibility for its working (and annoyance at their refusal to model its collaborative, inclusive goals). This is actually a position familiar to consultants – you may know how an intervention *should* be run, but you must sometimes recognize the limitations of your own role. It may also be helpful to see how conditions that are not ideal are not always detrimental to overall effect and impact.

By the time team leader Joe arrived and other Western experts who were to be the lead-instructors for the program began to dribble in, the first program was ready to start and the Institute Director had already announced two more for the rest of the year. Notwithstanding my success at influencing the design of SFET, I was (just) one of the six "consultant–instructors" who would be doing the training in individual areas, to be joined by Indian Ministry consultants as trainers as they completed the Institute training. Since the new Institute and the Ministry consulting service were part of the government, ensuring institutional continuity was not an issue, as it had been at Aloka. Ensuring an essentially collaborative nature within that setting would be.

Just as the individuals at Aloka had had their own cultural points of view, the international experts brought in to teach in this institute would have their pride in their particular disciplinary training. Although it was Joe's responsibility, I was hopeful that the team of instructors would gel, begin organizing training and intervention around a shared sense of purpose and role, and so also model collaboration for the Ministry consultant trainees and eventual colleagues in teaching. However, we international experts did not gel as a team. I believe this partly reflects the flaws I had already seen in the initial conception of the program, which had dictated the hiring of these experts based on technological expertise rather than collaborative skills or experience. Upon their arrival they found the programs already determined and planned for a whole year ahead. As we have seen, a large part of that time was taken up teaching "soft" skills and teamwork. Even before beginning, the other experts objected to having "too little time" left over for them to teach their own disciplines. Most had a sense that they and other Westerners "knew best," which was why they had been hired in the first place. Four were academics from the US and the UK, with little to no practical experience. All were strangers to each other and four were totally new to working overseas. All were men in mid-career with wives and small children or teenagers, and all came encouraged to ask liaison Dan for anything along the lines of material comfort that could help them stay.

It was clear early on that individualism and pride of specialty were going to remain stubbornly in the way of teambuilding among the instructor–experts. In their first week at the Institute, two team members began competing for more session time for teaching their own subjects. The most vocal and persistent, an American in his early thirties, specifically complained that too much time in the program was spent on interpersonal relations and building teams. Rebuffed by the Director, this team member then involved himself mostly in the three-week field placements. As the Indian consultants came and attended teambuilding sessions and absorbed the interactive and practice-oriented way of approaching the task, the Western expert–instructors complained that the "students" kept "interrupting" their lectures with questions and urging more discussion in their sessions, and also expected the "experts" to come with them into the field, which was, apparently, unheard of. Two Indian Ministry department heads complained to me that some of the Western instructors were treating them "like juniors or worse." Two instructors soon settled into minimal activities and involvement, and would best have been terminated right then. One was caught plagiarizing a standard text, another's "rather wild children" caused problems in the wider community; a marital scandal came to light. All of these things interfered with the work and increased distrust of one another and general disharmony.

Team leader Joe declined to intervene in problems or even call team meetings to consider live issues or the work ahead. Joe in fact discouraged discussion: we each "knew what we came to do." He did not ask for additional agenda items for his own trips to Delhi or for anyone else to go along. Essentially, he was a loner, tall, bent over, issuing weighty guidelines to one of us at a time or to the Director or Institute faculty or staff. He called together the "team" just three times in the first month, when Dan was due briefly from Delhi or to announce some new administrative arrangement at the Foundation.

It should not have been entirely surprising that the international team did not model the interdisciplinary working the Institute had made a core goal: they had been led to believe that their technical expertise would be central to the overall mission. The Indian consultants who attended the SFET program and would become the experts to carry on the program also were surprised to find their hierarchies less important at the Institute and that, unless they participated fully and did well, they would not be joining the faculty. But in spite of these conditions, the Institute went on as it had been designed, and the Ministry consultant cohorts not only honed their technological expertise, but also learned to work (and even embraced working) in cross-disciplinary teams.

This success may be an argument for the strength of the Director's vision and the importance of his firm insistence on the immersion of SFET attendees in teambuilding, a collaborative mindset, and a practical orientation toward their task. Perhaps some of them recognized how the earlier way of doing things had not been effective. It certainly affirms that the mindset of the Western instructors was less important than the things these Indian consultants were learning. In any event, I decided to minimize my attention to developing the international team and concentrated my efforts on developing my own designated department of Extension Education. With the faculty colleague from Aloka, I facilitated the three weeks of daily interpersonal and teambuilding sessions and took an active part in the three weeks of fieldwork at the end. And this work – and more – was strengthened greatly when already highly experienced and reputed psychologist Udai Pareek forewent his nineteen years of seniority in the Ministry of Agriculture to become my colleague and then department director.

A Leadership Change Threatens to Sabotage SFET

I feared that my good luck in influencing the design of the Institute and my attempts to engage and satisfy the stakeholders in leadership positions was for naught, when a new commissioner took over at the Ministry two years after SFET had been launched. This new principal stakeholder wanted to put his own stamp on the Institute, and almost destroyed it in the process. First and foremost, he condemned the omission of leaders' input into the design of the program and insisted on "taking charge," or else he would resign. He ordered the Institute to schedule "immediately" the original seminar of senior officers, insisted on replacing the current director with one from inside the service, and insisted that the management expert on the international team work directly with him. His goal in these decisions was to sideline the current director and also the team leader of the international team. All of this was potentially incredibly disruptive to the Institute which, in spite of its rocky start, was thriving.

The new commissioner actually failed on all scores and did resign. The Institute's mainstay was the Governmental Ministry Deputy Secretary, who backed the Institute, and the Director's vision for it, strongly. Essentially, it was the prominence and success of the Extension Education department that confirmed and strengthened the Institute Director's steadfast insistence that collaborative work be the Institute's vision, implemented by the emphasis on developing interdisciplinary teams and sending them into the field together. Regardless of whether the international instructors modeled teamwork, this vision had taken hold due to his leadership and the openness of the Indian consultants in training. And they were making a difference to small-industry development. Transdisciplinary teams in ever increasing numbers worked on factory floors and offered practical advice to entrepreneurs on the government's expanding industrial estates. The new commissioner had come close to jettisoning this for his own sense of outrage that he was not in charge. I hope that my own role in influencing and helping implement the Director's vision was part of keeping that from happening. It points to the importance of broad support for a development that introduces real change. I always strove to understand and nurture such strong support, but in this case it was the Director's ultimate responsibility, and a consultant can never be guaranteed that a change in leadership will not signal the end of a development.

Building Entrepreneurialism in India

The first part of the intervention – the teaching of Ministry consultants, increasing in their numbers, and sending them out to do practical advising – got under way and expanded fast. But after multiple sessions, the second approach to building industrial capacity remained unaddressed: we were not focused on drawing in and training *new* entrepreneurs in large numbers all over the continent, as the first commissioner had talked about in Delhi.

There were multiple causes for this hesitation. One was that this initiative was required by law to involve the Khadi Commission, a major planning agency, which continued to share Gandhi's vision of a primarily rural India and opposed the initiative. Also, identifying, recruiting, and developing new entrepreneurs would require states to become active partners in the Institute and fund officers for the new programs, and the Governmental Ministry leadership in Delhi would have to accept states as partners in this endeavor. At this time, the Indian states were a heterogeneous group, continuously evolving and not equally well integrated into power structures at the federal level. Indian states consisted of former territories of princely states and former governors' provinces of British India, all merged into existing or newly created governmental units. Several hundreds of different languages were spoken, and states had been broken up and reorganized around common languages over the years. Politically, the states varied widely: some had a leader appointed by the national or regional governor; some had an elected leader; one state (Kerala) had a Marxist government, and several others have also had (democratically elected) communist elements. In short, the states of India had not long been one unified country, and they did not act like one, nor did the central government consistently treat the states as full partners at that time.

Notwithstanding these structural issues, the Director asked team leader Joe to go to Delhi to explore how to work with states and take the next step in increasing entrepreneurism. The generally supportive Deputy Secretary was not immediately forthcoming, although I did not know why. He approved moving forward on three conditions: that we proceed with it *quietly*, that the Foundation (not the Indian government) provide any additional consultants for it, and that the Commissioner link it to his plans for spreading existing industrial estates.

It should have been a red flag that the Ministry Deputy Secretary, who I knew was a strong champion of the Institute, was not willing to back this next initiative outright. He in effect insisted that we tip-toe around to do it as if it were objectionable, even beyond what I assumed I knew about the political realities. Nevertheless, with this modicum of support in hand, we proposed that the Foundation support and the Institute invite two internationally known experts to help map and if possible help staff the new department in what was being referred to as "Area Development:" Fritz Schumacher – of "small is beautiful" and "appropriate technology" fame, and close colleague of Leonard Elmhurst, a British associate of Gandhi's – and David McClelland from Harvard, known for identifying promising populations for entrepreneurship and "achievement motivation training." The Foundation agreed to fund this expansion.

So, team leader Joe and I began developing a strategy for increasing entrepreneurism across India, based on discussions with McClelland and Schumacher and reading. Over several weeks of back-and-forth, Joe and I developed a three-pronged argument for how best to pursue this goal:

1. We would be most likely to find new entrepreneurs not among the poor but among the recently dispossessed. For example, among second and third sons of Indian landowners (who now were not able to buy more land because of new laws), and among Hindus who had immigrated to India from Pakistan in response to partition. Nowadays, women would be added to this list, like later-sons then, often dispossessed by hierarchical family traditions. McClelland's insights into how to motivate such populations to achieve could be applied strategically to build and support an entrepreneurial class.

2. Maximum expansion would be made possible if we considered "appropriate technologies" – not necessarily either the newest Western technological advancements or traditional un-mechanized manufacturing methods, but rather the employment of machinery new enough, but not expensive or difficult to be implemented throughout the country – not the latest models, and able to be maintained locally.

3. Connected with this with respect to technology, we argued it was important to acknowledge the economics of mechanization

in a developing country as opposed to a Western industrial nation. In the West, mechanizing was meant to save labor. But in India, we needed to employ more people, not fewer, and not necessarily get things done cheaply and quickly. Thus, what was unfortunately called "lesser" technologies would be best. This argument matched well with team leader Joe's training in both engineering and his recent first-hand experience of grassroots development in China.

This logic seemed self-evident to us, and it was hard for us to imagine it not carrying the day. We figured that if the Ministry and Foundation powers-that-be heard and understood our arguments, all would go smoothly and well. But these basic tenets, raised by us, touched off major push-back in the Ministry and exposed fault lines in its relations with the Planning Commission and the states. These were the very difficulties the Deputy Secretary had tried to avoid by minimizing our effort.

In our passion to clear away the cobwebs and solve the problem, we did not consider that the Ministry's and others' resistance to our ideas did not stem from the ideas' novelty: the Ministry, the Foundation, and the others were quite familiar with these arguments. They were most reluctant to express them and take sides because the ideas were extremely politically controversial, and that controversy had the potential to derail the operation. But Joe and I were fired up to actually increase entrepreneurialism, which in our defense, the Ministry did want to do, and we were confident of the logic of our methods for doing so. More important, we were naïve enough to think that if they only understood our points, they would come around. Joe and I decided to take a leap. We wrote a monograph describing our argument under our own names, published it privately and sent 2,000 copies out to stakeholders. With this act, we risked being fired on the spot, if only for the politically awkward position in which we put the leadership.

But we were not fired, though *everyone* was upset with our going so publicly forward. The Director did go ahead with what the Deputy Secretary and the Foundation had agreed: bring in the two international consultants, incorporate their advice, staff and start the new program, and develop Area Development as an additional department in the Institute. And though not "owning" the strategies we had suggested, the Ministry and Foundation allowed them to continue "quietly." Although not admitting to agreeing with our critique of the status quo, they allowed the status quo to give way to new ways along the lines of what we had described: finally forging equal partnerships with states, focusing on second sons of landowners, allowing for the value of increasing the number of employed over maximizing efficiency with the newest technologies.

We turned out to be correct about how industrialization was going and how to jumpstart Area Development programs in the new Institute: our logic and basic tenets were proved by the results. By the third year, Area Development became a fully fledged additional department in the Institute and opened to private persons as well as officials from any ministry or state. McClelland and Schumacher helped staff the new department, one by seconding a senior colleague to join the international team, the other by admitting an Indian faculty member to advanced training at Harvard. The Institute (finally) began connecting with individual states, started new programs for second sons of farm-owning families, and leaders in each state began recruiting local entrepreneurs and business owners for programs of training and technical assistance. The Area Development Program spread its influence and ways of working throughout India. In later years SFET also became regional and international.

At the beginning of my second three-year stint working for SFET, Joe left and I replaced him as team leader. For both the Foundation and the Ministry, I was Joe's obvious successor: already "at home" in India, my area of extension education evidently successful and lined up with Area Development. There was no change in contract, but my day-to-day activity increased because my understanding of leadership went beyond merely filling a slot. It included helping the client envision and implement the overall strategy. I now had always in mind the "bigger picture" and the need to ensure and maintain the overall cohesion of the team, while remaining (I may now say "stubbornly") active in my own professional expertise.

Thus, I was always running out of time, even with Udai right there, the so-competent, experienced, and nationally recognized senior colleague and director of the Department, and ever-closer family friend.

The Role of Recording and Reflecting

As always was my practice, I kept a record of the SFET development for reflecting and learning. From my first day in the Foundation office and Ministry in Delhi to my last day six years later, I kept notes about all the people involved, mapping the far-ranging stakeholders and meticulously recording all my interactions with all of them. This daily data became what I reflected on to plan, activate, and propose next steps. I mapped and updated the list of major stakeholders inside and outside the Institute (e.g., Ministry, departments, entrepreneurs, Foundation, etc.), scored all my interactions with them on a daily matrix as it lay open on my desk and then expanded my diary notes first thing the next morning. Using four columns for each stakeholder, I was able to track my interactions, what they were about, how well they went, and what difference I thought they made in the bigger scheme of things. Usually, I discussed outcomes with Ronnie and started the next day well-prepared. With this regular practice I also learnt some practical details about recording itself:

1. Even with over forty stakeholders, mapping and recording my interactions with them was quite feasible if done in the course of the day, and greatly helped my reflective planning.
2. Continuous practice with it helped greatly to keep all stakeholders in mind, the forty-eight of them eventually here and the up to 140 in future settings.
3. Keeping the daily matrix lying open on my desk signaled that there is nothing secret about this unusual practice; it is open to others to copy it and do likewise.
4. Three months sufficed to move from the first list of stakeholders to the lasting matrix, leaving one or two spare columns in each category for yet later additions.

The clearest lesson about recording taken from this period may be stated most succinctly: no matter what, keep notes! It is obvious from the story just told that I was not perfect in my understanding of all the stakeholders of the SFET Institute. Nor did I completely succeed at keeping everyone on my radar and (even harder) "on the same page." Yet, it is also true that an understanding of the core dynamics of this fast-moving environment, even in retrospect, would have been impossible without the recording in real time. This was a different kind of recording than we did at Aloka, but one perhaps more suited to understanding the dynamics of systems in transition and providing a basis for the consultant to consider next steps.

Family Development

As a family, Ronnie and I and our children also experienced big changes in Hyderabad in those six years. Prevented by Foundation rules from working directly with me at the Institute, Ronnie developed a new career in researching, writing, and publishing about the city and its history. She also participated prominently in public affairs. All our three children started school, and we became close with several Hyderabadi families in addition to the Pareeks from Rajasthan and our Ahmedabad family. Vikram Sarabhai and Kamla Chowdry routinely asked us to participate in national management events in Ahmedabad and, most memorably, introduced me to Eric and Joan Erikson as he researched "Gandhi's experiment with truth." When, after the end of our second three-year stint, my contract and those of my Western expert teammates ended, and the Institute went on without us, we decided to settle in India. We had bought an old mansion at auction and renovated it, and planned to return to it after the next sabbatical and start a country-wide (and possibly also Southeast Asian) practice based there, if possible together with Udai.

The Results Overall: An Inventory of Victories

First of all, my particular area, extension education, quite quickly determined the distinctive collaborative, practical image the Institute became known for in the world at large. This attracted highly regarded Udai Pareek to forego his senior position in the government, becoming director of it and attracting others to join the faculty, including several of his doctoral students. Udai is remembered as the "the Dean of Indian Social Science" and co-founder of the Indian Society for Applied Behavioural Science, which remains a major professional development organization across India. In the third year we also invited faculty members in India's new management institutes to join a two-week program off-site for facilitating interpersonal and group training, and the team leader of MIT's new school in Calcutta joined me in facilitating it. I take pride in having drawn in and engaged this team – including Udai Pareek, and consultants McClelland and Schumacher – to key roles.

So, this extension education department grew ahead of all others, developed active collaborations with other schools and institutes, and pioneered the all-country Society for Applied Behavioural Science, mentioned above, going strong to this day. Then, with retraining and expanding the service well under way, my department also took the lead on the Institute's second goal of attracting and preparing large numbers of new entrepreneurs. Area Development too took off as a separate department: the formally agreed activities started and continued, and the stakeholders joined in as and when they chose, as the hornet's nest calmed down. In this quite practical way, the Institute expanded into its full mandate. So, though without a directive or even authorization for it, I actually greatly influenced things – enacted "institutional development" – from my position as consultant, even ahead of becoming team leader of the international instructors in the third year.

Propelled initially by the successes of the Extension Education department, the Institute advanced as well. For the immediate purpose of upgrading and enlarging existing consulting service, the new Institute hit full stride with its very first program and then went right on to train more consultants every year. The program's design and implementation led to the Indian consultants changing their relationship with each other and with entrepreneurs, owners, and managers. This change was germinated by weeks in collaborative team-work training and was incubated by the emphasis on fieldwork where, in their weeks actually in the factories, we could see that their behavior truly had been developed and that they were having a real impact on the work being done there. Most of them left changed, from aspiring to rise within a particular disciplinary hierarchy into collaboratively working in interdisciplinary teams and aspiring to rise as a group. And surveys after their program promised its sustainability: most planned to continue working in these new ways when they returned to their central and state offices.

Long term, too, the SFET program and its strategy for developing India's industrial output and potential proved successful and added to the incredible emergence and growth of India over the last half-century. In 1972, the Indian Society for Applied Behavioural Science (ISABS) spun off, which added to the program's sustainability – a national society of behavioral scientists working as independent consultants, trainers, and community change agents to promote education, research, and development in the field of Indian applied behavioral science. In 1984 the SFET Institute was recognized as a Center of Excellence for its "meritorious performance," and expanded to serve all of India. Today, India is an industrial and entrepreneurial powerhouse. Perhaps SFET played a role in this development. Like all transcendent challenges, the need for employment in India is not "fixed" – the country is still two-thirds agricultural employment, many of those subsistence farmers. But the Institute continues, now providing training programs, degree-granting schools of enterprise, and global partnerships and influence.

The Results Overall: The Challenges Along the Way

Two critical interventions are described in this chapter: a) creating a fast-start, team- and field-oriented program design with the Director before the other faculty arrived and without consultation with Ministry leaders, and b) publishing (even with limited circulation) a design for Area Development that conflicted with the major, prevailing, Gandhian presuppositions on the one hand and the dominant Western industrialization paradigm on the other. Might it have been possible to achieve these gains without the crises and drama that accompanied the early days of SFET and nearly ended its upward trajectory?

Some may say that I would have done better to stay out of influencing how the Director designed the program. However, to do so would have deprived SFET of the successful approaches demonstrated at Aloka and Minetown, and would have failed to respond to the Director's direct request for assistance on how to make the training practical. In short, this would have meant withholding the major value I brought to the situation. How then to offer this help without incurring the problems that ensued?

The Director, with my support and inspiration, decided to go ahead fast with the needed new direction, but in doing so, he neglected the strategic need to involve stakeholders in the capital. The new Institution's formal autonomy did not ensure that it would survive if it lost their essential continuing support. It was the Director's job to think about this, but it was mine to help him do so. In the relentlessly fast-forward development of this training program (and most training programs are this way), I had failed to ask the Director whether the Institute's governing council had proposed a way to start the new Institute. As we have seen, they had suggested a seminar of senior officers to discuss best practices. The clearly successful programs in quick succession delayed the effects of this omission. When the next Commissioner took over at the Ministry and made this omission and its effects into an open crisis, the immediate response of the Deputy Secretary and Institute Director vindicated my efforts to understand and fulfill their goals. However, the initial neglect of the institutional landscape had left an opening for an attack by a new leader bent on establishing control.

Not giving these leaders a chance to be part of the planning at all disallowed any chance for them to experience a sense of investment in the program. The error came not in the initial plan but when the Director in his enthusiasm immediately scheduled more programs just like it for the whole year and indefinitely ahead, without involving the other stakeholders. If I had it to do again, I would discuss with the Director how to bring these stakeholders along. There might be a general principle lurking here: the consultant and the client need to work out a shared systems view and have a joint strategy about how they intend to approach stakeholders at multiple system levels.

The other negative consequence for this fast start was damage to the start-up of the international consultant team. When the other international experts arrived, they were understandably upset that major decisions had been taken without them, and some could not adjust. Was there a way to avoid these consequences? Perhaps not, given the contrary expectations that had already been set up, the team leader's reluctance to engage during the transition, and the Director's determination to go ahead. But doing more to recognize the impact of the imposed change on the international consultants, helping them work through their reactions, may have led some to recommit. It must be said, though, that in change situations, some will not make a transition, whatever support is provided. Under ideal circumstances the effective change agent will be able to smooth and humanize that transition, yet it may be that the resulting alienation of some of the international consultants was inevitable. Luckily this reaction did not damage SFET in the long run.

The second crisis in the development of SFET was the publication of the "offending monograph" which laid out for all to see conflicts with existing practices and political sensitivities, that major leaders were keen to keep out of the public eye. Where Joe and I saw a void in clear values and norms – and thus a need to explicate why the goals the key leaders and stakeholders espoused were inconsistent with the methods they'd chosen to reach them – they saw a minefield.

In retrospect, I don't necessarily recommend "taking matters into your own hands," as we did so boldly at that time. Instead, I suggest giving due weight to the political obstacles, roadblocks, and underlying attitudes where we meet them. I may have done better with paying closer attention to the messages being sent by stakeholders, their political realities, and a more mature understanding of my own (limited) role as a consultant.

Our monograph did many controversial things, more or less explicitly: it called into question the Ministry's current methods; it threatened to raise the specter of the old caste system by allowing that the poorest of the poor might not be the most appropriate targets for development; it called for decentralizing decision-making, deconstructing the governmental hierarchy and instead applying grassroots understanding of needs and solutions nation-wide; it questioned how the work of the Ministry was funded; it raised again the old debate of mechanized versus un-mechanized manufacturing and/or raised hackles by implying that "second best" was good enough for India. The list goes on. With greater awareness and appreciation for the resistance to our ideas, we would have at least been in a better position to do damage control when the memo came out.

Some might argue that Joe and I may have avoided a lot of conflict and more securely ensured our influence if I had urged the Director to spend time connecting and communicating with the powerful stakeholders, rather than developing an argument to radically criticize what existed. We could have proceeded instead with just the agreed-on parts of the effort in the hope that, unchallenged, stakeholders would join into this quite logical development quietly and in their own good time. There was some risk in making ourselves irrelevant if we insisted on what we knew best rather than what was politically more palatable to our stakeholders.

But it may be also that the project was a success not only *in spite of* our having stirred up controversy, but even *because of* it. Specifically, my and Joe's owning this issue, writing the monograph under our own names, and putting it out explicitly against the Government's and the Foundation's approval, allowed those stakeholders to enact change that they knew was necessary though not politically expedient. Seen in this way we were "secret partners," outsiders able to take stands that insiders cannot, and thus pushing the system to move in positive ways, against the ingrained preferences of some powerful but conservative stakeholders. However, it is good to recognize that the consequences of these types of actions may be significant and unpredictable, decided by the alignment of forces in the setting at the time. At SFET, taking a strong stance in the service of needed development worked out and was supported ultimately. In the South of the USA, the next setting, as we shall see, the strong push for change produced a backlash that reversed some though not all progressive elements of the innovative plan.

Taking a Long-term Perspective on Development Priorities

The SFET experience seems to encompass two major dichotomies found in much international development. First is the tension in relying on technical as opposed to human solutions: as the world looks more and more to technical/practical solutions and makes use of narrow metrics to measure success, we may tend to forget the human side of the equation as regards implementation. Thus, we may spend money and effort on the wrong solutions and endure much unnecessary failure because of under-engagement. Related to this is the emphasis on intervention as opposed to engagement: the tension between doing something to communities "for their own good" and truly engaging communities, which involves hard work of inclusion and collaboration.

SFET showed that even drastic counter-cultural developments are possible: even full-time salaried practitioners and officials steeped in hierarchical traditions with themselves on top will change when faced with clear, pressing needs for it and good ideas for addressing them. They will get colleagues to join in doing it with them, and will keep going with it even in such a long-established hierarchical system as the government of India.

The vignettes I describe in this book, including SFET, show how the tension between intervention and engagement may be resolved in many different settings. In some ways we were ahead of our time, and theory is only beginning to catch up with better practices. Most essential when facing such tensions is to recognize that organizations are fluid systems that require the back and forth, questions and answers, and at last a dialogue that leads to understanding. Coming to grips with understanding and working with institutions as systems became the focus of my next sabbatical and has continued to be my major interest.

CHAPTER 4

The American South: Re-tooling the Academy for Updated Public Service

"…each generation can and must revitalize each institution even as it grows into it."

Erik Erikson, *Childhood and Society*
(New York: Norton, 1950), p.279

Introduction

A planned one-year sabbatical in a prominent state university in the American South turned into twelve years in academia, in which I become a tenured professor and then founding dean of a field-oriented and then altogether unorthodox school of public health in a second university. In the first instance, I created a consortium of eleven international universities to help each other promote population programs and studies, and also helped develop neighborhood health centers in the American South. In the second, I piloted a field-oriented, interdisciplinary, mid-career school of public health. My work leaves a lasting legacy, but the special challenges of innovating in the university setting also suggest how change agents must learn to adapt to institutional cultures while also influencing them.

Chapter 4

Transition

So many new opportunities in my career have involved being in the right place, with the right people, at the right time. And, I may add, being open to the upsetting of best-laid plans in order to seize unforeseen, sometimes life-changing, opportunities. Near the end of my consultancy for SFET, I was again ready to take some time off to reflect on and write about my work, while Udai and I were also completing what would become *Training for Development*. At a monthly meeting of all team leaders at the Foundation, Max, the leader for India's program in family planning, asked me to come to the University of North Carolina (UNC) in Chapel Hill for my sabbatical and so also get paid to help him build an interdisciplinary population center there. So, that is where we went, and where everything then changed for me and my family in major ways. The time in Chapel Hill turned out to be a launch pad for what grew into twelve years' work in academia, in two state universities in the US South and part time in a prominent Latin American one. In these settings, my eye for innovative work would blossom into what co-author David Kiel terms *intrapreneurship*, that is, developing new programs and organizational structures inside a large existing institution. This would also lead to the pinnacle (though also, in some ways, a nadir) of my academic institution-building stint, as dean of the new School of Public Health in the next state south, and chair of the Department of Preventive Medicine in the also-new medical school there. All of this while keeping one foot in international consulting, for better or worse.

Transitioning to an academic career was more than just a different venue: it represented a sea change in the route my life was taking. This chapter tells the story of that change and also illustrates the differences and the commonalities between the academic setting and other consulting and institution-building projects I had taken on in my career so far. Although it may seem liberal and forward-facing, academia is also conservative and resistant to change, the tenure system and power structures fraught with hierarchical thinking, although individual faculty members may not be.

At the public universities where I worked, I also found academia to be political in ways I did not anticipate, dependent as it is on the political winds of priorities and funding at the state, national, and even international levels. It is also political in the sense that one needs to understand history to recognize the motivations and dynamics of the individuals and groups involved. This is true anywhere, but again, academia has a patina of being free from these types of dynamics, of being the proverbial "ivory tower." So in the end, I did not remain in academia; I went back to international development projects. But while I was there, I gave it all I had and had a hand in the establishment of institutions that stand to this day, though not exactly as I envisioned them.

Institution Building in an Academic Setting with Favorable Tailwinds

I did not go to become an academic; I went to reflect on my experiences in India and to help an erstwhile colleague build a center for programs to counter the world-wide challenge of rapidly increasing population. Even though it did result in my earning a doctorate, teaching, and writing for publication – and thus "taking the plunge" – I now consider my time at UNC as a sort of hybrid between consultancy and academia. My time there was a stepping stone to the deanship at the next university, which became itself a setting for major institutional development.

World-wide political tailwinds combined the US inclination "to lead" with a growing alarm at exponentially increasing populations across the developing world. The political winds included President Johnson's "War on Poverty", which had been introduced in 1964. This "war" included an expansion of the federal government's role in education and health care, including programs to increase wellness and prevent poor health outcomes in the population, which is the very definition of public health. Among other initiatives, the legislation resulted in the creation of the Community Action Program, Volunteers in Service to America (VISTA) and the Peace Corps, with which I would also become involved.

The political winds were only vaguely salient to me at the time. I was not intending to stay more than the academic year before returning to India. The new Carolina Population Center seemed like the kind of initiative I had always consulted for. It was created to facilitate research, education, and – to me, most important – service devoted to understanding and solving population-related challenges around the world. I expected to approach this task as I always had, with an eye toward action and transdisciplinary collaboration.

However, conditions at the Population Center were different from what I had expected. Max and the experiences he brought from developing family-planning programs in India were no match for how the university did things. For one thing, the Medical School's "representative" took over the lead. The long-time head of Reproductive Medicine, he assumed a medical man would run this public health initiative, and he also had the most plausible access to more outside funding. Faculty from sociology contested his leadership, and with their heavy-weight expertise in demography they did eventually win out. But while I was there, the leader's focus was on the traditional academic research endeavors and engagement with other research entities, rather than a focus on prevention in the field and health in the context of broad social systems. "Action programs?" – they would best be "contracted out" to institutions already out in the field.

But, as always, opportunities for practical engagement and intrapreneurship did surface quickly, even within this frame. For example, as part of the US Agency for International Development (USAID) response to rampant global population growth, the new center at UNC was asked to be a technical and informational resource for programs developing overseas. Inquiries piled up from start-up population centers around the globe: directors wrote for advice on a range of issues, and the Center Director turned to me to develop and secure funding for what we called the International Network of University Population Programs, of which I became Project Director. Centers in fifteen universities on four continents joined the Network, and we met annually to discuss progress and general themes. After the first in the US, these meetings continued in Ghana, Iran, and Thailand during my time there.

In this flowering of academic activism, there was opportunity to consult internationally as well. One of the constituents of the Consortium for Developing Population Programs in international universities asked for significant technical assistance. A prominent Jesuit university in Latin America requested the Center's help with making "Population" part of medicine and public health as the first of five most pressing national needs (I would call it a "transcendent challenge") around which to organize a new graduate school. I led this project, traveling there part time, supported by my university position, with a senior colleague in residence there. We created an interdisciplinary program in population and migration. This project carried me through my next academic setting, and foreshadowed the type of consulting at a distance that I would continue in "retirement."

Also on behalf of the Center, I joined an ongoing consortium of US universities to conceptualize institution development, out of which came *A Guide to Institution Building for Leaders of Technical Assistance Projects* in 1971. From this experience I learned how little academics and university system leaders understood or looked for collaboration with others, which was at the core of my institution-development practice. So, when listing "external linkages" (key outside relationships) for the work they were gathered to conceptualize, the contributing universities did not even mention collegial (peer) relationships. I added that. Subsequently, with institutional leaders looking for help for coping with increasingly turbulent conditions across the world, two of us added "personal linkages" to the list as well.

At the Population Center, I was able to keep my hand in international work in other ways that were "blown" by the winds of President Johnson's policies. Two of us, the other a full professor, planned and directed the first program for Peace Corps volunteers to work on population programs overseas and then also the first international summer program for population workers from eleven countries. We added Ronnie to the twelve-week international program staff in the summer of 1967.

I also became a faculty member in the School of Public Health. To do all this work I was required to have a faculty appointment, even though I only planned a sabbatical year on campus, and my earlier sabbatical in a state hospital made Public Health the most plausible appointment. I got a second office and administrative support in the School. I offered courses in consultation practice and in interpersonal relations.

The course in consultation practice quickly attracted participants from all over the Health Division and across campus (co-author David included, whose doctoral committee chair I then also became). And as an offshoot from the course in interpersonal relations, the School began requiring all new students to join for a day's program for quick-starting relationships with one another. From this a new faculty position opened up, and I added a colleague to be based in the School of Nursing. For the School of Education, we offered programs in interpersonal relations in school systems across the state. I also joined the staffs of other interpersonal relations programs offered by the Department of Psychiatry in the Medical School.

It was probably the eager response to my courses that prompted the Dean to make the offer of a faculty position that changed everything, delivering the impetus to continue my education through master's and doctoral degrees, and plunging me into the very heart of an academic career. It made professional sense to pursue that path; even at the Population Center, having the higher degrees would make a difference in how I was received and viewed. For I had found there, when I spoke at staff meetings, that it was as if I were invisible. Ronnie resented this even more than I, and reminded me that it had also happened during Foundation team leaders' meetings in Delhi: "When you have all the experience in the room, only no doctoral degree!" She had urged me to at least sit in on graduate courses, but instead I had concentrated on completing the book. Now, only halfway through the first semester, my "academic" role was taking over.

Family Life

I must pause at this momentous moment in my march into academia, to comment upon what all of this meant for our family. For my decision to pursue higher degrees was a commitment to this location for the foreseeable future. Now that our children were older, the decision to come to, and now perhaps stay in, the American South was a bigger deal than our earlier decisions had been.

When we had first arrived, we thought that the last sabbatical had prepared us well for this one: we would rent a place, preferably furnished, buy an old car to get around in, put the children, now ten, eight, and nearly six, in public school. It seemed simple and "easy" to be in a college town being *paid* to be here – not much, but *paid*. But returning to India soonest was certainly highest in our children's hearts and minds, Maya's most urgently. "We hardly had time to say good-bye to our friends!" our eldest complained.

We arrived just ahead of the Fall semester. Weary from driving from the Minnesota grandparents in the old car we had bought there "just for the year," we checked into a motel in sight of the campus, and planned for Ronnie to find us a house to rent and register the children for school in the morning, while I clocked in at the Population Center. But – "Rent? There is "nothing to rent," the realtor announces; and just *four* houses available to buy. We buy the cheapest, at the asking price ("no bargaining *here*," we assume, and the realtor does not correct us). Only much later will we realize that the agent's short list of available houses had stopped at the railway line with the "Black town" on the other side. It did not occur to us that the town was so rigidly segregated, literally, into "Black" and "White" sides of the tracks.

Registering the girls for school went all right: school buses would collect them and take them to their two schools and bring them back at the end of the day. But not for Devadas: he will not turn six until mid-December, that is, after the cut-off for first grade. "But he has done first grade already; in India, school starts at five!" No, not possible: "Next year," was the answer. That, we could not settle for, so Ronnie drove to the Friends' school, which tested and accepted him, for a fee, and no transportation provided. Once that decision was made, that part of settling logistics went smoothly.

We assumed also that we would fit into the culture itself quite easily. We were, after all, American and European by birth. But what we were not prepared for was the deeply ingrained racial segregation, which we found utterly strange. Ronnie had not been prepared for it by living in Minnesota and Boston, nor even by her war-time service in Washington, DC. And I was certainly not prepared, even having been half-Jewish in Nazi Germany, an enemy alien in war-time England, a British "representative" active in European "unification," and then an ever-so-proper Brit in only just post-colonial India. Neither of us could help our children when they asked why so many Black people walked in the road, and why there were none behind the counters in the post office and shops. The girls' teachers found their names strange, asking "Are you sure?" as they took roll that first day. At break-times the girls moved easily between Black and white groups, and got rebuffed by each. A week or so later the girls brought school mates home, both white and Black ones, but no return invitations came.

When I wrote about this later in a book about parenting overseas, I described the strangeness of seeing Southern American racial segregation for the first time:

> Blacks – were they like low castes as we first saw them in India – on the street but similarly furtive, separate, as sweepers or on other menial duties? ... We learn they live in the city across the railway track where the realtor that first morning had drawn the line against possible housing for us; she probably carried no listing for there, certainly not for a white professor.... Almost every day the girls report horror stories of racial tension at school. Though it is twelve years since the US Supreme Court outlawed school segregation, the Town Council here instituted desegregation only the very year we arrived. Our Maya and Nandani neither knew what this separateness could possibly mean or foresee "problems" when they ignored it. And our own dark-brown South Indian Devadas... when

he did change to public school the next summer, his sisters took turns to protect him.

This was all puzzling and troubling, but not life-shattering for us personally when we first arrived – we were here only temporarily, after all – until the Dean of Public Health opened up this new academic world for me and us, and we could not turn it down. We decided to stay on: taking this step would make our family finances secure, permanently, in India too and everywhere else. But getting the necessary degrees would take three years, minimum. The children strongly objected. Leave-taking from friends for even this year was quite dreadful, so for indefinitely long – impossible! "We miss our friends!" Maya, our budding teenager, continued the most upset. "A visit home at least?" But we were too financially strapped for that, and my doctoral studies were going to make it worse.

Ronnie found paid work while I combined the shortest-possible studies for the master's and then the PhD with my full-time faculty position, and even added some paid consulting here and there to augment our finances. For courses to count towards a degree I had to take them at another university; Duke was the nearest, though it required that I buy my own car. I paid full fees there, certain that scholarships are only and quite properly for students with no funds. When, after the master's, Duke turned down my proposed doctoral dissertation based on my just-ended richly recorded institution-building experience in Hyderabad, I applied to the new program in policy development at the State University of New York at Buffalo, led by my former colleague in India, Warren Bennis, and for the next two years I flew there for one week every month and covered the fees by intermittent teaching.

With the decision to stay on for at least three more years, but really indefinitely, we now actually entered this university world, lived in it fully. Needs and possibilities that any of us had merely noticed in passing we now explored and acted on, I at the Center, in the School, and presently also in the Division of Health Sciences and in professional societies at large and the choral society, Ronnie more widely in the community – the India Association, the museum, the Inter-Faith Council. In short, we became our usual selves as we had not been since leaving India: outgoing, eager to engage with others, make friends, and "improve things." Now that "we belonged here" – that wonderful Indian phrase – we reached across the racial divide quite deliberately whenever opportunity offered. That there always are such openings in and outside the university was confirmed.

This was the time and place of sit-ins to end racial segregation, so we played our parts, adult and children. We joined churches, protest marches, the India Association, the inter-universities' evening graduate seminar, made new friends and joined the children in theirs; presently, we built a house to our design, and took on a mortgage.

Practice, Outreach, and Workforce Development: Neighborhood Health Centers

So, I worked to gain the education and credentials I needed to "belong" in academia, and we began to make our home there. But I remained in many ways an outsider, and as always, this status was both a benefit and a challenge. One benefit was that I could take on projects that might seem controversial. This benefited me because I liked working on change, which is often viewed as controversial – but necessary – to the institution being changed.

For reasons that I came to appreciate only later, President Johnson's "War on Poverty" legislation brought me to the attention of top administrators of the Medical School and the university's health division. I was asked to help create new federally funded Neighborhood Health Centers, mostly in Black neighborhoods, and direct the program for training new health workers for these Centers. This grew later to include my developing an annual summer remedial program in English and Math for health workers otherwise ready to enter programs for professional degrees to further their careers and increase – and diversify racially – the population health workforce. I recruited Ronnie to join this effort and asked colleagues around the country to find another trainer, preferably an African-American, and succeeded, via an NTL Institute friend in Boston: Walter was a large, jovial, practical man and we became close colleagues and friends. Walter became the director and Ronnie resumed her writing interests in and about India.

Following from these activities, the Vice Chancellor of Health Sciences asked me what I thought about starting a degree-granting or certification program at the School of Public Health for practicing health workers. Many in the public health workforce were Black, and many had been self-educated or learned on the job – small wonder, given the cost and limited accessibility of post-secondary training for people of color, especially from low-income families. The idea had been raised at a faculty meeting but not discussed: neighborhood health centers were training health workers in a set of three intensive programs, six months each. What would happen if the School of Public Health carefully selected some of these workers and "leapfrogged" them up the educational ladder, admitting them to a two-year program of study, bypassing the bachelor's degree? He noted that he thought the Ford Foundation would be glad to support such a program. Within a couple of weeks, we had a committee taking up the possibilities of setting up such a program for experienced neighborhood health center workers, while at the same time expanding efforts to recruit Black students through the existing traditional channels.

Most gratifying to me as a consultant was the UNC President's leadership of this highly counter-cultural development and how I was supported while on a US campus organized on the usual disciplinary lines. Viewed from another perspective, these projects – the neighborhood health centers, programs for training Black practitioners, overseas development along progressive, interdisciplinary lines – all pointed to how, when this tradition-laden state university had to incorporate politically sensitive developments, an "outsider" could usefully take the lead but could also be disclaimed for not knowing any better. What could be better for leaders at the top than having a presentable and capable *outsider* lead some of President Johnson's "War on Poverty" programs and get the federal funds and national publicity for them, and then also be able to disown him if questioned by conservative legislators? So, *this* outsider was just what the university needed: British, plausibly senior, experienced, personally agreeable enough... and also dispensable if need be.

Indeed, those eight years in the late 1960s and early '70s stand out in my memory for the eagerness and support that accompanied the end of the post-world-war years of university expansion and the national legislation and funding that inclined administrators to support plausible new developments. And then, quite abruptly, my department was cut back and several faculty members, including me, were told to search for other employment. A sharp reduction in state funding folded my UNC department back into Epidemiology, and my tenure appointment came to an abrupt end. Here I was, back looking for a job and a living, even with a PhD! And just then I was recommended to head up a new school of public health in the university in the next state south. And so we moved again.

"Small is Beautiful" and Also Promising in the "Other Carolina"

In its variety and ever-increasing opportunities for professional growth, my work at UNC, locally known as "Carolina," profited pretty consistently by steady tailwinds. That condition would suddenly change in my second university, just one state south, also known locally as "Carolina," which I joined to head one major new institution and help start a second. The north "Carolina" had been founded in the late eighteenth century and the south "Carolina" in the early nineteenth, so both were steeped in tradition.

When the South Carolina Legislature decided that there should be new schools of medicine and of public health established at the State University, Racine Brown, Deputy Commissioner for Mental Health, recommended that I be hired as dean for the new School of Public Health and Chair of Preventive Medicine in the new medical school. Racine Brown was one of the confrères I would come to consider an "alter ego," a long-time professional colleague and family friend, and well respected in state and professional circles.

The long-serving President of the University was a man after my own heart. He had been educated in engineering at MIT and was known for innovative methods and ideas based in practical applications. The flipside of his personality, not so unlike my own, was that sometimes he grew impatient with "the way things had always been done" and ruffled feathers, by making quick (some would say impulsive) decisions to hire individuals he thought could help build the university he wanted Carolina to be.

So Ronnie and I sold our beautiful house "up north," saw the children through leaving their friends and schools – again! – and bought a home. But before we could even move in, this president so central to my plans for the new endeavor left his post, and a new one was named from the inside. It is my understanding now that the other president's leaving had nothing to do with adding the new Division of Health Affairs, being more due to a scandal in athletics not of his making and, more generally, the changes in political winds blowing nationally. That I had been brought in from outside the normal channels of academic hiring was just the latest example of his bypassing existing structures and procedures. In any event, he was out and replaced in the presidency by the former provost. So, when I arrived, I was welcomed by, and set to report to, the recently appointed and also innovatively inclined Vice-President for Health Sciences –recruited from the Medical University in neighboring Charleston, but originally from New Zealand – and to the Provost who was "from the North," so also both outsiders, like me!

On arrival I did not even meet the new president or learn how he viewed the decision to start the School of Public Health along with the new medical school. What I grew to understand came from Racine, whom I then asked to meet weekly with me and the faculty in the new school, both as my best professional advisor overall and my best link to the state agencies.

I found out that the opening of these two new schools was somewhat of a bone of contention between diverse factions in state government and the University and the medical profession. The University, much more so than the Northern Carolina, was a conservative bastion. Although its first Black students had matriculated in 1963, it was still threatened with the loss of federal funds for continuing racial discrimination. The President and the board of trustees had been trying to modernize and upgrade and, following national trends, they continued to promote increasing research funding at the University and expanding graduate education. Medical groups pressed for meeting the state's real need for improved health services in rural areas. There was already a medical school on the coast in Charleston, which made starting a new one controversial, but the existing one was considered a school for specialists, while the state needed family practitioners who understood the larger social factors in population health. So, when the US Veterans Affairs Administration offered $25 million grants to each of several states to add new medical schools, the state applied and was accepted. Advocates urged the Legislature to add a school of public health to develop and expand the public health staff already working in the field.

More cues to what I was getting myself into came from the state legislature's conditions for approving and funding the new schools: "at least cost" was of the topmost importance. So, the new medical school would be housed in the Veterans Affairs Building off-campus and, like the new School of Public Health, use the existing sciences departments on campus for all science requirements. In other words, there was no new laboratory space allotted, and no new departments were created, with the exception of Epidemiology, to be located in the School of Public Health. Personally, I prided myself on being able to do things without a lot of resources, and this condition was not a red flag for me (although perhaps it should have been, for reasons I will explore below).

Towards a Custom-built Frame for the New School of Public Health

I quickly developed a very active relationship with the Provost: we met twice or more per week and soon became personal friends. I proposed several suggestions to meet the Legislature's conditions for minimal funding. One, the faculty who had come with me would be members of their several disciplinary departments across campus, not the new School of Public Health. We would have only one bona fide department, Epidemiology, which would serve for both medicine and public health. Public health funds would cover their salaries as well as the costs of public health students taking the required courses in statistics, administration, and environmental studies, in those several departments. So, the only faculty members actually appointed to the School of Public Health would be me, the full-time director of fieldwork, and the epidemiologist(s) I still needed to recruit.

Beyond the Legislature's conditions, I based my proposal for the structure of the School on my understanding of what the former president had wanted. Above all, the School needed to make a difference to health care in the state as early as possible. This overarching aim required it to be practical and task-oriented, with close ties to state government, even jointly planned with state service agencies, as well as private and professional ones. It had to be an educational resource, having degree programs, certainly, but attentive to the needs of policy makers and administrators, as well as the needs of the public health workforce for flexible and practical educational programs. Finally, it had to be frugal and relatively small to stay within the budget parameters I understood to be in force.

I did my best to engage internal and external stakeholders in this process. The Provost readily approved my plans, and I met the deans and department chairs he suggested and also the heads of major state agencies. We created planning and advisory groups for each program (Health Education, Public Health Nursing) and for institution development, and two School-wide. These groups were made up of faculty members as well as representatives from the state legislature and other state agencies. Over the first several months, drawing on this local advice, many decisions were made and implemented:

- Admission into degree programs would be focused on students who had some work experience and also held positions in health agencies; most would combine work with study
- Public health practice would be included as a continuing component in all degree programs
- Degree programs would be designed to be of minimal length, to be followed up with continuing education programs as needed in various parts of the state
- Students would receive instruction in the basic public health disciplines: epidemiology/biostatistics, health education,

public health nursing, public health administration, and environmental health, graduating when they had amassed the requisite credits and had supervised field experiences
- Health planning and service agency staff members would be included in the teaching faculty and as mentors
- Departments that sponsored faculty members to offer courses or take on other duties in public health would be compensated with funds from the School.

Getting buy-in from department heads was not so difficult because of faculty interest, the support of the Provost, and the fact that on campus the extra funds were open to flexible use.

In terms of the founding faculty group, those most closely involved in the development of the School, three of the five colleagues who came with me from UNC joined departments in their own disciplines on campus. The long-time science faculty member recruited from the Biology Department on campus actually earned tenure there while continuing also in the School of Public Health. The fifth new faculty member, also from North Carolina but not UNC, became the School's full-time director of fieldwork. From elsewhere I recruited a physician administrator to combine appointments in Public Health and Preventive Medicine, "my" two schools. The yawning gap was in Epidemiology, and my attempts to fill it failed again and again over the years and threatened the School's full accreditation in its third year. If there were a next time, I resolved, I would engage a well-regarded and connected epidemiologist to find that essential senior colleague.

With the Provost's agreement, I made the rounds of state agencies and gave them first claim for places in the School's programs, to enhance the skills of their field staffs, including many Black workers, who had not had much chance for advanced training. They welcomed my highlighting the full-time faculty-supervised fieldwork and the special programs in interpersonal and collaborative relations the new School would offer. All agency heads expressed great satisfaction with this personal contact, and had staff ready to propose for the first program to start immediately. Of the thirty accepted into the first class, seventeen were Black. The Provost backed our accepting applicants with test scores even a little below the usual cut-off, on condition that their first-semester grades warranted their continuing. They all did; in fact, the marginal applicants did better than most who scored just above the minimal score. I also met the University's board of trustees to tell them about the new school.

Other than Epidemiology, for which I had still to find a chairperson, the programs were well staffed. David Kiel (co-author) was Director of Information and Evaluation, a half-time administrative job with a faculty appointment in Community and Clinical Psychology. The Director of Public Health Practice would design and carry out field placements and associated learning activities in each discipline. In a whirlwind of preparation, the core team, working with partners across the School and state, made ready to open the doors to students in a mere couple of months.

The first semester ended, and all public health students passed. Future programs filled readily. That winter, the question of off-shore drilling for oil was raised in the state, and I proposed, organized, and partly funded a long weekend meeting for about thirty faculty together with legislators and media representatives to discuss ways to address this controversial issue. The event was full. Discussion narrowed to the very practical issue of how impossible the piled-up oil pipes would be to hide on the crowded and major income-producing beaches. Publicity was wide, all strongly favoring holding similar programs to bring broad groups of stakeholders together to discuss timely issues of importance to the state.

So "Thinktimes" were born and became an annually recurring innovative public service initiative with the goal of building connections to the state government and addressing challenges faced by the state. They incorporated Search Conference methods later further developed in the US by Dick and Emily Axelrod and Marvin Weisbord, who became famous in our field for popularizing "large group interventions." Our "planning community" came to include researchers from major South Carolina academic institutions, policy makers from the state legislature and state agencies, national and state advisory group leaders, administrators, and others. Inclusion in these programs depended on whether an individual had some capacity to do something about the challenge, some expertise to bring to the discussion, and funding for his or her participation. In the next three years these multi-day conferences tackled issues with implications for healthy aging, rural health services, environmental health issues, and health measurement. Each was associated with one of the School's programs and led to months of committee work that resulted in proposals related to policy formation and interagency coordination, education initiatives, and ways to involve those directly affected by the challenge (coastal residents, the elderly, rural citizens, and others).

So, with that first Thinktime on "Public Health Implications of Continental Shelf Developments in South Carolina" (oil-drilling), the vision of a practice- and field-oriented School was taking form. Even as an old-tradition professor had stepped in as president of the University, all looked well set to start on the ground with a strong presence in this area of engagement with the practical issues of the state. However, in mid-semester the President phoned, the first direct contact we have had: "Several trustees have complained about public health students interviewing workers at the gate of the textile mill, and about others taking water samples to test for poisons in the river used for drinking water." I took note and shared the message with faculty, but nothing more: *of course* our mid-career students knew where to look and go for live issues to study for their fieldwork. These projects continued as courteously as possible.

Although efforts to create a practice- and field-oriented School of Public Health seemed to irk the new President (and, apparently, those trustees), the Thinktimes in particular were extremely well-received in the state and were associated with identifiable changes in policy and practice. Large amounts of work went into these events and the months-long planning and implementation that grew out of them, and the outcomes were remarkable. For example, a Thinktime on "Healthy Aging" was held in the Spring of 1975, planned in collaboration with the chairs of the Legislative Committee on Aging and the South Carolina Commission on Aging. It was chaired by the then-governor of the state and included representatives of ten public and private agencies, four leading universities and a technical college, geriatrician leaders from South Carolina, and a geriatric consultant from the United Kingdom, where comprehensive services for the aging had been developed in which local citizens gave as well as received services. That Thinktime influenced the development and passage of the 1976 Retirement and Pre-Retirement Advisory Council Act, creating a panel to advise the state directors of the Retirement System and the State Personnel Division on matters relating to retirement and preretirement programs and policies. The bill itself was informed by research done by a School of Public Health student, which recommended life-span education and activities around services and planning, deinstitutionalizing and housing, and transportation.

With the Vice-President for Health Affairs preoccupied with finding a dean for the Medical School, I readily relied more and more on the Provost for top-level support. We continued to meet frequently, both prearranged and spontaneously, on and off campus. When the state legislature voted severe budget cuts the following summer, he reflected that with the School's quick start and the state agencies' support, I may well have "saved the School."

Headwinds and Snags: The School of Public Health Organizational Structure versus Traditional Structures

The successes of the School and its rapid launch in the first few years were not the whole story, however. It was difficult to recruit a chair of Epidemiology, and this in turn created a problem in recruiting the core faculty in that department. On top of that, having faculty housed across campus actually was challenging in different ways. One difficulty came from that uniquely academic convention, the tenure track. The structure of tenure in academia is different from any structure I had encountered in my earlier consulting roles. Faculty are under intense pressure to earn tenure; departments confer it based on faculty's contributions to the discipline in the form of teaching, research, and service, but these elements are not always weighted evenly, and the decisions can seem arbitrary, particularly to jointly appointed faculty who must answer to two department chairs and two sets of expectations. When Biology voted to give one of the public health professors tenure, I interpreted that as a decisive advance, but it remained singular.

So my insistence from the very beginning that tenure be in disciplinary departments had become a major source of conflict and disagreement with peer deans and perhaps among university leaders, and administrators resented the complications of keeping track of public health funding. The departments appreciated the funds coming from public health for some of their faculty's time and for students taking classes in their departments, but they did not appreciate their faculty having "dual loyalties." Some of the faculty members also had more of a teaching load than either the School or their home department realized, and were anxious about how public health participation would affect their tenure prospects in their home departments. These situations were sometimes hidden from me, and I did not know enough at first to anticipate them or meet early with the chairs or other deans to forestall difficulties.

In another issue related, perhaps, to perception of the School, the two African-American faculty members I had recruited and placed just like the others in the departments of their disciplines were a living challenge to the long exclusion of Blacks. The idea that the School was a hot bed of radicalism or at least "difference" may have been furthered when a tall, assertive, incisive, and astute Black man from a medical college in Philadelphia, trained in the cool and distant Tavistock style of group leadership, replaced an equally perspicacious but quiet, affable, self-effacing (and also Black) man, as head of the Public Health Education group. The new faculty member wore a panther-claw necklace, well before it was a symbol of mainstream superhero status. As much to the point, perhaps, almost none of us in the central core had a real academic pedigree, and I myself was a newly minted PhD, although an unusually experienced one.

The greatest formal institutional weakness, though, continued to be my inability to recruit a prominent epidemiologist to direct and develop that core discipline across Health Affairs. Two promising candidates visited but decided against joining because starting from scratch, uncertain finances, and the unsettling presidency change were "too discouraging." The very best possibility came and passed: a prominent husband–wife pair of physicians, she for Medical School dean, he to chair Epidemiology. But the medical society found a woman outsider doubly unacceptable as dean. And with that prize opportunity, we also lost a possible foundation grant which, besides offering some additional and flexible funds to the School of Public Health, would surely have helped validate its new and so unconventional arrangements in the university at large.

There were also wide-ranging ways that the School, with its mission to help solve local health problems, rustled feathers in high places. In the example, described above, of students surveying at the doors of the textile mill, one was actually employed by the textile workers union and was doing a master's-level project to explore whether companies were warned (illegally) before state cotton-dust inspections. The surveys handed out at the door were to test this hypothesis. The company called the chief lobbyist for the textile companies, the chief lobbyist called the President of the University, and he called me. There were no school funds allocated to support this project, so we were technically off the hook in terms of formal policy violation, and the effort was protected by freedom-of-speech rules, but incidents like this raised eyebrows.

The School's new ways continued to offend many on campus, and in the manner of true Southern gentility, these resentments remained unvoiced and unspecific. I now recognize that our style did not fit well with the past-oriented, intimate, only lightly rebellious ethos of the town, the region, and the time. Yet I was convinced that only with an innovative design, such as we had developed, could the field- and action-oriented school survive and thrive in the academically oriented university.

I took the need to "face outward" to heart, in all of my roles, perhaps to model a cosmopolitan rather than purely local perspective. Along with being dean, I was also head of the Preventive Medicine Department in the School of Medicine. I also headed the new International Association of Applied Behavioral Science. I continued my work with the Jesuit university in Latin America, helping build an interdisciplinary graduate school. At my previous university, I had negotiated leave funds designated for action-oriented faculty. Now, such international contract work only further marked me as an "outsider," and not in any good way. Adversaries in high places and perhaps in the core group may have criticized me for "not minding the store," where a lot of attention and hand-holding were needed. Moreover, when I was away in South America or on another international commitment, that showed again how *other* I really was.

Looking back now, I could and should have done more to avoid such absences. They also added to the impression that I was "always busy," too busy for campus stakeholders. That, I learnt later, contributed to keeping dissatisfactions smoldering. I gave too little importance to meeting deans and faculty on campus and tuning into their agenda, including the unvoiced dissatisfactions and unspecified unease. Although Ronnie and I had made several personal connections, they did not give us early warnings.

A final way I was "too busy" and faced away from my role as dean was in continuing to head the required public health course in interpersonal and group relations. This did connect me with the teaching values of the institution, but it also took a lot of time, committing me to six set hours a week plus more for preparation, reviewing written work, and counseling.

Letting Go

I have not described at length my role or activities in the new medical school. The Vice-President for Health Affairs had left (and not been replaced) not long after I had first arrived. Now, only a few years in, the School of Medicine had gone through five deans coming and going in my time as chair of Preventive Medicine. A fellow chair drew invidious comparison with the "rapidly developing" School of Public Health and suggested I take on the Medical School as well! I let that idea pass, but my resigning the chairmanship in the Medical School would probably have been a better response. I did that only when the next several dean candidates insisted on having *all* teaching of medical students done *within their school*, preventive medicine and epidemiology included, "as all medical schools do," no matter what the Legislature required. And even then I failed to depart "clean" from the Medical School but turned my chair and office over to the physician I had recruited to direct administration in the School of Public Health, and retained the faculty appointment.

Back at the School of Public Health, programs were in full swing, state agencies were well satisfied, and provisional accreditation was expected, only three years after launching this massive effort. Yet the President concluded that the School needed "to be reconceptualized" and rather than speak to me directly, he asked the Provost to tell me this. Were they worried the School would not be accredited because of its untraditional structure and shoestring budget, and thus bring shame upon them? Were they worried that it *would* be accredited, thus institutionalizing this structure that did not support their "traditional values"? I did not know. I was asked to step down as dean, and, later, essentially erased from the official history of the School as it appears on the current website. My replacement was the one long-time Carolina faculty member from the Biology Department on campus whom I had recruited into the School to chair Environmental Sciences. She was the one who earned tenure during my deanship and went on to have a long, illustrious career of leadership at the School and University. I stayed as Professor of Public Health Administration, but not for long. After a three-month sabbatical, I started working in Indonesia, first on unpaid leave, and then I freed my tenured position. All faculty who had come with me also left when I did.

Perhaps in the exuberance of freeing themselves from foreign influence, the University and the state foreswore their previous commitment to frugality and committed themselves to investing mightily in a new school along more traditional lines. Under new leadership over the next several years, the School got its own building on campus, established disciplinary departments, and received a substantial endowment. It became, in fact, more like other schools, except that it continued to have Epidemiology and fieldwork at the core of its degree programs, which is something that the accrediting association now requires of schools of public health.

Interestingly, the next new school on campus, for environmental studies, led by the husband of my successor in Public Health, developed outreach features similar to those we developed at the School of Public Health when it was new. Did we lose the battle but win the war? In a sense the answer is "yes" in terms of the state's increased financial commitment to public health graduate education, but certainly the answer is "no" for adopting a radical model of public health schooling in terms of orientation to the field in South Carolina. Then again, the answer may have been "yes" in demonstrating a compelling model of interdisciplinary institutional development that influenced the development of other institutions on campus.

Looking Back, Learning Forward

The departure of the innovative president who had hired me essentially pulled the rug out from under my endeavors at the very beginning. After twelve years of rapid growth and change under his leadership, and the turning of political winds both nationally and in the state, the time had come for a return to more traditional ways of doing things. But by the time I recognized this, my family and I had moved there; drawing back was no longer practical, and hope never quite dies. Perhaps what I tried to institute was too much innovation from outside "to take" in the deeply embedded traditional culture of this old university, and in a conservative state. After a time, my outsider status became less a protection and perhaps more a symbol of the imposition of "alien" ways and approaches.

But much indeed went right, even so. With its novel highly collaborative design of the advanced degree programs, the School won provisional accreditation within a couple of years. By the end of its second year, eighty students were enrolled and twenty-two master's degrees had been awarded. The opportunity to get a Master's in Public Health while working proved attractive to those working in health. Every part of the state had been served by degree granting, continuing education, or service project programs.

The faculty who came with me or were recruited on campus and from outside were competent and effective and made an appropriate team, as their subsequent careers confirmed. Two of the six who left with me went straight into directing neighborhood health centers, one became state director of Public Health Nursing, and the other became head of continuing education and faculty development in a unit of North Carolina's Area Health Education System.

For me personally and professionally, several learnings have proved permanently significant. The biggest overall and basically most important learning, something I did not do sufficiently in "the second Carolina," was to test for, and (ideally) ensure enough support for, the proposed development. This lesson had informed me before in more familiar settings; academia was different enough that it proved ultimately impossible. But the pounding home of this lesson served me well for exploring the very next setting of my career, as we shall see. To end this chapter, I will suggest some lessons learned from this important "detour" into academic culture and the American South.

My experience suggests that in the most staid and confirmed traditional, hierarchical, discipline-organized universities, there are faculty members ready to join fresh efforts to collaborate more and develop structural changes to support this. These may be identified by some patient circumspection and testing of possibilities for collaboration. This holds also for developments across long and deep racial divides that put continued local funding at risk.

Even up-hill efforts that falter or "fail" as originally structured leave two kinds of advantages for the next change effort: some part(s) of "what worked" are adopted somewhere on campus (and the University as a whole did stay more actively connected with several state agencies, the Legislature, and the governor's office); and the experiences with having tried create a better-informed readiness to try again.

As we have seen, in my three years as dean, several new ways of organizing and doing things did take root in the University at large: the next new school to be developed, the School for Environmental Sciences, was also interdisciplinary and reached across the campus. The launching of this school may be a case in how a different way of starting an initiative affects its success: the environmental school grew from existing strengths in biology and marine sciences, while public health was seen as being imposed from outside and headed by outsiders. Environmental science had broad-based support; the School of Public Health had lost its one major champion when the President left. Although he left for other reasons, it may be that insiders were tired of "exciting, new" initiatives that did not look like traditional South Carolina values. In this situation, "shooting the messenger" may have paved the way for "getting the message."

Understanding the Requirements of Different Engagements

One difference between my two major academic stints was that I was hired at the North Carolina as a consultant to help develop a new program. At South Carolina, I was there to build the institution from the ground up. This difference in role had implications for where I could or should have directed my energy as founding dean. In a larger sense, it has implications for consultants transitioning to new projects and considering what may be required.

At UNC, especially during my three years of doctoral studies on top of my full-time teaching position, I worked *all the time*. At USC, too: the amount of work to take an idea and develop it into an institution made up of five degree-granting departments and several active programs of service to the state, to build institutional relationships, administer budgets and contracts, create and manage a complicated system of non-traditional students with a non-traditional structure, all on a shoestring budget and without a strong champion in leadership – I am exhausted to look back on it now! But unlike the first, I was in charge at the second university. I was building an institution rather than consulting for one. I should never have lost sight of that larger fact, but with that weighty task I was not able to attend to some of the individuals involved as much as I perhaps should have.

At South Carolina, even with the original President who hired me gone, I still assumed, wrongly, that the University was generally acquainted with and favored the establishment of the two new professional schools, and also with the funding conditions the Legislature had set. So, assuming support, I limited my early steps to specific practical ones, listed above: establishing the new core courses, finding potential public health faculty on campus to augment the faculty I brought, placing new colleagues from outside in their disciplinary departments, and channeling public health funds accordingly. While I am proud of the incredible amount we did accomplish, I needed to give more time to building a supportive climate within the institution for the School, and within the collaborating departments and colleges for the public health mission.

In this regard, particularly given the heavy hand of tradition which I meant to change, I needed to spend much more time moving about on campus, to support the public health faculty scattered across campus in their various disciplinary departments. But also, importantly, in un-programmed time with fellow deans and chairs, I needed to tune into *their* agenda and join and support them, get to know them personally, and become known by them. In short, I should have *become (more like) one of them*. A consultant can remain an outsider, but an institution-builder must eventually be seen as part of the institution. My getting seen as eagerly listening and tuning into priorities on campus could perhaps have warmed my reception there and encouraged the Provost to continue his support. Failing that, I myself may have shortchanged, perhaps even got in the way of, giving the counter-cultural developments a fairer chance.

Even aside from all of the academic machinations involved, heading any brand-new institution or team called for allocating my time very differently from being a consultant (or professor). As always, I wanted to "do it all," and freeing that time meant foregoing other activities – so, which? By far the most time-consuming was my continuing to head the required public health course in interpersonal and group relations. Although it did mark me well as a fellow academician and so aligned me with campus values, I persisted with it mostly because it kept me firmly anchored in my profession. This issue had arisen in the SFET initiative, when I should have eased up on my individual role when I became team leader. In both cases, but especially here, the leadership position was fraught with uncertainties and likely conflict, which I tried to avoid by anchoring myself in what I loved to do. Needs for such anchoring are important to recognize but also need to be met at much lower cost.

For even more compelling reasons, I could have reduced and even cut out the international consulting work I had brought with me from before. Elsewhere, such international and contract work might well have been prized, but here it confirmed me as different and exposed me to the charge of neglecting my primary duties. Few as they were and ever-fewer as they became, external responsibilities confirmed me as outsider when fitting in was much more important. That I simply persisted with these activities I now attribute most to my long-established ways of confronting change – *any major change*: confident that all will be well even along with everything else. Continuing to recognize and value my personal dispositions but also taking them into better account overall would now be high on my agenda, as my work in the next setting will show.

So, the task was heavy, I was over-extended and not attentive to some fundamental relationships in this setting. But appearing not to have any time for others is a risk even when the task is not so heavy, because most jobs will expand to fill the space available. I now encourage colleagues to warn me when I "look always too busy" to listen to their concerns or suggestions or to engage with their agenda. Identifying regular time(s) for being with others and open to others' agendas is clearly most urgent for improving my practice.

In general, it may be good for change agents to take some time to reflect about the differences between the role and setting of the new assignment and the previous one, and explicitly to determine what can be carried over and what should change. Sometimes the distinction is between two entirely different consultancies; other times, it's different roles within the same project. It requires, among other things, analyzing what the organization says it needs and what it *values*, explicitly or otherwise.

So, from my faculty position at South Carolina I put one foot in Indonesia, and then launched wholeheartedly to that multi-island nation. There I was to go next, to work with the Health Ministry to develop and then implement a plan to decentralize health services, reflecting local needs and cultural differences, and breaking down barriers left over from Dutch colonial rule.

CHAPTER 5

Indonesia: Creating a Health System That Serves the Whole Country

> "Unless we treasure our differences, we will never achieve interdependence.... It is difference that makes interdependence possible, but we have difficulty valuing it because of the speed with which we turn it into inequality.... [S]ustained attention to diversity and interdependence may offer a different clarity of vision, one that is sensitive to ecological complexity, to the multiple rather than the singular."
>
> Mary Catherine Bateson, *Composing a Life*
> (New York: Penguin, 1990), pp.104–5, 166

Introduction and Background

In early 1981 a US agency inquired if I could come help Indonesia spread and enhance public health services throughout the country, to ensure that the outer islands, in particular, had sufficient, modern health services and professionals to manage them. Twenty years into its angrily achieved independence, this so-spread-out, huge, old–young nation had just legislated for this. The legislation was provoked by the current state of affairs, in which most of the 3,000-plus islands had only limited services or no services at all. The Dutch had ruled their spice empire at minimal cost, without establishing universities (there were perhaps 100 college graduates in the whole country at decolonization in the 1950s), and without consideration beyond the largest islands, particularly Java, other than to extract spices. Indonesia had had a bloody civil war that included the massacre of Communist Party members and the Chinese minority in 1965. In the context, then, the development of its public health system could be seen as reparations and restorative justice for colonized and war-torn peoples, as well as a bulwark against communist encroachment.

The US Agency for International Development (USAID) had arrived, supporting efforts to nationalize services, increase educational capacity for doing so, and help create structures to sustain their widely dispersed administration. They brought me in to help implement that structural development for public health services.

As I understood the current health system and government in general, they were particularly ill-suited for such a geographically huge country. Not only were services lacking on the far-flung islands, but *everything* related to its administration was centered in Jakarta. Thus, decisions about staffing, training, promotion, and so on were made in Jakarta, based on traditional criteria of seniority and credentials, with no sense of what the provinces needed in regard to tasks or skills or suitable organization; similarly, budgets and priority services were "one size fits all," determined at the Ministry. With leadership dominated by and restricted to physicians, its focus was on classic medical treatment and individual care, with no sense of preventing disease, or targeting services to rural populations, or recognizing the wide cultural differences between islands separated by hundreds and even thousands of miles of ocean.

Coming straight from my dire experience of flagging support for creating a collaborative and practice-oriented school of public health in academia, I arrived determined to test whether there would be system support here for "decentralization." The one-year contract on offer was one thing that underscored my doubts. Another was that the Ministry of Health had already established residential training centers on the big islands, as if multiplying health workers to standard professional specifications were the essence of sound decentralization. They and I also had very different views of placing physicians in all supervisory and managerial roles, as Indonesian law required. If, as I feared, support for my understanding of how best to develop the national services was indeed lacking, I would not sign on for this work and would simply return to my tenured professorship in the US.

I was no longer the same young consultant who trusted that funders and organizational leaders knew what they wanted, and would only later find out that what they truly wanted (or needed) was much more complex and even quite different. At Aloka, I had set my own conditions for taking the directorship and gained more understanding of what a true, rooted intervention required. At SFET I had learned the hard way how to use the outsider's perspective to develop meaningful change, and now, on leave from my faculty position at the University of South Carolina, I came with fresh knowledge of what I could be up against *going in*.

I knew, for one thing, that one year was not enough time to create what they needed. Although the infrastructure already in place was impressive considering where they had come from, the decentralization they talked about required much more than massive training from the center out to "expand" what existed centrally and make it envelop all. It would mean changing the norms and structures throughout, and building service capacity and organizations that also suited the widely varying local conditions. I did not know yet what the new structures would look like, but I knew this was a true institution-building project, requiring developments that would take root in those "outer islands," be nurtured to grow and thrive *there*, and *also* join together as a national service with the Ministry at the center.

I worried too about the law that all supervisory and managerial staff would continue to be physicians. That requirement alone would make adding more staff extremely slow. Also, I had just left a position where the difference between a physician's focus on individuals and a public health professional's focus on population health had become painfully clear, not to mention the sense that physicians considered their work higher on the hierarchical ladder. In my experience, medical doctors started out focused on treating sick individuals instead of improving the health of whole populations and designing and managing institutions for that. This gets us back to the point that the training program here had to do more than share expertise: it had also to address the ways that managers and leaders think, and the challenges that might come from the diversity of cultures on these far-apart islands. This seemed to me so obvious that I questioned whether the VIPs thought decentralization would be possible at all.

But why not go and see? My erstwhile close public health colleagues were already dispersed from South Carolina, both our girls were married, and Devadas was in student housing to finish his degree. I was confident that I would not take the position if I did not think I could do it, and I had the safety net of my tenured appointment. Indonesia had personal attractions too. We had *liked* the Indonesians who came to Aloka, and stayed in touch with several and their organizations. We had a "feel" for how they thought and worked, from their years in the student armies and the struggle for independence, then through the years of Jakarta's pulling out the tiny number of credible candidates countrywide to create the new government in Jakarta while royal traditions continued to dominate Java. One Alokan who had also become faculty was now on the national Planning Commission, others headed the trade union federation and parts of the prominent cooperative movement, others directed the Moslem part of the Ministry of Religions, and up to twenty alumni still met regularly, more than two decades since Aloka. Indonesians figured largely in Ronnie's and my sense of the Aloka successes. Indeed, only the world-wide financial crisis in Aloka's third year had stopped our locating an urban program there.

So Ronnie and I went, and the one year turned into over six, with our ideas setting the conditions for the program. During those years we were able to challenge the focus on "exporting" expertise from Jakarta. I brought together an international team of full-time senior consultants and technical (specialty) consultants on call, and we realized success and development beyond all expectations.

Testing for and Finding Commitment to an Inclusive Approach

The primary concern on arrival was to check whether the Ministry would really back a development strategy other than the outer islands copying how things were currently done centrally, and to encourage instead developing the services *in each* that also drew upon and reflected the cultures, challenges, and priorities there. That would need the active participation of public health nurses, health educators and communicators, epidemiologists, and other practitioners, as well as the well-credentialed physicians the Ministry envisioned, and others who understood the local economies, histories, religions, and physical environments. All were stakeholders who needed to work together but for whom the very idea that they were all part of one nation was as yet fresh and unfamiliar. The Dutch had only recently left; after five years of Japanese occupation during the War had come renewed Dutch attempts to re-establish sovereignty, followed by the internal turmoil from gaining independence and creating a central government in Jakarta. It has been said that the post-war era was one of "wasting a lot of time... rather than training administrators, workers and doctors... and the illiteracy rate was 93%" (Ensor, 1979: 197). So even on the four larger outer islands, services varied from none to some, with none at all for the thousands of small but inhabited islands scattered over 3,000 miles of ocean.

The first person I met after completing the usual formalities at USAID was the head of Pusdiklat, the training unit of the Indonesian Ministry of Health, Pa Ibu. Unlike elsewhere, where training is usually a lowly unit in the organization, here the organization as a whole was eager for this work to begin, and Pa had been chosen to lead this major development. Pa was an MD, but known for taking larger action. We developed a close personal relationship from the very start. As he began to describe the new legislation and the ways ahead, I took the occasion to talk about several conditions that my experience told me would be necessary for success:

- We needed a flexible process of working, with provincial stakeholders and the Ministry acting jointly and on equal

terms; this meant multi-directional communications and somehow overcoming hierarchical norms
- We would need to hire very experienced organizational development consultants, who understood management, population health, and inclusive collaboration
- The consultants should come with their families and live, work, and be readily available on one outer island at a time, for as long as it would take to root suitable health services there
- Only I, the team leader, would work in Jakarta with the Ministry and travel to hold the whole effort together, to model the new decentralized national system we wished to engender
- Any additional training would best be done in short full-time programs offered to everyone involved in the effort, and organized such that all felt heard and recognized as full partners in the system. Residential training centers and funds already allocated for running full-time programs on the four largest outer islands and in all Java provinces could be well used for this.

I offered to find up to four experienced OD consultants to pry loose for full-time work on these terms, and also specialist faculty members to come as needed for short programs. I was confident I would find some among my professional networks – and already had some ideas.

To my delight, the Director immediately proclaimed his agreement with this battery of ideas, and then added something that revived my original doubts: as if it were obvious and worth mentioning only in passing, he said that all first efforts would *of course* go into the outer islands "because they need improving services most." But that, I immediately thought, would perpetuate the idea that the outer islands were merely "pupils" to copy and fit into the Ministry's ways instead of true partners in the program-building for the whole country. Working first only in the outer islands would set in stone this sense that only a remedial, piecemeal sharing of information was required, not a truly collaborative strategy to improve the health services nation-wide. At the same time, it would not be prudent to sideline royal Java, which did have the most extensive experience providing population health services, and so should be directly involved in helping build the program elsewhere along with upgrading and enlarging its own staffs.

So, to test what we were really talking about and confront my original yes or no challenge, I proposed that all work be done in groups of three partners: two provinces (one outer island plus one Java province) with the Ministry as the third partner, and that all of them would participate in all training programs. I believed that being part of these teams would help the Ministry keep abreast of developments everywhere and allow the "outer islands" to learn from actual experience in the Ministry and Java and consider ways already found to be practically feasible. At the same time, the outer islands would present challenges not confronted in central Java or imagined at the Ministry, and so the challenges of developing the national system would show up soonest and clearest with all three at the table.

The main reason for having a Java province take part in each trio I kept to myself from this bureaucrat whom I still hardly knew. He naturally would not see the Ministry itself as a potential stumbling block to real change, but as a newcomer I could see that only with Java represented in each trio, the most populated and organized island, and accustomed to taking the lead in national affairs, could we hope to affect the Ministry itself, when changing the system as a whole became the agenda. It was a gamble: Java would get pride of place, perhaps reinforcing the current hierarchy – but also, perhaps Java would become open to transforming as well.

To my relief and lasting delight, the Director immediately changed to exploring practical next steps to implement the detailed structure I had offered. He scheduled more discussions ahead and discussed how best to involve other department heads and the best connections to particular outer islands, and which Javan provinces to invite to take part first. In our next meeting we used the Institution-Building framework to map the categories of stakeholders to involve and the three best sets of three partners with whom to start the work. Pa himself undertook to identify and recruit particular colleagues into key positions. With these steps, we had begun outlining the overarching frame for decentralizing the services overall.

With the Pusdiklat director so well focused and actively in the lead, Ronnie and I decided to stay.

Framing the Change Initiative: Five Parts

Over several meetings, Pa and I identified the required sets of stakeholders and first sets of provinces, and roughed out these five essentials to frame the development as a whole:

1. The three principal parties in the teams would work together right from the start and keep working together over the length of the program.
2. The number of trio-teams we would work with at a time would be limited by the number of *very* experienced organizational development consultants I could find and recruit to reside and work full time on a designated outer island to help it develop the services there to country-wide standards. I expected to find and recruit, and increase the funding, for just three or four sufficiently experienced institutional development colleagues. Limiting the number of trios of partners in action at any time would also make the development as a whole more manageable.
3. Only when a minimum concentration of collaboratively inclined and technically competent physician–officials were in place, and all essential functions were working convincingly well, would external assistance end in that province and the senior consultant there be able to move on to the next island and its new partners.
4. As innovative ways of working developed, many new stakeholders and fresh visions and competencies would be included into the program. All along we would also link participants as they "graduated" into networks across provinces and so keep innovation going and create a national system of support and communication.
5. A major aim of the program would be getting the Ministry to formally recognize this expanding network of newly trained and experienced stakeholders and figure them into the regular

budget. It was not clear yet what form this recognition would take; it would depend upon how well we could spark and nurture trainees' engagement with and commitment to the program in the long term.

Most of that original one-year consultancy went into negotiating this very different and more costly consultancy with the Ministry and the funding agency, and finding and recruiting the three or four experienced large-system consultants from among my professional networks, contracting with a panel of short-term consultants-on-call to lead the short technical and managerial programs as needed, and selecting and initiating the first set of provinces and trios. Out of that effort also came the new contract for three years, which was eventually extended by another three.

Recruiting the Change Agent Team

First, we would need resident full-time experts in organizational development. The role of these consultants would be to develop training in the provinces, including staffing with full-time trainers and developing training programs in line with job descriptions, staffing plans, and production targets. The most obvious first candidate for me was Udai Pareek. After our six years of working together to develop the SFET in India, we had joined up again in academia and we had often stayed in each other's homes; he and Rama would come with one of their small twin grandsons. The other two were Jack Grant and Michael Norris from the USA. Jack, the African-American dean of a school of education in the American South, and his wife Joan, a long-experienced school principal, came all-too-well acquainted with racial discrimination and the challenges of working in an imbalanced system. Michael came with Amy, his wife, who had her own practice working internationally with independently active women. It was Udai's coming that took some persuading, a "senior consultant" for Indonesia out of next-door India in the 1980s? In the event, he became the one the Ministry would ask to stay an extra year to help develop services in one more outer island.

In the initial discussions with Pa and then more widely in the Ministry and USAID, we provided for six-month residencies in each province. That proved to be a gross underestimate of minimal time and also of the widely different times required in different provinces. Jack stayed in large out-of-the-way and very distinctive Tana Toraja for all of his two years. After fifteen months in large Sumatra, Udai moved to East Java and from there also joined up from time to time with Michael in Bali, *his* second location before moving on to North Java for the most advanced program, in which Amy then also did advanced work with Indonesian women consultants-to-be. In the fourth year, an intern from Vietnam also joined the team with her partner.

For short workshops on particular management or other administrative topics that came up as needed, drawing experts from nearby countries was clearly most practical. Most were Indian colleagues of mine from earlier work. Using Pusdiklat's residential training centers, we could rotate the two-week nation-wide programs, so officials in different provinces could also mix and get to know each other and so develop themselves into a coherent national service.

We consultants met as a team mostly in combination with the successive short programs and, after an early introductory visit, I joined each consultant on request. I stayed with them and their families and moved about with them there as needed. I joined Jack and Joan in Tana Toraja when he was in and out of court after his driver had an accident in Jack's jeep that killed a woman, and he was determined to clear his driver of having caused it (he succeeded). Routinely, my visits were in response to a request for extra support to make a strategic decision.

When I stayed with Udai and Rama, assessing the development in East Java, one day Udai reported a curious happening: in the open-air market that morning where he had gone to buy a lot of green mangoes for Rama to prepare and preserve for the winter, the village woman sitting on the floor limited his purchase to six. "What would I do all day if I had no more to sell?" she explained, and did not budge.

In Jakarta I joined the choral society and the theater group preparing Gilbert and Sullivan's *The Pirates of Penzance*. I made friends with the local AID head of family planning and got into the habit of joining them for weekends in the hills above the city. I also vividly recall the long, long night in West Java when our daughter Maya, back in the US, had sent a message that she had given birth to her twins but one had life-threatening jaundice. Before cell phones, we had no way to check for better news until her relieved, positive message the next morning.

Training for Development of the Health System

We aimed to use the short technical programs as vehicles for changing the culture of the health services. Currently they were top-down and largely formalistic training activities, which we aimed to transform into locally-appropriate-and-backed ways of analyzing and working with actual problems in lasting ways, leaving in our wake a more egalitarian culture focused on health systems improvement. Our strategy for this was targeted, highly interactive, problem-oriented, team-focused training.

Systematic task analysis for staffing, organizing, and running public services and *organizing and working in teams* became immediate candidates for the short nation-wide programs. *Recording* and learning from the actual program-building and -managing came next, and also researching and creating *cases* for reviewing in detail the actual experiences of managers. The case program would be used to help managers to analyze tasks and discuss best steps whenever an issue arose. This program was Ronnie's particular expertise. She spearheaded the effort to solicit stories from health officials, helped them to write them up, and created a detailed instructors' manual for using them to lead discussions and introduce useful concepts for visualizing next practical steps and larger applications for each case. All participants received a *Case Book* and manual in both English and Indonesian. The books came to contain thirty cases written by local MD-officials and represented a wide variety of challenges these officials had faced. For example, Case 1, "The Unwanted Prescriptions," concerned a new staff doctor who issued prescriptions to patients, despite instructions from his boss to give (free) medicines from the health center's own supply. A seemingly simple issue of needing to discipline the staff member elicited discussion of conflicts of interest (it turned out the doctor was receiving money from the pharmaceutical company), how best to communicate discipline (in front of others, or separately), and the problem of poor pay throughout the system. Other cases described attempts to set up formal processes to tackle absenteeism and other norms that weakened the workplace culture, how to run meetings and other mundane issues, dealing with administrative apathy towards new programs, perceived favoritism in the workplace, and what to do when you receive conflicting or contradictory assignments from more than one authority figure. They came to reflect wide ranges of cultural norms, priorities, and challenges from across Indonesia.

The model was cost-effective because it incorporated inclusive collaboration and support in all roles. The trainees brought the method back to their organizations, to allow all levels of staff to implement collaborative planning and management. As one Indonesian physician was quoted in the US funder's final evaluation, this way of working was like "going back to nature – to *'musywarah'* – decision by consensus." In short, it was an "appropriate technology" – a phrase we may remember from the chapter on SFET and Schumacher's contribution: not expensive, broadly applicable, and fitting with prevailing cultural norms.

One of the most significant lessons we learned was the importance of prototyping or piloting the program before fully launching it. As we have seen, this is not always possible, due to budget constraints or leadership balking at not "jumping right in," but in this case USAID and the Ministry were willing to let us try out the curriculum with small groups and also push ahead in a few provinces ahead of others. So we first piloted more rigorous task analysis with nurses in a hospital in Central Java, and then extended the pilot to two more provinces and developed trainers to staff programs there. The successive try-out took over a year, but it allowed us to incorporate, from the very beginning, inputs to address management situations and actions that these individuals had actually experienced and so began the process of using a real-world feedback loop to continuously improve the program for the duration. Second, this process institutionalized the "train the trainer" aspect of the program, which was part of the long-term goal to staff the program with native Indonesians from the various islands. In time several of these original trainees became WHO experts and developed competency education manuals which became popular also in India and other Asian countries. Finally, the strong basis created by patient and responsive piloting made extending the program to other islands much easier.

We used the Ministry's existing training sites, located around the country. This facilitated attendance by more individuals in this very large country, and also modeled the very decentralization we wanted to institutionalize. For, in many ways, "centrality" is a mindset. Each island is itself the "center" of its own universe, only "outer" in terms of the sense of some other place being more "advanced." To counter this mindset was a first step in helping the Ministry and provinces see themselves as partners. Another way of encouraging a decentralized, inclusive mindset was the grouping of trainee organizations into the sets of three described above, made up of individuals from a (central) Java province, an "outer" province, and the Ministry. These organizations were considered equals; even when the Ministry or a Java province brought good experience and insights into what worked and what did not, all three had a voice at the table.

The use of cases based on actual experiences was central to the goals with regard to training along inclusive, collaborative lines. Creating the cases had its own value: through the research and writing of these, health department managers gained keen insight into their own tasks, processes, and outcomes. Then analyzing the cases in groups made up of members ranging from health department staff and MD leaders to the top provincial officials allowed us to focus on actual events, problems, decisions, and actions specific to particular places in Indonesia. Cases allowed students to consider for themselves what *they* would do in a real – not theoretical, and not foreign – situation, in which there are often no "right" answers. The programs lasted three or four days on-site then, with a few weeks back home in between, students would return and continue discussions and move forward with training. Health staff members at

CHAPTER 5

all levels worked with cases from their own cultures, developmental stages, experiences with managing, and capabilities for leadership – and were asked *their* opinion of what someone else had done, what he or she might have done to produce different outcomes, what they might do in a similar situation. It opened students up to the give and take of collaboration and inclusion, ideally in ways they would bring back to their workplaces. The case method proved so successful that the agency head engaged Ronnie separately to add case programs to several other development efforts in Indonesia.

An important and wide-ranging outcome of decentralization along these lines was the greater and greater change (away) from traditional modes of promotion and career advancement based merely on seniority or educational standards, towards selecting and advancing participants based on performance criteria and broader support from their particular parts in the nation-wide system. So developing this way also helped build structures and better capacities into the system as a whole. Starting with choosing participants for the initial short programs, additional programs focused on training and consulting skills the participants themselves requested, and on to advanced programs that would lead to internships for consulting and (eventually) replacing the international consultants in the provinces.

Because of supportive leadership at the Ministry, we were able to flexibly fund these different levels and creative additions to the modules as needed to push everything forward. Within health service agencies, the training spread vertically from managers to practitioners, and also horizontally among the different service areas, such as family planning, immunization, and community health. The strategy was to keep developing innovative and competent individuals until there was a minimum concentration of them, all able and willing to continue working innovatively and inclusively throughout the country. A supportive network began to emerge that would be led by the Indonesians themselves.

Following Through

Along with the overarching ways the long-term consultants worked in their successive provinces and the three-fold working groups, the short technical programs moving from province to province, and the better-prepared candidates getting promoted throughout the services and the central Ministry, decentralized planning and working became ever more normal and reinforced the overall development strategy that Pa and I had crafted those six years previously.

Its goal had not been limited to reorienting and retraining personnel but meant changing the norms and structures throughout the entire system, and building the capacity to sustain it in these collaborative ways. So the international system consultants had moved from province to province, staying in each for however many months it took to identify and develop a concentration of individuals and develop systems that they could then run themselves. Having an international consultant live there confirmed that each was an important actor and even instigator of major development. And working in trios spread professional recognition nation-wide.

The Results for Indonesia's Health Systems

The strategy as a whole, the team, and our actual consulting on-site worked well beyond all expectations. Over the six-plus years, the Ministry spread health services to eight provinces, routinized joint planning with each province, and accommodated the wide variations of cultures and economic possibilities. Most heartening were the organizational competencies the provinces developed locally. This called for much longer consulting help on some islands than others, but the overall system that emerged was competent and capable, and also reflected the long-standing differences between the varied island provinces.

Very important – perhaps most important – was that these mostly young and only recently qualified physician–officials and managers turned out to be much more open to public health perspectives than most physicians we had worked with in the West. They welcomed learning the more systematic "job analysis" of tasks for which they had to recruit and supervise staff, and they readily came to use health statistics to track and evaluate their effectiveness. In the short technical programs and then in staff meetings on site, they routinely focused discussions on actual "problems at work" and referred to records they kept and actual cases. Case writing and discussion were especially valuable for participants from the very start, not only because they involved concrete issues, but because they allowed participants (and, later, their colleagues within their workplaces) "to feel personally heard" and open up, which is especially important in traditional hierarchical cultures. In the final evaluation of the program by the US funder, it was noted that although researching and creating full-length case studies would require further external funding, it would be well worth continuing.

Also, contrary to the rather discouraging experiences of engaging physicians in the West in public health measures and institutions, the medical doctors here wanted ever more programs to enhance their competencies. So we added several steps of career training to the original design, and of the 283 physician–officials from fourteen provinces who started technical programs, 253 came again for the programs we added on consulting and institutional development, 88 came again for the multi-phase advanced programs for extending their provincial systems and inter-provincial networking, and 41 from eight provinces became interns and consultants in the national consulting service that they themselves pioneered and anchored in the Ministry.

Neither the funding agency nor we consultants had foreseen these further developments. The local initiatives and sustained enthusiasm gave the whole effort a distinctive energy. Although we consultants could continue to nurture this ever-denser net of personal collaborations and eager participation, we knew that it would also go on without us.

Implications for Future Development Projects

Four decisions taken along the way suggest strategic guidelines for elsewhere: first, the decision to locate and have the consultants live with their families in a designated outer island and work there till services were established and/or upgraded, and no longer required most accessible assistance, had the immediate benefit of making the local trainees feel supported and even "championed" by a highly experienced consultant. When the consultants deemed it was time to leave, they and the local officials *knew* they were ready to take charge of their own organizations. And, as we saw when we became part of the community at Minetown, or lived equally with the Aloka participants, embedding in the community makes clear that learning is not just one-directional. The consultants learned from the provincial communities as well as the trainees learned from the consultants.

The second important decision was to make the technical training programs national and move them about to various parts of the country. This structure reflected what I had first helped institute at SFET, with our movement to different states and, later, different countries and cities for different programs and cohorts. In Indonesia, along with the grouping of different provinces into training groups, this structure underlined the geographic decentralization of health services, while also building a lasting body of active and competent executives, and *also* creating opportunities for officials in different provinces to get to know each other and collaborate across provinces and nationally. Thus, decentralization did not mean "dispersed," except for geographically: the individuals themselves became well-connected and mutually supported and supportive by the end.

Third, to build in flexibility, it was important to have financial flexibility to respond to needs that arose as the program progressed. In this, we were lucky in terms of our funding inputs, as well as with the overarching support from the central Indonesian government, the US funders, and the local stakeholders. The goal was to create a cadre of thoughtful, well-rounded officials, so we needed to firm it up at the beginning with pilot testing and then be continuously able to respond to their requests for additional training that would grow with them and their needs. As when we incorporated the women factory workers' ideas into the program at Minetown, responsiveness enhances a program and makes more certain that it will take root. In this case, it required constantly checking in with participants to know their challenges, and having available a number of potential trainers and the budget to bring them in for short, more advanced, or just different programs. It also promoted more robust programs in response to their desires for further career advancement opportunities.

And finally, it was important to build solid relations within the Ministry and with the funding agencies. This facilitated flexible and even additional funding when actual development required it, as described above. It also spoke to the need, which we have seen again and again, to keep aware at all times of the perspectives and contributions of the great diversity of stakeholders required for collaborative development. My close personal relationship right from day one with the well-respected division head, Pa Ibu, who led the decentralization for the Ministry was turned into a strategic advantage in this regard. He valued the big picture I sketched and proceeded with that in mind, in contrast to my recent experiences in academia where central leaders, used to being in charge and accustomed to seeing themselves as the experts, found it difficult to include other voices. Pa remained a strong, steady, and increasingly influential supporter of the initiative as he moved up in the Ministry and involved me in related activities. In the fourth year, for instance, when he led a delegation of senior officials to study neighborhood health centers in the USA, I accompanied them and, for their most sustained study, took them to a health center in mountainous Appalachia in the South, which was headed by a top alumnus of my school of public health.

In this context, favorable beyond expectations, the local cultures of these health services organizations changed in important ways. For example, in terms of the day-to-day running, they documented increased attendance, active participation at work, and improved work norms of health workers of all types and ranks. There was more working across department lines, and working in teams and inclusive planning and reviewing became the norm. In terms of the structures for hiring and career advancement, they established performance criteria for promotions and field-oriented training for career advancement within the organization. And in terms of the larger national organization into which they now felt fully integrated, there was a greater readiness to release staff for temporary assignments elsewhere, including the new consultant interns, who were readily assigned between provinces and Pusdiklat, as well as elsewhere in the Ministry.

These "domestic consultants" gained and demonstrated growing commitment to and ownership of *their* health service. They formed a national association that the Ministry supported with office space and working funds. At its second annual meeting this association detailed rigorous criteria for members to advance to *independent consultant* status (a recognized classification that carried financial benefits) and took steps to institute formal registration and official backing by the Ministry. The Association also had recommendations for the program going forward as follows, based on their keen understanding of the conditions in the provinces:

1. Increase membership to reach minimum concentrations in all specializations in all provinces. Many provinces were still understaffed compared to needs; the Association recommended continuing the training and expediting technical assistance and fellowship programs.
2. Contain and limit the pressing demands on the health services organizations to increase and upgrade services. Budgets were tight and crises were constant; while staffing was still inadequate, quality suffered under the added pressures of continuous growth.
3. Introduce working in pairs and teams and ensure adequate funding for that. This would help alleviate the stressors of dealing with crises and expansion.
4. Simplify procedures by which local training centers secure experienced trainers from more advanced provinces. These regional linkages would help alleviate stress in under-staffed provinces, as well as strengthening the network going forward.

The fact that this association was formed and took such a strong role in improving the program demonstrates their commitment to and investment in it. It highlights the enormous benefit of having local actors in the lead in the charted development, and then also in pioneering and carrying forward the plans.

Implications for My Career

Probably the most important element for me personally and professionally in this project was the support I received from the Ministry of Health. As it was at SFET, the decision-making at the very beginning depended on personal relationships at the top level, relationships dependent on shared purpose, values, strategy, and style. In a way, then, I was "lucky" that Pa Ibu and I hit it off, that we trusted one another. But beyond the strengthening our interpersonal relationship, his decision-making style promised success. Decision-making is a core feature for organizational culture, and the realities of what, when, who, and where decisions are made provide a good indicator of organizational health.

My immediate next contract made even more starkly clear how important this was: the funding agency's director in Indonesia was so pleased with the outcomes that he urged his counterpart in India to ask me to help decentralize the health services there. So to India we went next, with the additional advantage of already knowing and being known there. But the Indian government official in charge of state relations was against letting any of her own power go, and so turned down any meeting to discuss which state(s) to start in. When a state government took the initiative and asked me to start there, the central government official ruled that all travel outside Delhi had to have her approval. Thinking perhaps she found me personally unacceptable, I asked her to meet Indian colleagues who could do the work in the field. She met eighteen local colleagues, but kept her rules in place and nothing developed. Happily, the USAID director in India had other projects with which I then helped. And our connection with India resulted in one last, successful consultancy of my career (or, really, post-career, since it arose during our early retirement), helping scale up PRADAN, one of India's premier anti-poverty programs, as I describe in the following chapter.

In Indonesia, meanwhile, we had met our goals. Our colleagues there had moved from decisions about staffing, training, promotion, and the like being made in Jakarta, to decisions made in collaboration with the provinces, based on performance criteria, training, and organizational needs. They had gone from a "one size fits all" budget determined at the Ministry to a system by which the provinces proposed budgets for their work based on their needs and capacities, from priority services determined centrally to priorities customized to each region. A focus on classic medical treatment, based on a Western, urban model of individual care, had transitioned into a focus on population health, targeting services, prevention, health communications, and so on, based on their impact on rural populations. "Decentralization," it turned out, did not mean "expanding" what existed centrally and making it bigger, to cover everyone. It meant changing the norms and structures throughout, and building capacity and collaboration everywhere.

CHAPTER 6

North and Central India: Up-scaling Rural Programs to Help the Poorest of the Poor

> "We should... live towards the other man, who is not framed by thought but bodily present before us; we should live towards his concrete life."
>
> Martin Buber, *Between Man and Man*, trans. Ronald Gregor-Smith (New York and London: Routledge Classics, 1955), p.32

Introduction

In this sixth setting, I worked with Professional Assistance for Development Action (PRADAN), an organization devoted to reducing rural poverty in India, helping the poorest of the poor across the northern and hilly central swath of this vast country. As we shall see, this engagement was different: I was a wholly external consultant, and the organization was not new (as were Aloka, SFET, and the USC School of Public Health) but was expanding greatly; and in so doing, it embraced with practical fervor the broad challenge of rural poverty. Working with long-time PRADAN consultant Deepankar Roy, I had an opportunity to help with people who were already making a difference in extremely difficult circumstances.

CHAPTER 6

A Productive Interregnum

As noted at the end of the previous chapter, after the work in Indonesia was completed I was asked to go to India and replicate the process in the health system there, but I was not able to develop the key relationship necessary to launch that project, so the USAID director offered me other assignments. Ronnie continued writing and delivering workshops for various ministries in the Indian government and educational institutions. These activities kept us busy in India for another year, and – now in our sixties – we decided to retire "home" to the US, to central North Carolina, returning to the environs of our first innings in US academia.

Back in the States, Ronnie and I did what retirees do – reconnect and expand our social networks, enjoy our growing family of grandchildren, and generally relax. But I think by now an attentive reader will know that a true consultant – one who loves the job as much as I did, anyway – never really stops working. In fact, that may be one of the reasons I have loved my profession – for the variety of challenges forever precluding boredom, as well as the possibility that around every corner there may be another person to engage with, another problem to explore and help to resolve. The fact that institutional development was an inner calling was made clear at the beginnings of things (such excitement and vision of possibilities!) and at the end – when, even in retirement, Ronnie and I continued engaging with that world.

All along, Ronnie and I were asked to do various short projects, and chose to do some of them – for example, two programs in Africa to "train" top health administrators in Botswana, and then also in Lesotho. The largest projects during these years were in India, where Ronnie led case writing and teaching workshops, and our one-year residency at the new Indian Institute of Rural Management, where I formulated some of the key ideas about social-change interventions that reappear in this book. In one of Ronnie's social forestry case workshops was Deepankar Roy, an international consultant in organizational development. We had known him for years, since he had attended a training program run by the Indian Association for

Applied Behavioural Science, which Udai Pareek and I had helped to found. Now he was consulting for PRADAN. Also during this time, we continued our long-time connection with Vijay Mahajan, the co-founder (with Deep Joshi) of PRADAN and pioneer of micro-loans in India.

We also took on many professional activities back in the States, including some consultancies with our several professional societies. I continued reflecting, writing, and commenting on scholarly work in the profession. Ronnie traveled regularly to Hyderabad and London, leading workshops and writing (over her career she wrote books on management, a social history of "our" state in India, biographies, novels, and a memoir, along with the case studies and other educational materials). I continued corresponding with colleagues all over the world, and attended meetings and conferences. I celebrated my seventieth birthday in the mid-1990s with an international conference of thirty colleagues here in Chapel Hill, which co-author David Kiel secretly organized and Racine Brown from South Carolina facilitated. This conference fed into my book about our family life during all our moving around.

Although I never stopped engaging, I was not expecting a new paid assignment back in India when, in mid-June 2007 (and now in my eighties), Deep Joshi asked me to come to work with PRADAN the following winter. PRADAN had been laboring in some of the poorest states of India to reduce rural poverty for more than two decades by then. It had been internationally recognized for using innovative methods to make the poorest of the poor agents of their own rise up from poverty. They recruited, apprenticed, and then employed master's-level university graduates to live in communities and help families develop new livelihoods to add to their subsistence-living incomes. Vijay Mahajan, the first CEO of PRADAN, and I had worked together several times over the years, on organizational issues related to bank micro-loans programs. Seeing the need to develop broader capital resources to fund and multiply micro-loans and growing village enterprises, Vijay had launched the BASIX Social Enterprise Group about ten years earlier. This was the first micro-finance institution in India and among the first in the world. He had been able to affect changes to Indian regulations and also attract commercial equity investments internationally and from within India and build a critical mass of opportunities for the rural poor, which could give financial muscle to PRADAN and other similar NGOs' anti-poverty activities. Vijay was (and is) internationally recognized for this work. I was proud to have been a part of it.

Now, with their major funders agreeing, they wanted to take PRADAN to scale across a vast region of the north and central part of the country – growing from under 100,000 to over a million people served. Deep asked: "Could I help them do that?"

The Special Qualities of PRADAN

Beyond my familiarity with and trust for its founders, I was drawn to PRADAN by several ways that its methods matched my own sense of how best to serve community development. First, they relied on native Indians who were familiar with (and to) the people they served, and spoke the local languages, rather than on foreign experts. Also, these young professionals were screened not only for their education (often a master's degree) in technical fields such as agriculture, forestry, water management, engineering, and business organization, but also for their social conscience, empathy, and spirit of commitment to the cause. These PRADAN field staff helped develop new family incomes among women and also nurture the villages in self-determination and self-management; they transferred technical skills; and then they moved on to other villages.

In contrast to Western versions of long-term community service dating from the same era, such as VISTA or the Peace Corps, young professionals working for PRADAN opted for an entire career with PRADAN. After a year's apprenticeship to examine their suitability and commitment, new recruits were posted to a local team and immersed themselves in chosen villages and, with access to a team leader, contributed and learned all they could. This process – both its thorough dedication to community agency and its use of embedded consultants, understood and trusted by those communities without "taking over" – reminded me especially of our work in Indonesia.

Second, PRADAN engaged most directly with women. PRADAN chose to work with the women not only because they were most dedicated to the well-being of the family but also because they were the most marginalized in the intersection of caste, class, and gender. The PRADAN method was to help women form self-help groups (SHGs), and to create small "collectives" to develop their own skills and ideas with the technical guidance of the young professionals. Women's SHGs met regularly to discuss common concerns, help each other, and access micro-loans to develop "new livelihoods" – income-producing additions to subsistence living. These SHGs launched micro-enterprises in areas such as poultry and silk production, the introduction of new crops and agricultural methods, the improvement of water supply, and soil preservation. As the women empowered and supported each other, they also initiated new activities and became more involved and influential in their villages and in improving social conditions there. As the small enterprises grew, PRADAN helped build larger-scale production and marketing collectives for various agricultural and artisanal products.

Finally, I was drawn to PRADAN because of its laser focus on poverty. After the climate crisis, which threatens all life on the planet, there is no more important transcendent challenge than global poverty. This is, again, the type of problem we all readily agree in the abstract that we want to solve, but which most of us do not get to address in our everyday work lives, whether because it seems too complex or large, or requires too radical a change from the status quo, or we do not have the institutional or stakeholder support to address it. I encourage social-change practitioners to be attentive to cues that a transcendent challenge might be present and to gain clarity about the possibility for transformation.

PRADAN was clearly committed to addressing such a transcendent challenge. When PRADAN began its work in the mid-1980s, almost half of the world's population lived in extreme poverty, defined then as living on below $1.00 per day (today it is defined as less than $1.90 per day). Extreme poverty correlates with hunger, lower life expectancy, lower educational attainment, with health disparities, gender-based inequality, and many other risks to individual, family, and communal well-being. PRADAN, with its theory of "communities as drivers and professionals as catalysts," was attacking this problem at its root and also at the point most apt to have an impact on individual lives. By the time they called me in 2007, with the women's self-help groups up and running well, and over 80,000 new livelihoods under way, PRADAN was effective. Just the year before, in 2006, PRADAN had won India's first NGO-of-the-year award. PRADAN was (and still is) also a uniquely egalitarian and idealistic organization, offering a living-wage starting pay with increases based only on seniority, not position. Now, PRADAN would "go to scale" – grow from a successful program launch to serving a much larger area and many more people. Knowing they already had Deepankar Roy as their primary organizational consultant, there was only one question I needed to ask: "What does Deepankar think of this – about the idea, and about my joining the team?" Deep Joshi assured me: "We both think it would be useful… come via Delhi… two days at least…. Should we book a double room for you at the India International Centre (IIC)?"

A Different Type of Consultancy

From the outset, this engagement was quite different from some of the others we have described. At Minetown, at Aloka, with SFET, in academic settings in the US, and in Indonesia, I was embedded in the innovative institution itself and had an established role as a full-time organizational member for several years. In all cases I was *also* an outsider, although we have seen what varied forms that "outsider" status can take in different situations. Except for the academic institutions, unlike regular employees, my contracts were time-limited, up for re-negotiation every three years or so. In the academic settings, I was a different kind of "outsider," and we have explored the ways that outsiders, even those with central roles in the organization, can sometimes enact change as true insiders cannot. But notwithstanding my erstwhile outsider status, my commitment to those organizations was long-term, my sense of responsibility all-encompassing, for better or worse.

Working with PRADAN was basically different. Although I had long-time relationships with the key leaders and stakeholders and was deeply committed to the cause, I did not anchor the consultant's role. I would not work full-time, and I would not be the primary driver of the initiative, on whom all pressure and decision-making would fall. And, I was not building a program from scratch: I would be helping an already very successful mature organization that was in very good hands.

In short, at this point in PRADAN, I was more like the "typical" external consultant, one with power and influence for a time but not with overall institution-building responsibilities and, most important, one whose lasting contribution would be in affecting the actions of others, through intensive but relatively brief encounters. I was not unfamiliar with this role; in fact, I had taken on this type of assignment many times, even before retirement, including in the early 1970s to help the Latin American University form its new graduate school, and later to help the Tibetan Government in Exile work through some internal issues, among other examples. The point is that Ronnie and I were aware that this was a "hit and run" type role and determined to act our part effectively within that framework so as to help these long-time friends and colleagues who were laboring so earnestly and so long, and with such passion, to lessen a major global problem on a grand scale.

I was eighty, Ronnie a bit older. She had had some illnesses that were now, happily, over. We could continue for half of the year staying in our beautiful and convenient house by the little pond in North Carolina, within driving distance of our children and grandchildren in the southeast US. And – best of both worlds – we could resume our winters in India, visiting, writing, and working on this and other projects here and there. The fee would be the same as Deepankar's: I felt no need to discuss or negotiate. We decided to accept Deep's offer for the winter, leaving aside, for now, decisions about how long it would last and what Ronnie's part might be.

CHAPTER 6

Coming "Home"

Over my life and career (so far!) I have lived all over the world. This book covers placements in the United Kingdom, Sri Lanka and South India, the southeast US, Indonesia, and back to India. I consulted in central America and several African countries, and also spent time in other parts of Europe, and this (all) does not even take into account the fact that I was born in Germany, moved to England during the War, and had my own family and in-laws in the United States. Perhaps it was my early life, or perhaps just my personality of always wanting to connect with people and see what life will offer next, but I never felt adrift or "homeless" as a consultant. I was used to "making myself at home" wherever I went, and to having several places where I felt at home, in the sense of its being familiar and its people like family. Probably no place embodied this sense – for me and for Ronnie – more than India.

Going back to India felt like a reunion of like spirits. This was partly because I was known and respected professionally – so different from earlier beginnings, where I had to build a trusting relationship with the person at the helm, prove myself, find out whether stakeholders would be open for exploratory discussions or were set on their agenda. Ronnie, too, was respected and valued in her own right. We had been in touch with all of these people for twenty years. I had attended annual conferences with them, kept up with their work, and read and commented on their writing. Deepankar and his wife had taken the lead in training small-group facilitators in Ronnie's case programs earlier and he, but for a last-minute death in the family, would have been a consultant with me for the work in Indonesia. Now here he was PRADAN's consultant-on-call, long-time friend of Deep's and also of PRADAN's head of human resources, working frequently with the organization's management committee on institutional design and training programs.

And our familiarity and feeling of reconnecting with an international family in Delhi went beyond the PRADAN leaders. The Ford Foundation, which had funded and anchored me while I helped set up SFET forty years before, was up the lane from the India Cultural

Centre near where Deep Joshi had launched PRADAN twenty years previously. And here also was Tom Kessenger, who backed Deep Joshi's launch of PRADAN; Tom had been our neighbor and friend with his wife Varyam in Indonesia (when he was with the Ford Foundation), and we often now stayed with them when in Delhi. Sheela, Deep's wife, now headed Tom's office in Delhi, and I often stopped by to say hello to her on my way to the Lodhi Gardens and the wondrous tall stone tombs there that lit up so strikingly at night. The lane itself was named for our friend Jo(seph) Stein, the architect who had designed the India International Centre and the half-dozen other public buildings along one side of the Gardens. With him and his wife Margaret we had become good enough friends to spend holidays together. And Kamla, Ronnie's friend from Harvard and then our colleague for Aloka's second program, had proposed us for membership in the IIC. Now, I passed her some mornings walking in the Gardens and nodded – no talking was the unspoken rule for early morning walks. And at IIC itself, our active alumnus and colleague Abad Ahmed was now the India head of the Aga Khan Trust for Culture, and responsible for exhibiting the renovation work on Delhi's Moslem temples and palaces.

It was a small world, full of like-minded people; a home-coming, indeed!

Three Challenges and Three Interventions

PRADAN was (and is still) an award-winning civil-society effort to place trained professionals in the field to work with families in the poorest conditions in India. The ruling philosophies are that communities are the central agents of their own change and all change processes must be democratic and transparent. PRADAN recruits from a dozen campuses across India to create cohorts of apprentices (AKA "Pradanites") and introduce them to development through an organizational culture that includes ample space and freedom to learn based on individual interests and support for experimentation, risk-taking, and playing helping roles from day one in the communities. When I arrived there, PRADAN already had more field workers than any other non-governmental organization in India. The organization was led by a governing board (Management Committee) made up of independent members with distinguished records of public service. The organizational chart included the CEO and a few central staff, the Management Committee itself, program leaders, team leaders (the primary mentors and coaches of apprentices and field staff), and field staff (placed throughout the countryside). The plan to expand the reach of this organization was a function of its past success, and of a consortium of Indian and international organizations offering to fund going to scale. It was going to be a massive undertaking. Our two-day preparatory meeting at IIC focused mostly on mapping the expansion and setting priorities for moving forward. Three far-ranging challenges that the Management Committee would need to address arose from these discussions.

The first challenge was enlarging PRADAN's conception of and response to a vastly expanded "outside world." The number of stakeholders with an interest in the organization had already greatly enlarged, and would grow even more: first, by the growth from three to seven state governments, more funding sources, and other stakeholders scattered over thousands of square miles. PRADAN leadership would have to spend time identifying and connecting with these new stakeholders, learning their priorities and norms – even, in some cases, local languages and cultural codes. A larger PRADAN would also be expected to participate in many more high-level consultations, and governmental policy- and decision-making. Attending to these responsibilities would require significant time and attention of PRADAN's most senior managers, and this would be taken away from their heretofore primary *internal* concern with mentoring staff – and just at the very time when they were coping with expanding work in the field, greater diversity, and increasing numbers of staff.

The second challenge was helping staff adapt to new territories, customs, and working arrangements. Expanding PRADAN meant including areas altogether new to this development. The norm had been that Pradanites worked in their own language and remained near their families, so PRADAN would have to find field staff prepared to go to areas with which they were not familiar, and it was up to the Pradanites to understand and accept the communities, not the other way around. I knew that building capacity for this would have to be a large part of the intervention. How severely it would affect the current apprenticeship year or cut into future recruiting was unknown.

Following from both of these challenges, a third was that PRADAN's middle management would need great strengthening – and fast, even at this extra busy time. There were thirty team leaders for about 200 (growing to 300 and more) Pradanites. The organizational culture made these team leaders' jobs complicated. Foremost was the fact that during their apprentice year and beyond, new Pradanites were given space, time, and support for reflection and learning, as well as the freedom to choose how to focus their learning. This innovation continues, and is considered valuable – in evaluations of the program, it has been called "essential" by participants – and yet it is labor- and time-intensive for both staff and team leaders/mentors. Second, from their very first day on the job Pradanites were the "voice" of PRADAN in the communities in which they were stationed. Thus, they worked immediately with community elders, local governments, and community service organizations to design and execute programs based on the communities' needs. With expansion, team leaders would have to be ready to support new staff as they navigated this active engagement.

Finally, all PRADAN staff were prepared to assume any role. It is worth saying again, because it is so foreign to the way Western companies and even NGOs are organized, that starting pay was a living wage, increasing only with seniority, irrespective of position or function. So staff could (and still can) shift roles as needed without financial consequences for themselves or for PRADAN. But the low pay ran counter to India's burgeoning economy and its many openings to high-paying professional positions and, for many recruits, also upset the expectations of their families, which could intensify their need for professional and personal guidance. What all this means is that mentorship – support for experimentation, reflection, and risk-taking, and coaching through a wide range of ever-greater responsibilities, was a never-ending process for team leaders.

This would all be par for the course, all things being equal, but with the new focus on a larger constituency of outside stakeholders *and* increased challenges of isolation and difficulties communicating, team leaders would have to double down on their support for field staff at the same time they were increasing the time spent on administration and institution-building.

The First Intervention: Envisioning and Engaging the Outside World of Scaled-up PRADAN

With these broad understandings in mind, Deepankar and I led the management team through a discussion of first steps for the organization to go to scale. The organization had labored to establish effective patterns and ways of working over more than two decades. Now, abruptly, they needed to take the time to visualize just what the new, expanded PRADAN might look like and plan the pacing, phases, and steps to achieve that vision. We asked them to visualize what the staff and organizational structure would have to be like at ten times its current size. Based on their envisioning "expanding ten-fold over ten years," we asked the Committee to explore the agenda of work and the sequence and pacing that the vision suggested, and then map the outside relationships that this massive expansion would require.

As we have seen, keeping stakeholders in mind is a key job of change agents and organizational leaders. The range of stakeholders always includes the board, staff, and those served by the new institutions, but also funders, regulatory and facilitating agencies of government, sources for specialised technical resources, and the general public and media, in order to support the development. Sometimes it is not possible to know who the stakeholders truly are, but in the case of PRADAN, their experience and success had fully apprised them of the types of stakeholders they would need to go forward; the expansion would need to engage with local banks, governments, and others in the new geographical areas. Finally, in areas where PRADAN lacked historical ties and where conditions on the ground were different from those in the regions and states it currently served, a more complex response was required.

In an intensive brainstorming session, we helped the Management Committee create a map of thirty-two key external stakeholders which became a lasting view of PRADAN's partners. They then discussed which relationships mattered most, both currently and in the future: for example, banks for making micro-loans, markets for the new livelihoods that would be developed, universities and technical institutes for recruiting apprentices and staff, local political figures and public media connections, state and union ministries, and corporate, governmental, and international funding sources. The linkages (channels of communication) for relationships with the external world are important for any intervention, but for PRADAN they were especially varied and integral to the workings of the program. Visioning again, this time we considered: how the relations with these external stakeholders might best evolve, how "rivals" could be turned into colleagues, how "helping" relationships with villages could be made more interactive, how links with universities could become more continuous, and what connections would best support the needed funding growth.

Program directors paired up to plan meetings with stakeholder groups to introduce the organization and talk about the "ten-fold over ten years" concept. They were nervous about the reception they might encounter for this expansive vision, including the suggestion that stakeholders be involved in planning and implementation. So, in anticipation of complexities, they decided to add an extra day to their next session to report the results of these meetings and discuss ideas for next steps. To the program directors' surprise and pleasure, the external stakeholders without exception backed the ten-fold expansion and supported it. Yes, indeed, they would welcome a more sharing relationship, one in which they, the outside stakeholders, could also raise questions and suggest next steps and priorities.

With the confidence that comes with a clear, consensually held vision, backed by leadership and a strong scaffolding of external support, "one million new livelihoods in ten years" became the rallying cry. The Committee considered practical steps to developing these more collaborative outside relationships. They decided to open some regular meetings and internal discussions to key external stakeholders, and welcomed opportunities to join meetings and events outside PRADAN. With this discussion, a major shift in the relations with other NGOs was envisioned – and took place over the ensuing spring. Instead of regarding other NGOs as competitors for the same funds, PRADAN involved them in discussions about extending their intervention. With these new partners, the livelihood target was raised to 1.5 million. The executive director got the board of trustees' approval for proceeding with the envisaged ten- to fifteen-fold expansion of families served.

The Second Intervention: Helping Staff Make Sense of and Adapt to Changed Conditions

"Give someone a fish and they eat for a day; teach them to fish and they eat for a lifetime," the saying goes. What if the "fish" in question is the ability to adapt to changing circumstances? The ten-fold expansion into highly diverse settings and relationships would affect *all* staff, executives and team leaders most of all and soonest. And as in Indonesia, this was not just "making bigger" what was working elsewhere, although it was originally implied that they could do just that. The new regions into which PRADAN was sending staff occupy much of India's mountainous and forested center and include the very poorest, least accessible, and most severely marginalized villages. Some of these villages are also among the most restive and violent in the nation. Expansion severely tested the original mandate for staff to involve themselves directly in village life and do whatever they could in an open-ended fashion, with maximum agency among the participants, and maximum transparency. The expansion would challenge the staff's sense of capability and focus, and its morale.

To engage and support staff members most actively and concretely, and allow them to express and analyze the challenges they were facing for the next phase, we proposed a case-writing-and-teaching program for field staff. Our experience and (especially Ronnie's) expertise with this method, as used in Indonesia and in her practice more broadly, taught us that a focus on actual events helped individuals "learn to learn" and could potentially lead whole systems to be better learning organizations. As we found in Indonesia, having practitioners create their own detailed descriptions of their work helps them understand their needs better. These cases then teach others by allowing them to discuss actual events and specific problems, decisions, and actions taken by people in similar circumstances, rather than theoretical examples created by academics. The process of creating and then studying these cases also creates a nucleus of trainers ready to coach and mentor new recruits and others, a highly prized feature of PRADAN.

We designed the program for two cohorts of twenty staff who also regularly trained new recruits and executives. Each program had three phases of five days. Phases one and two focused on discussing cases we brought from elsewhere, and on case research and writing. These phases were separated by a month so participants could absorb the learnings from discussions, observe their daily work behaviors, select one or two experiences and "write them up," and send them to us for comment and revision. The two capacities we intended to develop most across the whole system were a heightened respect for actual hard facts, as fuller, more correct, and more detailed than individual memories or theoretical situations, and habits and support for routinely keeping detailed records of new events and unfamiliar interactions. These two skills would facilitate ongoing learning and create the capacity to develop and teach cases to new executives and other staff. I recommend this type of process for any great organizational change.

Exceeding all consultant expectations was the eagerness with which team leaders and executives took to this way of sharing their experiences. Typically, participants wrote about tough change situations in which they had been directly involved. By emailing both ways, some drafts received several rounds of faculty comments and so became ready for open discussion-in-the-rough in the second phase. At the end of the two case-research-and-writing programs, forty-seven drafts were in hand, twice the number we had expected, and thirty cases were close to being ready for use in sessions in PRADAN's regular programs. Many draft cases were on outstanding and heretofore unresolved institution-wide issues. Examples included abiding impasses and dilemmas in entering and leaving village communities; female–male relationship changes occasioned by women's greater freedoms and new competencies fostered by PRADAN; a new competition in a village occasioned by a producer cooperative that PRADAN staff had helped develop; reconciling the strict output demands and schedules of funding bodies with the more fluid dynamics of sound community development; and more.

We were pleased to see that the cases that were developed came quickly into regular use in the apprentices and staff training programs. The participatory approaches we modeled in the case program sessions also influenced PRADAN's training methods and designs in general, including especially the trainers holding back from responding to individual comments and letting the discussion proceed in an all-to-all pattern. Ideally, then, the organization as a whole would begin to regularly use detailed attention to crucial events to anticipate and understand the challenges that come from rapid change and be a "learning organization," that is, an organization that can acquire and reflect on new knowledge almost organically. During my time with the development, however, no new cases were added or more case instructors developed. We had helped the individuals in those sessions, and their improved observational, recording, and analytical skills may have had longer-term impacts, but we did not yet see an institution-wide commitment to these methods of helping Pradanites understand and cope with their new challenges on the ground. I reflect on this apparent outcome below.

The Third Intervention: Strengthening Mid-level Leadership

PRADAN's team leaders were pivotal to keeping the widely scattered work coherent and accountable and were chosen and placed with special care. Each was responsible for helping his or her team of up to ten "executives" plus current apprentices at any stage of their highly varied work in villages scattered across a district of one to two million people. Each project was exacting and required creative responses – and was often also frustrating and discouraging. With the expansion beyond familiar areas, the team leaders' best functioning became even more challenging. And because program directors and other leadership were now attending to the new larger array of external stakeholders, team leaders found themselves left more and more on their own to meet their assigned targets while coping with the uncertainties that go with rapid expansion. All this, easily understandable but also unstable for the long term, led Deepankar and me to revisit the vision for change and the needs and sequences required, and urge instituting a special program just for team leaders, to focus on how to handle their role at this particular juncture. This special program was approved at the end of our first winter's work, and instituted the following year.

To fit best into the team leaders' prevailing work and travel patterns, we planned a program of two four-day sessions, three weeks apart. In line with the PRADAN work culture, participation was optional and the participants were able to identify their particular learning interests. Responses to our query indicated pressing practical concerns, such as time management, financial accounting, managing meetings, dealing with conflicts, and interacting with the central office. So these became the program contents, distributed, as usual, in advance so participants could reflect before arrival and be ready to discuss them from day one.

As they assembled that first morning, we were prepared for discussions of these concrete management-related concerns. But it was immediately clear that the team leaders' *real* need – and joy – was to talk with their peers, many of whom were long-time colleagues. And at every turn, no matter what the *stated* topic was, more heart-felt and immediately pressing topics took over. That their current challenges varied widely between pairs and groups caused no concern.

So, we let these more clearly topical needs drive the agenda. This meant shifting from leading "content-based" sessions to facilitating the team leaders' efforts to build more robust and continuing contact among themselves. Instead of discussing ways to run team meetings better and the other issues they had themselves proposed, they considered and agreed upon how best to become much more completely and continuously engaged with each other in mutual support. They developed firm agreements about the best spacing, initiation and timing, and mixed methods of staying in touch.

One form of mutual support would be to present agreed-upon ideas and recommendations to the Management Committee and PRADAN as a whole, rather than as individuals. The participants spent time figuring out how to overcome the practical obstacles of time and space to make this happen. Another desire was for mutual assistance and practical feedback in the field. To meet this need, team leaders together created and planned a program of videotaping and discussing the regular meetings they had with their own teams, and then showing and discussing these meetings in new, regular consultations with their peers, to allow the team leader-in-action to analyze how he or she handled the situation and engage with the others' suggestions.

By the end of the first four days, team leaders had made detailed plans to do several things that would benefit both their morale and performance:

- Travel to another team leader's district to "sit in" on each other's team meetings and then stay an extra day to process it together afterwards
- Arrange with headquarters for just team leaders to meet together for an extra day or two in conjunction with the annual meeting of all PRADAN staff
- Identify geographical clusters of team leaders so headquarters would deal with them in groups for many communications and requests, instead of individually
- Videotape at least one regular team meeting and bring the video to the next session of the team leaders' program for discussion and learning together.

These decisions involved much discussion but all were made smoothly. Eight videos were brought and four discussed at the second session. The discussions confirmed that team leaders were ready to be observed by their peers and welcomed their advice and support – clearly supporting a growing culture of mid-level collaboration, a creative self-organizing subsystem in place of the now-missing mentoring and nurturing from above.

Thus, the program that all originally thought should comprise a curriculum of enhancing leadership and management skills changed spontaneously into an experiment in self-organization. Interestingly, one of the processes they organized was a type of "case study" – different in format from written cases, and not as broad in its focus, but with similar ends of analysis and mutual support based on actual work circumstances and challenges. We consultants found it an exercise in rolling with the unexpected, such that what the client really needed was exposed and then met through a new agenda. It illustrated the difference between being a teacher, who shares expertise with an audience of learners, and being a facilitator, who helps groups discover what they need and what actions to take based on shared understandings.

Reflections on the Three Interventions

Visioning the Future Scaled-up PRADAN and Engaging with Stakeholders

The leaders of PRADAN used visioning to decide how to go forward with major organizational change. Visioning helped them gain practical clarity about where PRADAN wanted to go in the future, how relationships with key organizations might change and grow, and how they needed those relationships to look and perform, to be successful. This in turn raised institution-wide confidence to set about the internal and external changes the expansion called for. This process had positive results and suggests an approach that others might consider for any large change. This was in essence a "test hit" – the unusual result when a new initiative finds its target on the first outing. The process may have worked because it was a more intentional and systematic, yet still action-oriented, "look before you leap" approach to planning, taking into account the whole organizational network that must work together to bring about the large-scale change intended.

The key steps of this process included our "worry beads" of imagining what the organization would look like in the years ahead if successful, mapping the network of key stakeholders essential to making the work of the organization happen, and making the map as inclusive of appropriate partners as practicable. The next step was to hold conversations with key current stakeholders and potential new stakeholders systematically, but expeditiously, within a set time frame. The goal of stakeholder conversations is generally to reach a firm "go or no go" decision on the major change envisioned. Then (if the decision is "go") to come to an agreement within the organization's leadership about how the current relationships would best be developed to support the envisaged change, now informed by any new information gained from the conversations. If the decision is "no go," the time is not wasted – the discussion can be turned to how the visioning and lessons learned might support a different approach to addressing the needs that motivated the original proposal.

This process overall worked very well for the Management Committee, in terms of the external world they most needed to consider as they started out. We saw above, however, that one area of stakeholder engagement was not sufficiently attended to in these early discussions: the internal stakeholders, those Pradanites who worked in the field and in middle management. PRADAN had institutional "doctrine" (core values, policy choices, and practice guidelines) that had developed (in practice) over time. Some of those practices involved intensive mentoring responsibilities and a culture of learning, and all of those internal actors were stakeholders in how the program was organized and run. Ultimately, we consultants realized that these cultural norms would need attention, but it is worth questioning why we did not consider the internal stakeholders as candidates for this first round of consultations. In retrospect, this would have been an excellent basis for one or more visioning conferences with participants from various parts of the organization.

Helping Field Staff Build Their Capacity to Understand and Adapt to Change

The reader will know that I am devoted to recording and analyzing concrete details of my work and that of others, to keep learning why something worked or not, what or who was instrumental in the success or lack thereof, or how I could have done things differently for better outcomes. I do not trust memory and I believe that having more specific data, recorded in the moment and reflected upon later, makes for better diagnoses and outcomes. I have looked for opportunities to encourage organizations to adopt practices that use these methods and approaches to build insight and capacity.

The case development and teaching program experience showed that participants engage enthusiastically in paying detailed attention to concrete complex situations like those they know closely, and with guidance and support can develop many cases and also facilitate case-based teaching sessions. This approach made PRADAN's training more relevant and, more generally, also showed practical approaches to "training for transformation" in which the content is not a set of "how-to's" but the discussion of real, well-described dilemmas and situations that members encounter in their work of promoting major social change. Rather than teaching "best practices" in emergent and experimental situations, this method develops the critical thinking, organizational analysis, and skills participants need to work problems and issues through as they arise. In short, it helps participants react to novel situations with their own "field experiments." Beyond that, however, our wider expectations that the leadership as a whole would develop habits of intensive recording on which to base decisions were disappointed. We had hit upon a successful intervention for the individuals, but PRADAN did not institute case recording and reflection on a continuous basis.

The idea that organizations of the future must be learning organizations became current with Peter Senge's book *The Fifth Discipline*. But how to accomplish this? This may be more possible today than when Senge was writing (1990), since new technologies have made recording and discussing experiences easier and more inviting. The experience of the team leaders suggests that technology can play a role: in videotaping their team meetings, they essentially produced "cases" that their peers helped them reflect upon. This does suggest then that, when timing, attractive recording technology, and the very practicality of getting advice are all in place, recording reappears as a good investment and habit, at least for staff who have similar roles and trust one another.

Institutionalizing this practice more broadly, though, will likely require investment in training on case recording and analysis, staff to oversee the process, and sanctioned organizational fora where cases are reviewed for their implications for practices, programs, and policies going forward. All this would have required a much greater mandate for investment and follow-through than we had negotiated, and as outside consultants, once we had left the organization, the impetus for continuing with case writing or other forms of institutionalized individual reflection and organizational learning declined. However, further inquiry may uncover impacts that we are not able to see from this vantage point. From the perspective of this book, however, there is no type of organization where it is of greater critical importance to develop the capacity to learn and adapt than those organizations tackling transcendent challenges.

Helping Mid-level Leaders Cope with the Lack of Support from Above
Our experience with the team leaders highlights the likelihood that institutions undergoing major transformations experience new demands *at every level* of the organization, and these demands have wide repercussions. Often, interactions *between levels* get crowded out, narrowed, and strained in such a situation, because each level becomes so preoccupied with coping with the new conditions and adjusting and safeguarding their own roles that they loosen or even lose connections with the others. And, at every level, shortchanging the dealings with those "below" becomes easiest. So, just at the time the "lower" levels are feeling the greatest need for guidance and support in the novel circumstances and tasks, they get deprived of them and feel "deserted."

In these situations, old ways of thinking about interventions or appropriate trainings do not promise at all well for repairing deep organizational rifts and/or for creating the continuing support needed to cope with major institutional change or to accomplish the desired goals. PRADAN's team leaders (at all levels) may have needed to develop core skills of management and communicating under these conditions, but they needed to shore up their peer work network even more – and *before* they could be expected to address those technical skills. Fresh thinking and new ways of organizing and empowering the various levels of the institution were needed to address the challenges that flow from "going to scale." We may recall here that Barry Oshry, writing in his evocative book *Seeing Systems* (2007), argues that the key to improving large organizations lies in strengthening the ability of middle managers to communicate and problem-solve. This appeared to be what we did, unintentionally but quite willingly, in our mid-level training program. Participants left empowered and followed up on their own thereafter.

Our advice for consultant–facilitators is to be flexible to the extent that the organization will allow, welcome the initiative, and change the program to let emerge what will. Do not be afraid to revisit the "worry beads:" ask again what is envisioned and needed, and map new sequences. We let the participants articulate their challenges and work them out as best as they could in these quite new conditions, rather than the forceful alternative of sidelining their agenda and taking over again. Deepankar was PRADAN's long-term consultant, and I also had had close involvement with PRADAN's leadership development staff over many years. In a way, that made us part of this same culture and so we could readily work with the real needs of the participants and not even think of trying to thwart them. In my experience, a collaborative, participatory culture which permits, even encourages, self-organizing is preferrable for large-scale social-change organizations to be able to deal with order-of-magnitude growth.

So the planned training morphed into an unplanned but apparently much-needed self-organization of team leaders to support new practices that *they worked out themselves*. Unlike the foundation-supported external instructors at SFET, these individuals trusted one another, knew one another very well, and existed within an organizational culture that seems to have nourished these conditions, though it had not gone far enough to institutionalize them. Our intervention with team leaders gave them space to go one step further – caused, in John Lewis's famous formulation, "good trouble" – disturbed the system such that it rearranged itself subsequently in a more adaptive way. This seems consistent with emergent change theory.

Reflections on Organizing and Managing Large System Change

In PRADAN, the prevailing conditions already favored team leaders acting on their own behalf and for their new self-organization to evolve. PRADAN's whole culture was highly participative, so its top leaders and also funders could be expected to tolerate even major shifts of agenda and priorities, even welcome them, on the understanding that it was important to be maximally responsive to the "conditions on the ground." Not all organizations have this cultural norm in place.

But even with these cultural norms, PRADAN struggled with this change. The challenge may have flowed from the fact that only external stakeholders had been considered at the beginning of the intervention and maybe before that. Whatever the reason, at the early planning stages we did not address how the great expansion of the program would draw senior leadership away from their current practices of being available to support team leaders and mentor new staff. Underlying the Management Committee's difficulty as the expansion was under way, was the assumption that these same leaders could, and should, "do it all," despite well-established institutional norms of joint decision-making and collaboration that were considered essential (though never formal) doctrine. A lesson for organizational development consultants is to help leaders recognize or make formal these types of institutional norms as a way of opening them up to discussion and modifications that would better address emerging conditions.

The Management Committee continued planning and directing the expansion and tried to manage it alongside its ongoing responsibilities. The change agenda, then, fell more and more behind, and the Management Committee lost its accustomed interpersonal ease and openness. It was a downward spiral: just when maximum clarity, best functioning, and highest-level flexibility and support were needed most, the Committee functioned less well and with lower expectations from meeting to meeting, and issues piled up. We have seen that the team leaders reached out to one another in response, but they still needed steady organization-wide support.

In trying to do too much – not only continuing their regular work of running a large organization, but also instituting larger changes – the Committee lost sight of facts on the ground that affected the actual change work going on. For example, even in the poorest villages women were now coming to self-help groups with cell phones as well as their babies, and with current experiences with contacting banks and participating in markets and public events. What they might need and expect from PRADAN was surely transforming as well. Also, official and funding arrangements kept changing, requiring more attention. The sitting Management Committee could not see which changes in current practice would be most appropriate in these settings on top of carrying on with the day-to-day functioning of a large organization.

Program directors and other Pradanites on the Committee withdrew into their own particular concerns, involvements in their own state government and bidding for state projects in their special competence, like water management or forestry, or getting a new university to start a professional degree program in community development that could also be a next professional step up for field workers and team leaders. Several members left for positions elsewhere.

In response, the Committee established a new horizontal role of "integrator" to take responsibility for one major function across the whole of the organization, such as *all* self-help groups, not just in one region or another, and to experiment with ways of grouping the self-help groups into "clusters" or "federations" and helping them get more technical support. This new role took the constant monitoring of "conditions on the ground" off the to-do list of the Committee as a whole. But looking at the system overall with the reflective lens, a much broader and well-defined structural change related to implementing the expansion itself may also have been needed: an *innovative subsystem* to detail the massive expansion and best ways to manage and incorporate it into PRADAN. This need, hard to see and to manage from inside, is for the change-agent consultant to propose. Some self-chosen high-level staff with carefully chosen outsiders could have done the spadework on the expansion, identified time for it, including, probably, consultant time, and worked out orderly procedures for sharing insights with the Committee. This separation of duties could have made sure that the issues arising from rapid change could be faced straight on, unburdened by outdated habits or competing priorities. That group of senior staff could also have developed special expertise in institutional design and management, and perhaps become a cadre of candidates for the organization's future leadership. An internal consultant might have had the staying power to pursue this.

Reflections on the Role of the External Consultant

Some of the shortcomings of the consultation, and perhaps some of the successes too, can be attributed to the dynamics of the external role which I played, the stage my career was at, and the history of the organization. At least some of the impact I had within the power setting and external world of PRADAN came because it was known I would be in and out and would not stay around to meddle. I was secure enough to let the mid-level leaders "take over" their training programs, without fear of unfavorable long-term repercussions, but I was also unable to follow through with habitual recording, case writing, and other reflective practices, and to institutionalize them. Deepankar Roy and the Management Committee would continue their progress, and the Team Leaders Group was organizing itself in ways that would outlast my consultancy, but the lack of an imbedded "champion" or "container" for institution-wide continuous reflection may explain why the case practice did not take off (apparently), while the other two interventions were catalytic in the sense that they led to consequential and enduring changes. In a future intervention, perhaps, I would push for co-leaders from within the organization who would serve as the sponsor and advocate for the group's continuing use of case writing as a means of continuous training and development of managers and future leaders of PRADAN.

Another way this episode reflects on the nature of the "outsider" consultancy is that I was not there to assess how this practice may have actually become part of individual Pradanites' practice *and* had lasting impacts on the organization as a whole. So although it was not apparent to me that using cases had become part of the organizational practice, that does not mean that the skills taught in those sessions did not do so, for at the time many individuals took to and grew from the process.

In Aloka, SFET, and Indonesia, I was in a position by luck, by design, or through my own perspicacity to influence initial conditions, and had the staying power to respond to changing conditions, create the needed containers, and influence the required support for agreed-upon developments. In Scotland, the initial conditions were already favorably disposed at the outset because of the influence of the Tavistock Institute on the decision-makers. At the South Carolina School of Public Health, the container for innovative development was in place initially but was then dismantled, and so although the new institution prospered, several of its basic innovative features were discontinued.

With PRADAN, we had a long-standing successful system that opened itself up to major change. As a team, we consultants were well experienced and long connected with the organization; our own openness was rooted in the realistic call for innovation in novel conditions. My particular openness and flexibility were also rooted in the fact that I was neither able to set the conditions for interventions at the outset nor responsible for the ongoing work after I left. Many questions one might ask when in this self-limiting role have more to do with one's own career choices than with the project in hand. These questions may include how much feedback, un-requested, the consultant would want to give, to what degree he or she would push back against the tendency to envision the consultant as an external problem-solver as opposed to an integral team member, and other questions about how one may wish to work and what might be the organizational possibilities.

CHAPTER 6

PRADAN Proves that Collaboration Can Make a Major Difference in Community Development

Poverty, the challenge on which PRADAN has been focused for over four decades, is a complicated, stubborn problem that persists. Although in recent decades the number of people in extreme poverty has been falling, it is not falling as fast as it must, and there are still many millions who live in slightly-less-abject poverty, and not just in the poorest countries. But the transcendent nature of a challenge does not stop those who are truly committed to making a difference in the lives of individuals and communities, and PRADAN stands out as a leader bringing replicable change and measurable progress to individuals, families, and communities.

PRADAN stands high among the pioneers of organizing women into self-help groups as an approach to mobilize poor communities and improve family livelihoods. PRADAN's work is essentially different from that of external aid agencies that inject innovations into villages. Rather, its work is inclusive and embedded, as in the case of Minetown, where the manufacturing company had learned that placing a new factory in a town and mandating new norms for hiring, training, and working did not make a new initiative actually take root, which required the community's involvement. These two experiences showed that communities do not relish and truly adopt external aid if it does not reflect their own agency and their own needs and goals. On the other hand, where communities are recognized for the experiences and strengths they already have, they can take the assistance of others and use it in their own ways and to lasting effect.

The expansion described here began in 2007; by 2010, PRADAN was working in some 600 development "blocks" in over 100 districts across seven states, spending that year about 400 million rupees or about $8 million USD. (This $8 million spent in rural India has several times the purchasing power of that amount in Western countries or even in the fast-urbanizing parts of India.) During its 2009–10 fiscal year, PRADAN's 300 staff helped an additional 99,000 families develop new livelihoods. Now, according to the PRADAN website (accessed April 2021), PRADAN works directly with more than 848,400 families across India's poorest states, generating a gross yearly output of $80 million for participating women and communities. The livelihoods promoted today in sectors such as silk, vegetables, fruit, and poultry have helped community organizations become leading players in these business sectors. The program to link the self-help groups with banks is the world's largest microfinance movement, with more than 70 million women having bank accounts for their businesses. It has been replicated around the world and is now the central strategy of many grassroots NGOs and public programs. Most recently (as of November 2021), PRADAN was actively engaged in long-term consultation in several African countries, with Tanzania and Kenya the readiest candidate countries, and forty current Pradanites preparing to go there. And alongside direct economic development of the participants, PRADAN supports Women Federations, an associative tier of self-help groups that support members' engagement to fight exploitation and violence.

In closing, let me end on a personal note.

This is the last of my "case chapters" for this book. Although I am still active professionally – even attending international conferences and annual meetings, thanks to modern technology – I no longer take on this type of intensive consultancy. My Ronnie passed away a few years ago, my children, grandchildren, and great-grandchildren are all around, and I live by my little pond in North Carolina still. I keep in touch with many of the people mentioned throughout this book. One of the most important elements of my career has been the making and keeping of colleagues-become-friends everywhere I have been. For a modern reader, this may sound like "networking," but this is not what I mean by it, and insofar as it is "teachable" at all, I would like to impress the importance of developing and keeping these types of connections. I loved returning to India – there was so much to do and so much energy among those doing it – a perfect combination for me! But the main reason I was able to return was that I arrived "known" – I had over the decades made and kept these deep, rich connections of mutual respect and lasting affection. I persist with these deeper personal connections and have learnt from them, grown from them, over these many years. I am used to having several homes that are not just geographically apart but communal. So, I hope the reader has found helpful the experiences I have described and the methods and generalizations that I derived along with keeping up my continuing professional education. The next chapters will outline some of the lessons I learned over my long career – but most of all I hope the reader gets an encouraging glimpse of how to live a life that is open to and conducive to real connection with other people. That is where true happiness – and opportunity! – exist.

CHAPTER 7

Sustaining Life and Learning in Collaborative Development: Career Strategies

Introduction: The Life You Create

As I look back over this long career, several important patterns emerge that seem worth sharing with fellow practitioners committed to working on transcendent challenges in various settings, to increase our profession-wide understanding and to help manage the challenges we all face. In the next chapter, we will share some of the technical basics of actually working with clients. But before we go there, I would like to reflect on the *inner* experience of my career more broadly, and perhaps draw into action the many people I meet who wish to work at "something that really matters" but do not know how to start it or how to mesh it into their daily lives.

I start with three twentieth-century writers who introduced specific terms I have used to think about making a difference in the world.

"*Transcendent challenge*" is economist Robert Heilbroner's phrase for what "faces humanity within a thinkable timespan [with] an utterly new condition of caution and constraint on a civilization whose historical thrust has been in just the opposite direction." (1989: 98) In other words, it describes those grave trials of humankind, problems that are urgent and of vast import and require leaders to change their customary ways of thinking and acting. They are not necessarily the central focus of the actual intervention, but the need for the intervention, as well as the potential impact, grows from these challenges. In my own career, examples include the challenges of "realizing human potential beyond mere survival;" "bringing lasting peace;" "empowering and including women and others often excluded from power;" and "addressing poverty and economic injustice." These are the type of problems we all agree in the abstract that we want to solve, but which most of us do not get to solve in our everyday work lives, because they seem too complex or large, or because they require too radical a change from the status quo, or because we do not have the institutional or stakeholder support to address them. It is my goal that social-change practitioners look for opportunities to address transcendent challenges and know how to assess the possibilities when they arise.

"*Vital involvement*" is analyst Eric Erikson's term for the highest engagement such challenges and reversals of direction call for (Erikson et al., 1986). It is also my goal that social-change practitioners enact and encourage dynamic, active engagement with these challenges – as if their very life depended on it.

And the "*sound of sense*" is poet Robert Frost's phrase for what we need to hear and see to create (poetic) art – the music in the notes, the forest for the trees – in other words, the *whole* of the parts: "[artistic expression] begins with a lump in the throat, a sense of wrong, a homesickness… [I]t is a reaching out toward expression… an effort to find fulfillment." (1963) He hears it only faintly yet, from the sound in general, he is sure that it is *friends* talking, not strangers, and certainly not enemies. I am not an artist, but in my career, it has been my goal to include these "parts" of the whole, "friends," in all we do, people who are most affected by the challenge and have the greatest interest in the change to be brought about; others with the means and will to bring about change; others who know the problem and ways of addressing it from the inside out. These are the colleagues and advisors, who know processes that work, and locals who have lived the problem and tried to solve it. We must pay attention to their insights, intuitions, traditions, histories and not try to impose our own.

My practical aims for this chapter are to take those ominous "sounds" to heart and reflect upon how to collaborate closely with others to deal with transcendent challenges, and how to survive and thrive in the life created through this career. I wish to encourage many more people to join this top-priority work, to record and reflect on it for further learning, and to develop their "inside" self at the same time as they develop their attention outward – both, and both together.

Nine Key Lessons Learned

As I reflect on my life in working on these major challenges, several lessons stand out as most important to pass on and they have become the structure for this chapter. These include lessons for choosing and moving forward with major consulting engagements that address global challenges, lessons for surviving and thriving in a long career of such engagements, and finally, lessons for learning from these encounters and sharing these learnings with the wider professional community to encourage and inform future generations of colleagues. In all I list nine key lessons for a career in supporting inclusive transformative change in international settings:

1. "Listen to" and value highly your own life experience: what you *bring* to a next opportunity
2. Choose clients thoughtfully and test commitment early
3. Proceed with confidence
4. Join the communities where you live and work
5. Prize and attend to your closest relationships
6. Build life-long colleagueship
7. Take time to refresh and reflect
8. Record your experiences in a disciplined way
9. Share learnings with the wider professional community and future practitioners.

1. Listen to and Value Highly Your Own Life Experience

I do not assume everyone reads "personal prologues," so I will summarize here the basics of my early life as told in more detail there. As the middle son of three, I grew into extra awareness and solid experiences of "managing" upward and downward, from the very beginning. Born in Berlin, my part-Jewish ancestry made escaping Hitler's Germany imperative. My father left for the United Kingdom; my mother followed with us children. At our new school we learnt English fast and passed exams well, and I joined local life, as became my lifetime habit. Essentially, I was abandoned by one country and embraced by another, and then and forever learned the benefits of being included, especially when the threat of exclusion loomed.

During World War Two I turned sixteen and was the only one in my family to be considered an "enemy alien" and interned behind barbed wire on the Isle of Man with no outside contact, books, or writing materials, among thousands of men of all ages. I was freed after four months and resumed my schooling, and through school contacts found suitable work. Working in a factory during the War, I also studied for a basic degree (by mail), passed my BSc Econ., then studied and kept notes about the strange, ineffective management I witnessed in my factory, and wrote and published a book. This writing and a connection I had made in school landed me a position in the new British Institute of Management as a field research officer, and I was engaged as a junior fellow in the work in western Scotland, the first setting of this book.

I was also sent to study the repeated and hugely damaging strikes in the London docks and guide the new Labour government in what to do about them. While driving through bombed-out dockland, quite clueless about how to set about "studying" it, I noticed a sign for the Young Christian Workers HQ, went in, and found them interested, well-connected, and eager to join my enquiry. I stayed connected with their top team. Only weeks later, they asked me to join the UK delegation to the first World Assembly of Youth meeting in the USA and then become the UK representative on the board of the European Youth Campaign, headquartered in Paris.

So I headed into my life-long international career, armed with the lesson to always – *always* – pay attention and take every chance to connect with people. The importance of this last maxim is explored more below, in the lesson on building "colleagueships" – those unpredictable and often serendipitous human connections I have made throughout my life.

2. Choose Clients Thoughtfully and Test Commitment to Transformative Change Early

As we have seen, a commitment to work on a transcendent challenge constitutes a serious life commitment and often entails career risks for the practitioner and serious adjustments for the practitioner's family. It is important, therefore, as much as possible, to ensure that the possibilities for success exist in the situation in terms of the commitment and capacity of those who will be closest colleagues, sponsors, and partners, and in the setting itself.

Several questions have proved to be important to ask before or right at the start of a potential project:
- Do the key leaders genuinely aim for transcendent goals?
- Do they embrace (or at least accept) the values of collaboration and inclusion?
- Are they willing to collaborate with me (the consultant) right from the start?
- Is the chemistry right between me and the key leaders I will work with: does the initial tone promise a constructive long-term relationship?
- In the broader "power setting" of the institution, are there sufficient support and resources to give the new venture a chance to grow and show its promise?

The first questions above are very important (and central to this book): how to assess the potential clients' transcendent goals and values of inclusive collaboration. To address transcendent challenges and effect transcendent change, we must know what to look for and how to assess the possibilities when they arise. So, when choosing whether to take on a project, it is very important to test the client's readiness to address this type of change in ways that will work.

So, I assess: "Do these clients intend to work on the new or onward development by effecting change that is significantly different from a mere incremental alteration of the status quo?" Traditional leadership training, personal counselling, updating technologies, and merely changing the organizational structure do not do this. What counts is a readiness to work in different, perhaps unheard-of ways and to include and respect those whose participation is essential for success, but who may have been excluded in the past. Will the client include those most affected by the change in all decision-making and goal setting? How far is the client disposed, able, and willing to include others? How ready is the client to work with me to create an encouraging climate for people to interact comfortably across generally prevailing lines of status and rank?

Accepting maximum inclusion is so momentous a shift in most settings – the very idea of it and then also its implementation – that it becomes synonymous with openness to true transcendent change. The first useful indicators of this openness can be the client's attention to local particularities, their engagement with live connections already in place and functioning, their readiness to reach out further, and how they talk about their intentions. The client's approach to our first interaction is often a good indication of their openness to a "bottom-up" approach to action; for example, do they choose a one-to-one meeting with me or include others? The level of involvement both of levels of the organization and of parts of the community may be indicative of the client's willingness to be inclusive.

Making the widest inclusion and collaboration the very heart of development is indeed very different from the usual setting of goals at the top and getting "others" to implement them. If clients begin by including various stakeholders in collaborative working together, more may also come into view as the development gets under way, beyond "those at the table" at first, such as the neighborhood-at-large, a tribal chief, a local women's group, business leaders, the whole institution, and even larger systems; that is, other stakeholders with an interest in the outcomes. Including me, the consultant, in decision-making is part of this inclusiveness, and a history of calling on experienced consultants and inviting them into the decision-making process is an indicator of whether that project has best promise.

Regarding the question of chemistry with key leaders and the broader power setting of the organization: ideally, we know all the leaders, funders, political and financial stakeholders, and other organizational or community stakeholders, before beginning. Chemistry can be easy to assess (as when I first met and immediately connected with the leader of SFET or the president of my second university in the US, who hired me and gave me my charge) but not always easy to guarantee (the SFET leader was a very practical engineer looking for clear, concrete results; the university president left before I had even taken up residence!). Information about stakeholders can be very difficult to know at the beginning. Examples of being blindsided by powerful stakeholders abound in this volume. In any event, try to make a list when you start out, continuously expand it, and work with that information to advise your clients when necessary.

So, what does readiness look like in practice, and how do I test commitment? Some examples from the cases in this book follow.

In post-war Britain, maximum inclusion of stakeholders had already been made: the hosier company directors had had discouraging experiences with setting up two branch factories in the traditional ways on their own, then engaged the highly reputed Tavistock Institute to improve the HQ mill operations; seeing the greater effectiveness of inclusion and collaboration, they *then* invited them to help set up this third branch factory in Minetown. They had also already secured national agreement from the trade union for training the workers for the new branch factory. The other consultant, John, and I then underlined our collaborative intent by meeting the town council and working happily with its suggestions for where to stay, for the location of a workshop to start training and local workmen to fix it up, for how to recruit applicants, and, perhaps most telling, for finding a manager locally.

For directing Aloka, there was only a US foundation to propose my name and a world-wide meeting to approve my directorship. So I set eight then-unusual conditions for establishing a radically different form of training center in then-Ceylon. If these had not been accepted, I would not have taken on the project. When the board accepted these conditions, these conditions were all Ronnie and I had for working things out and taking our first large assignment overseas. Two years later the new nationalist government of Sri Lanka was no longer so welcoming, but by that time Aloka had proved its value, so it continued in India and elsewhere.

For introducing extension education into the Indian government's new institute for upgrading and greatly expanding its small-industry consulting service (SFET), the director and I happily hit it off from the very first meeting. Even more happily, he asked department chairs to join us every morning thereafter, which I took as a very promising sign for his inclination to work together with others. I realized three years later that more Ministry leaders should perhaps have been at that table, but by then the larger system power configuration was such that the innovative effort was able to survive an attempt to reverse changes.

In our work in the South Carolina School of Public Health, the early indications were indeed promising, but when the traditional administration replaced the original president, the circumstances of the situation changed. Much was still accomplished but not in the ways we had foreseen or wanted. This is the setting in this book that most dramatically shows the need for fully scoping the dynamics of the consulting situation beyond just the primary contact.

In Indonesia, the readiness for collaboration was unclear, but after extensive preliminary discussions, the Ministry made the necessary commitments to turn an initial one-year project into a three-year and then into a six-plus-year assignment. The Ministry's commitments included giving time for piloting of the program and allowing me to hire consultants to undertake a uniquely collaborative intervention.

With PRADAN, not only did I already have long-term relationships of trust and mutual respect with its founders and some leaders, but the whole Executive/Management Committee then met with local consultant-on-call Deepankar and me from the very beginning. Their enthusiasm, combined with the availability of major funding, favored their ambitious plans and promised realistic possibilities.

3. Proceed with Confidence

"Nothing great was ever accomplished without enthusiasm," wrote Ralph Waldo Emerson. Once I have chosen a setting to work in, answered these questions, and reassured myself on these and other lines, I plunge into the work with passion, discipline, and energy. In the second "lessons learned" chapter to follow, we will discuss practical ways to anticipate, map, plan, and altogether engage people to help them undertake interventions (and periodically revisit their readiness, needs, and sequences). However, it is of the very essence of transcendent change that although we seek certain outcomes, conditions on the ground make results inherently unpredictable. Sometimes plans do not work out, and conditions that promised success can change. It is particularly important, therefore, for practitioners to take the long view, confident that their efforts will have important impacts even if the originally mapped ways do not go as planned. In short, be undaunted by the many obstacles, twists, and turns you will face. If you work effectively to make significant change, results are likely to follow. Sometimes these "spin-off" results even multiply the original effect, creating a cascade of positive change.

There are several reasons that confidence is warranted and necessary. My experience shows that if key stakeholders are truly committed to significant change, have identified promising possibilities and contexts, engage in a participatory approach, pilot test change initiatives, pay attention to results through recording and joint reflection, adjust to events as they occur, and constantly work to grow resources and supporters, *significant change will happen*. If pursued consistently with the values of inclusion and collaboration, that change will be in the direction the world needs.

For example, in Scotland the plan was to help a prominent hosiery company create employment for women in areas of the country where they did not traditionally work outside their homes. Locally the need was evident, we encouraged the community to participate, guide, and co-create the methods, and as a result we made change together, despite the fact this sort of effort had been unsuccessful before.

Even when an intervention ends prematurely, as with Aloka's moving to India and then not receiving support for expanding there, in its six years, 250 young leaders from twenty-three countries participated in the twelve-week residential programs, seventeen became members of faculty, additional programs organized by alumni took place in five Asian and African countries, and senior officers came to additional short programs at their own request and cost. The effort was not lost: the individuals trained at Aloka went on to be influential in many nations and regions for years to come.

With the experience I brought from Aloka, I was then also able to offer a compelling way of moving forward with SFET and develop programs that made real differences in the field. And although we took great professional risk by challenging current policies for increasing employment, we were able to bring in short-term consultants and actually institute changes originally deemed too controversial by leadership and funders. In this setting perseverance and risk-taking paid big benefits. SFET evolved into an institution for supporting change projects in countries besides India, and local leaders created India's Society for Applied Behavioural Science, an independent training and development organization that continues.

And even without its original sponsor, we did create and launch the new field-oriented School of Public Health over three years. After I left the deanship, and the School reverted to a more traditional orientation, important innovations survived and became adopted more widely, the student body across campus continued to include many more African-American graduate students than before, and some programs continued active connections with state agencies. The interdisciplinary design we had worked to establish also influenced the design of the next new professional school (for environmental studies). So, even in the clearest "failure" of my career, significant change followed and became lasting.

Indonesia included an unexpected boon: the mostly young and post-independence physicians were much readier and even eager for administrative and organizational training and duties than we assumed they would be. They in fact took the lead in attracting additional stakeholders and advancing their own training beyond our plans. Of the 283 physicians who came for the first round of programs, 255 returned for hands-on additional programs for planning, staffing, and running the services. And 88 asked for yet further training in consulting, which we designed, staffed, and ran, and 41 of them pioneered the in-country consulting service that the Ministry funded and provided office space for. This "tide of learning" continued to flow across territories and communities long after the consultant team returned to the US and India.

The next few lessons learned concern surviving and thriving while undertaking major change efforts, with all the attendant uncertainty and stress. For consultants to continue to be successful, it is essential that we tend to our key supports in the community, family, and workplace. So I suggest that practitioners of social change, and particularly those who are working in a country not their own, join the community, protect and nurture family, and build strong relationships with colleagues. In the next few pages, I consider each of these prescriptions in turn.

4. Join the Communities Where You Live

Into these pages I have woven snapshots of the importance and significance of my family, growing up in these far-flung locations. In my book *Between Past and Future: A Field Guide for Fathers Overseas*, I give more sustained attention to this. I return to it here and add more examples because it is key to the well-being and continued capacity of those who want a life helping across the world or intensively in their own communities. In his book *Career Dynamics* (1978), MIT professor Ed Schein describes how stress builds within careers, partly because of stress points within the person due to personal dynamics and career-related transitions, but also when families are under stress as in times of birth, major transitions, and illness. Of all of these we had plenty. Reflecting on what is required for the family, I have identified the following guidelines. These points are paraphrased from pages 200 to 203 of *Between Past and Future*.

CHAPTER 7

For raising a family in a new and different culture, it is critically important to be accepted, and to be accepted it is critically important to be *accepting*. Everywhere we went we were welcomed and helped by those we interacted with, and we were told that the reason for this is that we too were outgoing, welcoming, and broadminded. Work to accept and reconcile and even ignore differences – of religion, of behavior, of dress – even when they are antithetical to your own customs. Visibly and genuinely honoring the ways of others is key to making the family part of the community. Even in situations in which it was important that we modeled (and program participants learned) "Western" concepts of equality and inclusion, as at Aloka, where men and women were to be included and treated equally, we still evinced respect for their local customs and sympathized with how difficult it might be for them to change.

We also always followed up on opportunities to connect to others, even if they were not directly related to the consulting assignment. In many cases this actually did further our work – you never know how or when a connection will become a lasting colleague – but more importantly, it created a *life*: a genuine and growing circle of friends and acquaintances, built on mutual respect, interests, and attraction.

Relationships of trust and mutuality are paramount. During our time in Asia, we had many adventures, including illnesses and other travails along with the demanding and exhilarating work of building new institutions and tackling major social issues. Through it all we felt buoyed by our relationships with one another, and with people in the communities where we lived and benefitted greatly by their help, often unasked for. A shining example of this was when Vikram Sarabhai offered to collaborate and house us for Aloka's first urban program when Ronnie was also pregnant with our first-born. She received the same care and extra help as his own family. We became lastingly close, a "joint family," over the generations. At the same time, our family unit retained its own sense of what worked for us when this was different from local custom or from the urgings of the expat community or the ever-solicitous sponsoring institution. Having one's own preferred practices and habits does not preclude also accepting others' norms, beliefs, and customs. We did not encourage people to copy us in large or small ways, and discouraged excessive deference, even when this became more difficult when we returned as elders. It takes discipline to be at once authentic, welcoming, accepting, and egalitarian.

5. Prize and Attend to Your Closest Relationships

For me the closest relationship was in the context of a traditional family, and the same was true for Ronnie, my true partner and helpmate at every turn. She loved to travel and live around the world as much as I did, and indeed continued traveling to India for her own research and writing after we retired to the States. For me it was second nature to live in many places; I had done so since young childhood and "made myself at home" wherever I went. But uprooting and change can be stressful. For Ronnie, it often meant changing roles, becoming a full-time mother where she could not join in my work until she created her own projects. Communicating about these changes, what we were experiencing and what we needed to thrive, allowed us to make accommodations that held us together *and* strengthened our family.

And as our family grew, understanding the effect of our life choices on our children also became important. For example, at times, our being so open and inclusive with others became stressful for the children. They seemed to wonder whether they were truly special in our eyes, or just part of the extended "family." Ronnie and I learnt how to show our children that they were truly ours and especially deeply and irrevocably connected.

There was a lot to balance: the retention of our family unit's own beliefs and ways, while at the same time encouraging the children to take in, accept, and acknowledge the differences they encountered. For example: in religious practice, one group sings at worship, the other does not; one uses prayer wheels; another separates men and women during worship. In these and other realms it was important to help the children develop a broad and accepting framework for what must have been at times a dizzying diversity when they were trying to figure out what was right to do and believe for themselves.

CHAPTER 7

As they grew, our children had their own ideas, and like children everywhere they asserted those ideas about transitions that affected them. The first time it strongly arose was when they were five, eight, and ten, and we took them from their home in Hyderabad to the very different world of the Southern United States. At first, they did not want to leave their friends and accustomed home; and once in the US, they themselves felt alienated and "strange" for the first time in their lives. We all found that that move affected us all to a greater extent than we had expected. Ronnie had grown up in the US (though not in the South), and I had spent significant time there. Nonetheless, returning in the late '60s after more than a decade away, the Southern US felt alien. After years of living in inclusive, collaborative situations we were suddenly witnesses to shocking racial prejudices and the struggles of tradition-bound institutions in the throes of change. That is not to say that India and the other countries where we had worked did not have their own traditions of prejudice, of course. It is just that at that moment in the US the struggle was front and center in a way we as a family had not experienced in the earlier settings. The children, grown so accepting and inclusive of others, were suddenly ostracized because of that central value so important to us all.

And on top of all that, my life away from my family became all-consuming and extremely stressful for the next three years! I combined my assistant professorship with, first, getting a master's degree at another university ten miles away, and then travelled monthly to the State University of New York at Buffalo to complete my degree in its new program for policy development, and added some clinical teaching there to pay the fees. All along we were very short of funds, having unexpectedly had to buy a house, buy a second car, put our youngest child in private school because his age and earlier schooling in India did not match with the local first grade, and more. I hardly saw my family, and all this was hardest on our children, dismayed as they already were about missing their Hyderabad friends and caught in the racial stand-offs in this first year of school integration. And violence in public schools led to more private schooling and also periodic therapy.

But those years too passed. After I received my doctorate, I was promoted to associate professor with tenure. So freed, I soon developed new connections, colleagues, and programs. And when we finally committed to stay, we all became active in our own way to live by our values within the community, which did after all have room for us.

A life in international development is suffused with many comings and goings. We found that attention to both of these processes is critical for maintaining a sense of well-being and connectedness. In the closing of my "field guide for fathers," I wrote: "For the children leave-taking is especially important, for their early years and friendships have made cornerstones for their lives. [With a good leave-taking] they can head into the next phase of their lives, unencumbered by business unfinished elsewhere." Nowadays, with social media and other instant communications, this aspect of life may be somewhat easier, but I expect the sense that we can "always be in touch" may also complicate matters. The leaving of day-to-day in-person relationships is still wrenching for any family, and sensitive attention needs to be paid to leave-taking and the feelings associated with that.

6. Build Life-long Colleagueship

A bit farther from home and more directly tied to the work are the professional relationships that grow when people are engaged together in meaningful and inspiring work. I have coined the term "colleagueships" to combine the idea of friendship and work partnerships. From the very beginning, an openness to connecting with others has furthered my career and expanded every horizon, often in unlooked-for and unexpected ways! My friends in school in England helped me find my first job. My marriage to Ronnie, so opposed by our families because of our different religions, actually made us the best candidates to lead Aloka.

Over the years, with each new potential project I thought of possible colleagues who could help me assess the project and, in some cases, join with me in the work. This finding, maintaining, and

CHAPTER 7

deepening of professional relationships – *colleagueships* – is probably my most important learning over the years. Colleagues further the work, but are also essential for self-care: working for transformative change is complex and often stressful and exhausting. Identifying and nurturing deep relationships with people in tune with this work is of lasting importance.

In retrospect, I group these colleagues into loosely defined categories based on how closely our work and lives intertwined. The category of "alter egos" (or "twins") contains those who turned out to share my own style as well as my life-long interest and action in social improvement. You know them when you see them, and keep working with them in places and projects that turn out to matter a great deal.

Udai Pareek became one in India, from SFET on. I had gone to Delhi for Erik Erikson's first public lecture in India, and this total stranger came over to ask about something I had said in the open meeting and also what I was doing in India. With just that, Udai resigned his already long career in the central government and became my "twin," a life-long colleague, co-author, and alter ego in Hyderabad, and then in Indonesia and world-wide. Together we built a national trainer network and we co-authored a best-selling book on training. And when I finished and left for Chapel Hill, Udai followed with his family; he it was who broke the ceremonial coconut on our new house to bless it there, and so on, till death did us part.

Racine Brown became "my twin" in my unexpectedly long years in academia in the American South: we met for work with the NTL Institute and continued to do that for year after year, driving together to and fro, creating new programs, and getting to know each other's families. He it was who recommended me for dean and department chair in the new schools of public health and medicine in South Carolina and then also quasi-parented our next generation when Ronnie and I resumed our careers overseas.

David Kiel, my second author here, is still going strong now as my latest alter ego. Originally my doctoral student, he joined the new faculty in the new school and, after my seven years in Indonesia, we resumed our virtually continuous professional dialogue, joint projects, and shared writing.

Sometimes the most random meetings initiated significant connections. We only connected with Vikram Sarabhai, a major influence on Aloka's urban programs, because Ronnie's being the only woman on Harvard's faculty, and thus not invited to faculty meetings, meant she was the only one in the office when Vikram, world-renowned astrophysicist, stopped by to explore possible links for India's first school of management, which he was creating in Ahmedabad. Everything else followed from this chance connection, not just for Aloka's urban programs but for our lives: our Maya was born while we stayed at his home and named into the family, and later when Vikram suddenly died, I advanced to quasi-father to his family. With all generations we continued visiting to and fro, and Ronnie and I were with them for his wife Mrinalini's last days and for floating her ashes down the Sambarmati river in 2016.

Participants in Aloka courses became colleagues and lasting personal friends, and followed us to future assignments: at SFET, Fritz Schumacher came as short-term consultant and joined the institute faculty; another connection from India, Warren Bennis, took my doctorate in his new program in policy development at SUNY-Buffalo; and John Thomas had worked with Warren in developing the management institute in Calcutta and joined the inter-institutional faculty development program. In Indonesia, "my twin," Udai Pareek, brought in Michael and Alexandra Merrill and Jack and Gloria Gant, Jack and Glo having the additional advantage of being African-American and prominent in the educational system of the American South. Indian colleagues at PRADAN, Vijay Mahajan and Deepankar Roy, had first joined Ronnie's case program for social foresters in the 1980s.

I set out this list in some detail to illustrate how haphazard this "finding" of one's closest colleagues can be, as well as how important it is to be open to all kinds of encounters that may lead to lasting collegial relationships and true friendships. Looking back, to set out my successive tasks over my long career without this network of close colleagues is really quite unimaginable to me. They furthered the work and made it possible to find senior colleagues willing "to rough it" with family in out-of-the-way locations and to move again every half-year or so.

Those deep relationships become the mainstay of a life in international consulting. "Networking" would be too mechanical a summary term for it. Insofar as it is "teachable" at all, I would like to emphasize the importance of truly developing, through openness and also respect and acceptance, and nurturing these key relationships, and convey at least a glimpse of how to live a life that is open to and connected with all kinds of people.

7. Take Time to Refresh and Reflect

As many academic researchers will attest, full-time sabbaticals are certainly most productive for major reviews and learning. From Aloka onwards I have inserted a sabbatical before I go on to the next setting. Each has yielded much fuller understandings of what led to what, allowing me to analyze choices and processes for including others for better and longer-term outcomes. Each also gave me time to understand how particular experiences augmented my competencies and how they might contribute to the general state of-the-art. Sabbatical "time off" can intensity personal development routines, recharge capacities, and altogether generate more readiness for the next contract.

This broader purpose of *personal* development was clearest following Aloka: for blocks of time, I had asked an Indian psychoanalyst to monitor my facilitation of interpersonal sessions. Then, by delaying my own next contract by six months I was able to accompany him to *his* next destination, continue my personal analysis with him and also help with the creation of the first therapeutic community in the USA, in a setting that matched Aloka's. Many complaints in the community meetings concerned how occupational therapy was run, so I offered to reorganize it, and this led to my becoming a more accepted member of that (for me) temporary community. My time there foreshadowed many conditions for the coming next work in India, which involved helping the large ministry and its staff work differently, and also addressing the highly specialized and separate traditions of the participants' several professions.

This first sabbatical was unpaid. Funding my subsequent three sabbaticals proved to be easier: the next, following the six years' work with SFET in India, was combined with an easy-paced faculty appointment in my first academic stint at North Carolina, where reflection and writing were part of the work. The third was regularly paid time off after my deanship in South Carolina, and after my work in Indonesia I have been retired, with the usual pension and other benefits. Projects like PRADAN, done in retirement with others at the helm, were the icing on my proverbial career "cake."

The change of venue and pace of sabbatical times allowed me to recharge my batteries and so bring my full Self to the next challenge. That each time I also had a trove of contemporaneous records from my previous assignment greatly grounded the reflecting and writing. So these sabbatical periods not only resulted in working through and letting go of the previous intensive engagement but also led to insights that would prove helpful in addressing the transcendent challenge in the next.

8. Record Experiences Fully and in a Highly Disciplined Way

Recording to learn from and improve practice is quite different from the recording of "outcomes" that most funders ask for, like increases in crop yields or numbers and costs of program participants. It is also different from recalling events for teaching, such as researching and writing up cases. For recording actual practice, contextual details are important, such as which and how different stakeholders participated, how collaborators responded to different ways of communicating, and how the work built continuing relationships and future readiness.

The importance of the meticulous, detailed recording of experience has grown on me over these many years. It is essential for institution-wide learning and ensuring that the right stakeholders are included, as well as for planning next steps and strategies. Memories may augment the record but are simply too partial and self-serving for reliable learning and onward action. I identify four milestones in my life that led to my recording in a full and personal way:

- When, looking over my machine into the vast World War Two factory, seeing quite dysfunctional supervisory practices go on and on, I kept a pad lying open on top of my grinding machine to jot notes on, and used those observations years later to guide further reading and writing. It all connected me with the Tavistock Institute and so also with helping develop the new hosiery mill in Minetown.
- Then, in the early 1950s when on the board of the European Youth Campaign, I put the supposedly "simultaneous translation" aside in favor of attending to the body language of the speakers and kept notes for guiding my own reactions and responsibilities.
- When we used the (laughably small) UNESCO grant to write up the Aloka program and tape-recorded the whole next program, working through the piles of typed-up records was so stimulating and insightful that I resolved to keep *complete* records from then on.
- At the new small industries institute in India (SFET), full recording encouraged the clearer identification of stakeholders and the standardization of a daily matrix for concurrent recording. This provides for recording *all my interactions with all identified stakeholders* and, maintained over my years there, informed major writings on developing institutions. I also keep copies of all correspondence.

So, my complete recording is not only for sharpening academic hypotheses and discourse for building general theory, nor for coming up with recommendations for decision-makers to consider acting on (as in my earlier studies of coal-mine management in Scotland and of strikes in the London docks); nor is it for looking back and reconstructing past situations to write teaching materials about, although it does allow one to do all these things. For me, it is most important for reflecting on and improving *my* practice, clarifying questions I need to discuss with colleagues and personal advisors, and for including the "right" stakeholders in the next steps and onward plans.

Reluctantly, I must add that my regular attempts to urge colleagues and outside stakeholders to keep their own detailed records have been mostly discouraging. "It's just too much on top of all that's going on" is the common excuse. So I leave my matrix for the day lying open on my desk and refer to it when questions arise and we consider concrete actions.

After these many decades of working with institutions in a wide variety of conditions, I have found sampling my interactions to suffice for most days, and reserve complete recording to times of crises and the moratoria that go with them. Four kinds of interactions continue to be most important to record most fully: the presence and absence of individual stakeholders; whose initiative led to action or failed to do so; indications of interactions among stakeholders outside of meetings; and how well I anticipated these specifics and then coped with them. I would normally start the day by looking over yesterday's matrix, augmenting my notes as needed, and thinking forward, refining and advancing ongoing patterns, adding practical ways to incorporate them, discussing them with Ronnie. I also have regular times for broader reflecting and I add more whenever I can, usually during train or air travel and long car-rides (with a driver!).

9. Share Learnings with the Wider Professional Community and Future Practitioners

Rabbi Tarfon said, 2,000 or so years ago, "[We] may not be permitted to complete the work of healing the world, but neither are we free to desist from it." Part of the work is to leave a legacy of learning for colleagues and the next generation of practitioners. In the next section I recount my experiences in sharing what I have learned, hopefully to encourage readers to record, reflect, discuss, write up, and teach about their own work on transcendent challenges, and thus help the community of reflective practitioners dedicated to this work survive, grow, and thrive.

Through Writing

Scholar–practitioners have a distinctive way of knowing because they are deeply involved in the processes they are writing and thinking about. Well-read in the literature of applied behavioral science, and usually with a broad knowledge of history and culture as well, reflective practitioners are indeed in a position to generate insights, understanding, and useful frameworks to guide upcoming practitioners in the art and science of helping major social change. These lessons can support the next rounds of innovation for relieving human suffering and nurturing better societies. If we do not take advantage of this perch, much could be lost in the flow of history. I have made it a practice to write up and publish my experience with each of my major development settings. The meticulous recording discussed in the previous section creates "the data base" for this serious reflection and learning.

Sharing and spreading the learnings then completes the cycle. But sharing them "enough" to make noticeable inroads in a transcendent challenge with work on a particular development remains the practical issue. It involves questions of what stakeholders beyond those immediately involved have been drawn into its wider ambit, what kinds and "amounts" of learning really matter for enlarging the effect, and how best to encourage and broaden the change. This is not to say these kinds of publications are sufficient to spread the innovation, but they can certainly sustain and foster it.

Each sabbatical has enabled me to step back, reflect, draw out significant learnings, and work them into books (twelve before this) or other publications, in addition to case books and other training materials. From Minetown, useful learnings about involving a whole community became one of the *Three Studies in Management* and part of *The Community Factor in Modern Technology*, published in 1951 and 1952 respectively. *The Tide of Learning: The Aloka Experience* detailed how cross-cultural, multi-ethnic men and women lived and trained together with faculty for personal and leadership development, as well as institutional transformation (1960).

Training for Development grew out of the extension experiences at the new SFET Institute and was published first in the US in 1967 and then in India, and there elaborated into *Training for Organisational Development 1* (for policy makers and change agents) and *2* (For trainers, principals, and consultants), both in 2000. My mapping of stakeholders and full recording of my interactions at SFET was the basis for my doctoral dissertation in the new program for policy development at the State University of New York at Buffalo, in 1969. Developing the Population Center in Chapel Hill also became a book (1968) and also contributed to a wider-ranging "A guide to institution-building for team leaders of technical assistance projects" (1971).

From the large Indian anti-poverty effort, PRADAN, the learnings included how scaling up requires significant changes in an existing institution's culture and practices, as well as the stresses and strains and required adaptations related to size. These were discussed in 'Practicing social change' in the practitioners' journal of the NTL Institute for Applied Behavioral Science, a three-part series (2011–14) which continues to be a good guide.

As wider generalizations and themes have emerged from across my major consultancies, they too became books, including *Social Science in Actual Practice: Themes on My Blue Guitar* (1998) and now this current volume. And another book was focused on our experiences with growing our family as we relocated again and again overseas: *Between Past and Future: A Field Guide for Fathers Overseas* (2009).

All these are additional to the often book-length compendia of cases and other training materials we developed and published in the course of the particular consultancies, and some of these too became books for the outside world, for example, *Asican Cases* (1961; with instructors' notes), *Agents of Industrial Development* (1963), and the whole series of case books with instructors' notes we used in Indonesia and for the programs for social foresters in India.

Through Teaching, Mentoring, and Leading

For me, a major way I "shared with the wider professional community" was in spending time in academic and professional institutions mentoring, teaching, writing, and program-building. Many practitioners will not have the opportunity to spend much time in leadership roles in academia. It was certainly a detour in mine, though a natural next step.

At North Carolina I represented the Population Center in a

four-university group for conceptualizing institution development, joined a workshop on that with the Food and Agriculture Organization (FAO) of the United Nations in Rome, and became part-author of a book published through USAID. My courses in consultation and in interpersonal and group relations became regular, and the latter spun off a new opening-day program for all public health students. In the Medical School department of psychiatry and in the School of Education, I joined faculty groups to plan and facilitate programs in interpersonal relations, first in the School and then also in school systems outside.

The national "War on Poverty" legislation opened several new federally funded opportunities. In the School we developed a multi-state program for training workers for the new neighborhood health centers and in the Medical School teamed up with physicians to start several centers in surrounding counties. When the training programs spread to other states I turned the leadership over to Ronnie, and we recruited an African-American to take over from her. For the Division of Health Sciences, I headed the funding and development of a remedial summer program for mostly African-American public health practitioners who needed more math and English skills to enter professional degree programs and qualify for higher positions. In my profession at large I also became active in the National Training Laboratory institute (NTL), staffed training groups every summer, joined the board of the fledgling accrediting organization for applied social scientists and then chaired it, with Ronnie as secretary.

Overall, at least since my time at Aloka, teaching, training, mentoring, and building programs to spread learning and development have been a big part of my work in the world. Sharing learnings and creating experiences by which others may learn must be of equal or greater importance than writing and publishing, and as practitioners we have different inclinations and gifts in these regards. I have been fortunate to do both.

"The Life" and "The Work"

So, do the personal settings and consequences of childhood, family, and later "explain" my "so interesting life" that others comment on? No. And I would not wish several of them or their like on anybody – emigration, internment, war-time London, and round-the-clock nightshifts in the factory making airplane parts in thousands – all unchosen.

And yet these, along with all the other serendipitous meetings which I write about in the rest of this book, have fostered the awareness and readiness to "go with" whatever comes next, freeing my full attention and energy for connecting and coping and making the best of what comes. With that comes the basic confidence that things will work out, that other stakeholders will rally around, feel included, and tune in. This generally positive disposition and staying engaged and connected seem like the essence, and letting confidence in them develop along with the competencies of actually doing them.

I have thought often of the continuities in my life and, specifically, how to keep this personal core to the fore as I recount my so long, wide-flung, and absorbing career in helping social change, while inclusion and wider empowerment have become ever more critical for twenty-first-century leaders and social-change consultants. My best attempts for conveying how my life's work emerged are to keep telling how it affected my family and our habit of including so many others; to show how I tried in practical ways to choose work that would feed my inner Self and let me remain consistent with my values; and to introduce the many important "Others" who, knowing it or not, opened particular vistas and concrete choices for me.

Perhaps most influential to my own journey, and underlying my own "vital engagement," is my personal history of uprootedness, migration, war work, and other experiences "baked-into" my coming of age and perhaps epigenetically "hard-wired" into my personality. This is probably the greatest inner resource I offer potential clients ready for wider inclusion and collaboration. Such a background as mine is not necessary – consultants bring their own unique experiences and assets to their work with others – but mine did foster the eagerness to face transcendent challenges and include others all along the way. Including all stakeholders and working together then *did* develop institutions and more effective communities.

And that work is urgent. Generations have passed since Heilbroner's call to alarm, Frost's to hear, and Erikson's to engage. So that now, decades later – from European anti-immigrant backlash, from school shootings in the USA, violence in Central America, threats and all-out shooting wars in the Middle East, persistent world-wide poverty and health inequities based on race, gender, class, environmental degradation, and yet other unrelenting disasters – developing in ever more encompassing ways has become even more urgent and complicated. Yet the world of *organizations* continues to go in the opposite direction: ever new versions of "the right way" to do things, fear of the unknown, measuring everything, harvesting all possible data, all in the service of heightened competition and profits. In that maelstrom, some of us remain committed to social change, and with these I have made my stand.

CHAPTER 8

Building Collaborative Institutions: Frameworks, Mindsets, and Approaches

Introduction

The six settings described in this book illustrate our collaborative, experiment-as-you-go approach to addressing significant global challenges. We were practicing this emergent change approach to organizational development before "Dialogic OD" became a term of art in the field of applied behavioral science. On the way, I learned lessons about choosing where to work, negotiating decisions, harmonizing purpose with process, and altogether making inclusion the touchstone of my practice. I grew as a practitioner and matured in my sense of Self and what constituted success. I share the lessons in this chapter for a new generation of OD practitioners who see the need for far-reaching social change and want to devote their careers to this mission.

If there is an essential formula to my career, it has been: 1) to find, or be found by, people who are willing and able to bring about real and lasting positive change in an issue of global importance; 2) to build relationships of trust; and 3) using the skills of a social-change practitioner, to help them take positive steps for change. The previous chapter dealt with the first two of these elements and described how organizational development practitioners who see the need for social change might be able to devote their careers to this mission, connect with others, and contribute to the learning of the profession. This second "lessons learned" chapter will be more focused on theoretical frameworks and the skills directly related to the work itself, with illustrations from the six settings.

Model Inclusion and Collaboration

The bulk of this chapter will be organized roughly around the "worry beads" introduced earlier and used throughout this book to illustrate what I think about when working with clients. But first, let us set the scene by reiterating ways I try to model the type of non-traditional and anti-hierarchical behavior I would like to promote. Previously, I discussed how I test early on for the client's willingness and ability to include others and to think non-traditionally and expansively as indicators of whether the organization is ready for transcendent change. But even when pioneers of a new or ongoing initiative show openness to change, their thinking may remain abstract, and once I have taken on a project, my job is to consider how to define, facilitate, and most important, to *model* inclusion. In my experience, this requires three major areas of attention: the consultants must be positioned (or position themselves as much as possible) as close colleagues, not distant authorities; collaboration must spread across the many dimensions of hierarchy embedded in traditional as well as modern societies; and ever-widening inclusion must be a condition for continuing the consultancy. Change-management consultants often argue that better decisions come about "when the whole system is [represented] in the room." We are saying yes to that and in addition: only through a thorough-going *and continuous* commitment to inclusion can we expect decisions and actions that advance the cause of equity and fairness.

At Aloka, Ronnie and I lived with, and similarly to, the participants, which was contrary to then-prevailing professional norms of group training. We modeled collaboration between a husband and wife, and we also showed ourselves to be human and approachable, which was very important in what was sometimes a politically charged atmosphere. In Indonesia the senior consultants and families were located in designated "outer" islands and living among the people there until the local services were well-enough established, as opposed to being centralized in Jakarta. It mattered that the consultants really understood the communities and had the chance to be understood and trusted. In India, helping the rural NGO scale up, I joined the local consultant-on-call instead of "coming in different and fresh." Over the different projects my actual consulting activities and even my formal roles and titles varied widely, but whatever it took, we chose inclusive and collaborative ways to work with the particular communities and institutions, and they then (mostly) continued to work that way on their own. For example, in the new national institute for small-industry consultants in India (SFET), programs along disciplinary areas were planned, while extension education on participatory, collaborative lines with existing staff forged ahead and became the distinguishing culture of the new institute, even as the area program for attracting new entrepreneurs was delayed.

Practically speaking, one of the things I often do to ensure that all participants are fully and personally present is to start meetings with a round of personal check-ins. With the available space and seating arranged so that participants can easily see each other, I encourage those "higher" and "lower" on the rungs of power, men and women, insiders and outsiders, first and old timers, to mix, and encourage silent members to speak. Going "around the table" or in some other quite straightforward way, I encourage each speaker to indicate where she/he/they are "right now, personally," as a way, I explain, "for all of us to understand better what we are bringing to our work here today." Are we elated/upset/rushed? Have we just been reprimanded at work or are we preoccupied with someone sick in the family? Did someone just learn of a "joyful prospect"? In the interest of inclusion, I too check in, preferably not first, but in my turn, so participants interact from the very beginning and begin to treat me like one of themselves.

This all leads to a culture of encouraging collaboration across traditional boundaries. Just as we encourage all helpers to stay close to the action, we encourage the stakeholder–actors to stay and work together and so transcend traditional divisions in the search for solutions to common problems. In a broad sense, for example, traditional male-dominated Minetown had to visualize and make room for the very notion that wives and daughters might work regular hours outside the home, earn wages, and spend many hours mixing with others. The entrepreneurs in the distant parent mill had to learn to deal in fresh ways with the branch factory developing on new lines. The hosiery company included local leadership and input into its manufacturing processes, and the linkers themselves had a voice in conditions and decisions made at the factory.

For PRADAN, I was able to draw on the already-robust organizational structure which encouraged continuous learning and shared leadership; however, even there the organization had to be flexible and let go of some control from the top as the massive expansion got under way. Major change makes new demands on every level of the institution, and interactions between levels get crowded out, narrowed, and strained. In that case, staff at each level became so preoccupied with coping with the new conditions and adjusting and safeguarding their own roles that they risked losing connections with others and shortchanging those "below" them on the organizational chart. At these times a different kind of inclusiveness is needed, one that empowers the affected stakeholders at whatever level of the organization to act on their own behalf, and to create new and more functional organizational arrangements that allow them to effectively carry out their roles in the newly emerging institution. That is what the team leaders in PRADAN began to do when we worked with them in our second engagement with PRADAN. In Indonesia, the medical director of the decentralized public health services on "his" island learned to share responsibilities with a newly trained planner–administrator, and then, together, they learned also to take their position within the national system not as "peripheral" contributors but as just as "central" as those in Jakarta. In these concrete ways – living with, "jumping in," dialoging with, being part of, not apart from, taking the point of view of key stakeholders at various levels, and encouraging people to take action on their own behalf and in service of the vision – we can enact and model collaboration and inclusion, and in a broad sense, equity and valuing.

These are but a few examples of putting collaboration and inclusion into practice. This is the subject of the whole book, after all! The following section delineates how and to what end the consultant stays abreast of the many moving parts of an inclusive and collaborative intervention.

The Consultant's Frameworks for Planning and Action

While the professional helper is first of all a part of, sympathetic with, and partner to the key stakeholders up and down the change-oriented institution, they also bring special skills and insights to share by dint of their training and experience. To come in as the "expert know-it-all" will not do at all, yet still consultants have knowledge and practical skills to share, so the consultant must strike a delicate balance between a stance of equality and knowing things that are worth sharing. In my practice I have found the things worth sharing are ideas that are generative in the sense they help participants understand their current reality better and then generate specific and effective action steps to move toward the shared vision. As it turns out, these helpful frameworks orient the consultants as well as the clients. My own framework, developed around 1991 for the Centre for Applied Behavioral Sciences and Action Research at the University of Delhi, has long been a touchstone for me in this regard and in this writing.

Referred to in the Introduction as our "radar" or "string of worry beads," this framework helps the consultant lead the process of addressing transcendent challenges by keeping in mind the necessary elements of change. Throughout the book I have tried to remind readers of what I was, or at least *should* have been, thinking about in each of these settings.

After using key questions to decide whether to take on the assignment in the first place, I try to turn my attention to all key components of institution development as the work unfolds, some of which are continuously vital, whilst others are in and out of focus. For example, up to deciding whether or not to accept the offer, *Recording and Reflecting* may merely require penciled jottings,

CHAPTER 8

but these must become comprehensive as soon as I decide to stay with the project. *Client Readiness* was particularly crucial for the success in Minetown, *Assessing Possibilities* was key to the design of Aloka and SFET. *Mapping Stakeholders and Engagement* is important everywhere, but arose prominently in PRADAN because of the wide-ranging and interdependent nature of that massive expansion. In the following pages we will share examples for each of the elements of the transcendent change diagram from the six settings we have just explored.

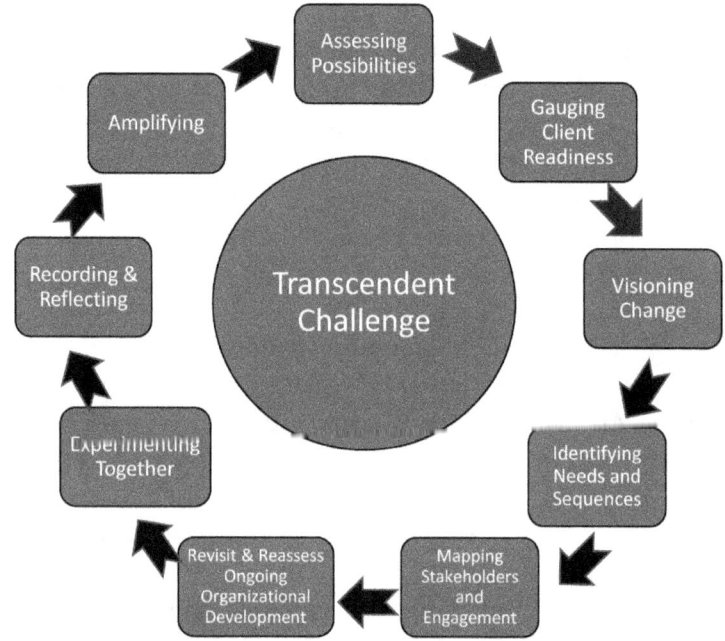

Figure 1.2: Transcendent Challenge Worry Beads

Assess Possibilities and Gauge Readiness

A first step is to explore the realities of the organization and the possibilities already present as the intervention begins. The first level of "possibilities here" is my own assessment of whether the leaders have embraced inclusion and brought all the important voices to the table. The focus on people present leads readily to looking at whether we have the right people here for the agenda. If not, what can we usefully do here together today, and whom should we add to future meetings? When first starting out, one cannot always know who should be at the table. At SFET, for example, I was somewhat blindsided by the opinions of other Ministry stakeholders as the project got under way, such that it would have been good in retrospect to have had them at the meetings with the Director and the others during the initial conversations. Participation in the planning could have given them "ownership" of the process, and helped them support it, even one so different from what they would have planned.

Beyond having people literally at the meeting table, some projects on offer have much in place already that influences how to start and carry out the engagement. When nothing was yet in place, as when beginning Aloka, I set my own conditions for taking on the project, whereas at Minetown we could just step in and begin to plan action, with the community, company, and trade union ready to go. PRADAN already had a thirty-year history of success, and our first intervention involved bringing new stakeholders on board to make the expansion successful as well. I knew the leaders very well, and as the program progressed and I grew familiar with the team leaders farther down the organizational chart, we consultants were able to flexibly take their needs and insights into consideration when designing their training programs.

In the case of planning SFET's fieldwork, I determined the possibilities for action through what today would be called "networking," in Ronnie's and my earliest days on the ground. Through state-level leads and small talk at social gatherings, I easily found local factories to host participants' three-week field placements. Factory owners needed help with investment decisions, factory layout, and engineering tweaks, as well as accounting and marketing and overall organization and management. By the end of the first year's programs, these owners competed for participant teams to come to them for their fieldwork. And for the new school of public health, I started by canvassing the deans and faculty in the institution to determine their interests in the new school and the faculty and other resources they had to contribute to the process.

Chapter 8

Help the Client Envision Transformational Change

Envisioning change is a means of preparing the client for actions that can make a big difference. In our experience the vision can come from the consultants as in Aloka or from dialogue with the leadership as with SFET, PRADAN, and Indonesia, and it can and should emerge from various stakeholders as the process unfolds. What is important, though, is that it is a shared motivating sense of direction that engages, links, and mobilizes stakeholders. In Aloka, my work to set conditions was done with the board of the sponsoring foundation. They agreed happily, and so the project went forward for six years in five countries. However, without this early assessment and negotiation, and without that connection with funding stakeholders, Aloka would not have had the same innovative and radical form, or the same impact and continuing influence. In the case of SFET, a key action was to convince the Director to institute a highly experiential and inclusive form of training from the beginning, drawing on the Aloka experience, in contrast to the didactic and abstract form of instruction that he was primed to expect. This set the pattern for SFET programs, and its prominence and influence beyond. I took another risk later, when team leader Joe and I published the "offending monograph" about how best to implement area development. I believe it was the right decision, and in fact the suggestions were implemented.

In the university setting in South Carolina, we set clear conditions for a field-oriented, interdisciplinary, highly efficient, problem-centered model of public health training and public service. The leadership of the University enthusiastically endorsed this vision, and pursuing that vision led to the initial success of the School. When University leadership abruptly shifted to a more traditional mode, the School shifted to a more traditional vision. In a sense though, this experience actually proves the rule in our six settings. Setting out a clear vision gives stakeholders something to work with, or in this case react against. In the end, though, they owned the change they wanted to see, and I moved on to other, more-receptive settings.

In the case of Indonesia, the client wanted to hire us for a year to undertake a complete overhaul of how medical care was delivered across the country. I was *conceptually* clear that it could not be done by and from the central ministry or in one year. Decentralization of such a system is complex, and the physician leaders needed help visualizing it differently in the first place (it was not just a "cut and paste" from the center to the outside) and administering it, in the second (hierarchical tendencies die hard). So, in the very first meeting I tested the Ministry's readiness to work toward a longer-term vision and their readiness to lengthen the initial contract to three years (which then expanded further to seven years).

PRADAN's leadership group had already adopted the new vision, so the initial work was helping them to imagine and then act on their idea of what an expanded network of supporters and partners would need to look like. Later on, we helped to create conditions in which team leaders could fashion new ways of working for themselves. The point is, most clients need strong consultant support for doing things in new ways, and putting forward and/or co-creating a challenging conceptual picture is key to this process.

Identify Needs and Sequences

It is at the very beginnings or at major turning points that organizations most often look for outside help. Consultants provide significant assistance at times like these, and can help them awaken to their situation and understand its meaning and ramifications. Often relevant and well-developed conceptual frameworks that are general across many situations can help clients better understand their own situation and needs.

In the Introduction (Table 1.1), we presented the **Crises in the Life of an Organization** chart based on Erik Erikson's life stages in individuals, presented as revised for organizations in *Training for Development* (Lynton and Pareek, 1990). Throughout my career I have used this chart to help clients understand where they are and what needs to happen for them to get to where they want to be. The table not only identifies a predictable dilemma and puts it in context, but also provides a big-picture strategy for resolving this and future ones. This identification encourages a more nuanced and sophisticated response than might be the first impulse of the embattled leader. In fact, the "theoretical" nature of the exercise – we begin by merely placing the organization on a neutral chart, and learning what crises and activities may accompany that placement – can alleviate defensiveness and resistance.

For example, the SFET was in a start-up *crisis*; I drew on my Aloka experience to help them drastically adjust what they had planned for training, staffing, and contracting the Indian consulting service. At Minetown, the hosiery company was clearly in a stage of *growth* and had attempted, but failed, to meet demand for their product in traditional top-down ways. They had also studied the Tavistock Institute methods, and together these two conditions had made them ready for an inclusive approach, focused on their objectives and priorities, and embracing new ways of approaching the establishment, staffing, and training in the new factory. The difficulty with the new school of public health in the US was that the organization was in the throes of both *maturity*, with its age-old academic hierarchies and conservative values, and *further development*, which set the stakeholders at odds with one another at times, their goals occasionally conflicting, and made my route difficult to navigate. In that situation, the institutional life crisis model suggests that rather than grapple with the dilemmas posed by the new design, the new conservative-leaning governing coalition chose to revert to traditional forms.

The **Institution-Building (IB) Model**, which you may recall from the Introduction (Figure 1.1), also helps clients gauge the current strengths and weaknesses of their system, looking at the internal components and external linkages all institutions need at all stages of development. Again, the *internal components* provide a guide and checklist for which parts of the organization need attention to address the issues implicated in the current crisis. The *external linkages* describe the types of linkages necessary for success and help map the external environment for development. Some elements on both sides of this table are taken for granted or sometimes not even recognized by the clients at first. Their "mental models" of what is possible may be the very thing that is holding them back. A framework like the IB Model helps bring these concerns to the fore and awakens the stakeholders to new possibilities. For example, the organizational leadership structure may seem to be set in stone (or, conversely, an "easy fix"), or the problem of resources may seem intractable and not worth exploring. Working through the categories of the IB Model with key stakeholders can lead to revelatory insights and action.

The consultant's job can also be to help leadership see the very values they take for granted but which are not in fact codified. In Minetown, the parent company was trying to make the community trust that their input mattered to them, but they had not set any concrete operational policies around this value. My colleague John and I consistently chose local options (for example, the council's recommendations for the factory site, local word-of-mouth for recruiting workers, and the consideration of family and friendship relationships in factory seating arrangements). We declared "local first" as our doctrine when asked, notably for finding the manager, which greatly aided in avoiding conflict over individual decisions. Although the company had thought their values were clear, they still needed to be stated as "doctrine" to best affect actions and decisions.

Often the most useful recommendation a consultant can make is for leaders to examine the prevailing doctrines that they think of as so established as to be not needing attention or nurturing. For example, the great expansion of PRADAN drew senior staff away from their regular practices of being available to support team leaders and mentoring new staff, thus putting at risk the well-established (though never formally codified) institutional norms of joint decision-making and collaboration that had been considered essential. We consultants proposed making these norms into formal doctrines, which then facilitated decision-making about how best to support senior staff in their multiple roles and/or draw in other staff.

Identifying needs involves determining who and what are key to the success of the venture, and building the necessary organizational underpinnings, understandings, and relationships among stakeholders to support the next stage of development. Developing the sequence of steps to address these needs is an ongoing process. To be good enough, the initial sequence must meet three criteria: 1) it aims the development clearly at a transcendent challenge; 2) it is open enough for the creativity and playfulness that allow major innovation to go where it will; and 3) it demonstrates the client's readiness for (or at least awareness of) uncertainties and the ambivalence that major innovations involve. With the extensive early sequencing process, I also demonstrate my readiness to help with whatever paths forward they choose, solidifying my role as part of the team determined to see the development succeed.

Map and Engage Stakeholders

We have seen throughout how important is the right-hand column of the IB table – stakeholders and the qualities, strengths, and perspectives they bring. The range of stakeholders always includes the board, staff, and those served by the institutions, but also funders, regulatory and facilitating agencies of government, sources for specialized technical resources, and the general public and media to support the development. Keeping stakeholders in mind has proved to be one of the most important elements of doing meaningful and important development work. Sometimes it is not possible to know who the stakeholders truly are, as when powerful entities are hidden behind the sponsoring foundation, for example, or when what they truly want or their motives are not made clear. I found that when my perspective did not regularly include the stakeholders, short-term goals were met but longer-term goals stayed elusive. As a result, I learned to be rigorous in identifying stakeholders and keeping stakeholders in mind, even if they were not physically present. Stakeholders should also be part of the decision-making about how best they can be engaged, if possible. For example, in PRADAN, we were surprised and thrilled by how eagerly the external stakeholders – bankers, political figures, business people so central to PRADAN's success – embraced the expansion and agreed to help steer it.

Sometimes working through these frameworks with clients can

lead to additions to the models themselves, and in that case the clients own the analysis even more. For example, in working through the important support linkages with clients, my colleagues and I added two to the standard list: "collegiate," that is, peer networks; and "personal," those who provide support and guidance to key stakeholders (for example, family and coaches). These many considerations make me treat the initial mapping of stakeholders and continuously updating the list as very important indeed.

To build the cadre of engaged stakeholders, it is useful to examine the resources available and the ruling doctrines of the organization, and then develop the external linkages that could add to the resources or help make the doctrines functional. So, in Aloka we made participants' senior officers at their home institutions party to the training we offered, adding sessions especially for senior officers. This not only furthered our mission person-by-person, it also built support for our programs at the home organizations. At PRADAN, the Management Committee quickly identified the development of new stakeholders as the core current challenge. So, we helped them visualize the staff and organization at ten times its current size, and they used the Crises in the Life of an Institution chart to map an agenda of work and the sequence and pacing, and then (using the Institution-Building chart) mapped the outside relationships this massive expansion would require. Their discussions resulted in a star-shaped diagram with thirty-two rays to external stakeholders for various purposes and accorded varying levels of importance. This "awakening" activity gave form and purpose to the early stage of scaling development and also encouraged innovative reaching out to fellow NGOs to take part in the work, which succeeded in greatly expanding its eventual impact.

The public at large is also a stakeholder, so communication with the general public is always important, keeping local journalists informed and using many ways to connect with the local population. In the true meaning of inclusion and equity, the local people most affected "own" the project.

Revisit and Reassess the Ongoing Organizational Development

We have seen how, before even taking on an assignment, I assess the client's openness to transformative and inclusive change, present my ideas for moving forward, and gauge their reactions. If I choose to go forward, together we map the development further. But that is not the end of the planning. Particularly at turning points after significant goals have been met and new challenges arise (or at the point of an unforeseen impasse), it is important to go back and revisit the questions with the new circumstances in mind: what are the possibilities for *further* change? Is the client ready to go that *next* step? What would those *new steps* look like? What are the *updated needs and sequences*? Who might be some *new stakeholders* to help carry it forward? The answers to these questions help us decide whether and how to continue the development, and may be revisited multiple times over the course of a long-term engagement.

The need to revisit/revise pertains to any long-term development, and it is not always easy. For example, in complex, multi-phased development projects we may lose track of stakeholders and the need, sometimes, to attend to existing stakeholders or add to their numbers. During the course of Aloka, the funders became quite distant and as the program matured and expansion was necessary, it became clear that their motivations were very different from ours. In retrospect, it seemed that they aimed to establish democracies, while we aimed to help collaborative leaders in the newly independent countries. Their goals were large and *abstract*, ours were also large but *concrete*. It turned out the goals were not compatible. Had we realized the extent of this incompatibility earlier we might have worked to arrange alternative funding sources, just as we arranged another venue in India three years in, when the new Sri Lankan government took a nationalistic turn.

Experiment Together

Another important role of the consultant is to propose and help organize real-life practical experiments to realize abstract ideas. Every potential project starts with abstract ideas about how the world could be. Change. Freedom. Safety. Health. Democracy. Even more specific goals like "women in the workplace" or "decentralize health care" are largely abstract unless and until you consider *where* and *how*, *what* it will entail, and other concrete questions. So, an important step is to put every principle and idea into practical steps and try them out, a process also known as "prototyping." Among other things, experimentation allows us to improvise new next steps from the lived experiences of participants, and particularly stakeholders whose voices may not have been taken into consideration before.

The bottom line is, these efforts are all contingent, and their success requires a process of collaborative learning and flexibility. Transcendent projects are designed to make progress real, and often a "first draft" solution develops into a more lasting method or program. For example, in Indonesia, what initially amounted to a one-year sabbatical from university to develop a plan to decentralize health care became a seven-year full-time engagement as the realities on the ground became clear. I was lucky the leaders agreed to start by testing the elements of the intervention among nurses and other internal stakeholders, because it helped not only with creating case studies for teaching but also with understanding the challenges we would face in the far-flung island provinces. With four highly experienced OD colleagues we worked from Jakarta and the provinces simultaneously and worked to break down barriers between regions. The consultants stayed in the areas long enough to establish the intervention and train local people to carry it on.

As we have noted, the initial success in Aloka's first year led to versions of the program in urban venues, for leaders of development organizations, and for educators. Some of the programs worked and were further amplified, others were abandoned after the first trials once we discovered that there was a lack of fit between the program and participants' learning styles.

Experimentation is important at all levels of the change institution. In Minetown, women on the production floor were encouraged to self-monitor, measure and adapt and implement changes that led to increases in productivity. Part of experimentation is being open to opportunities and going with what works. For SFET, early clients for the entrepreneurship consultant training were recruited in an unplanned way from contacts made at social events that Ronnie and I joined in Hyderabad. And in the whole effort to extend PRADAN's reach across North India, many small and large adaptations were required.

"Relentlessly" Record and Reflect

When prototypes are launched and consultants and clients are set on amplifying a transcendent change and supporting it with successive experiments and improvisations, the fullest detailed recording of ongoing practice is essential. In the current parlance of implementation science this recording might be called "developmental evaluation" to distinguish it from other evaluation methods. But this is not developmental, formative, or an outcome evaluation, and it is neither implementation (of a proven method) nor science (in the formal sense), but a collective, thoughtful, and thorough pragmatism. The practitioners record what is actually happening on the ground. They review and assess. They ask, "Is the effort measuring up to the intent?" If so, they continue and expand. If not, they assess and adjust. An important by-product of this activity is that it spreads a learning-organization approach throughout the initiative and engages the spirit of inquiry of each participant.

I described in the last chapter how this approach informed my personal practice and developed my understanding of how to work most effectively with others. My emphasis on listening, taking notes, recording cases, and using these to reflect back on what worked, may seem alien to the reader who may be more used to operating in the here and now, drawing only on remembered personal experience for decision-making or learning. I learnt, sometimes bitterly, that relying on personal memory is simply not complete and reliable enough for reconstructing situations, actions, and results in the detail required for onward practice. Taking the time for detailed recording of settings, meetings, outcomes, the "who, what, where, when" is key to helping to bring about emergent change because it helps one understand "why" things happened as they did. It is key also to keeping stakeholders involved, key to systematically identifying, including, and amplifying the voices of those not often in charge, key to understanding and nurturing collegial relationships, and it is essential to keep it all going.

Keeping records has also alerted me to potential or even existing problems in working with clients, sometimes too late for one project but in time for the next. For example, in my *post hoc* analysis of recording after the SFET project, I uncovered a major neglect of sponsoring agencies on my part, which led me to renew emphasis on including distant external stakeholders in future projects. This emphasis then made me more successful in my work in Indonesia, connecting the ministry to the decentralization process and recognizing the local practitioners as stakeholders, and then later helping PRADAN leadership build new external partnerships to support their big expansion.

The other client-relevant use for reflecting has been creating cases for teaching and learning. Usable "cases" for teaching can often be written from memory, and PRADAN staff did that for training new staff. But creating from memory is not good enough for ongoing practice; it is too partial and often deceptive. Moreover, the *research* and *writing* of cases by program participants serves many purposes. From the very first, we asked participants to keep their own records and to research and write up cases for their own benefit and that of their fellow participants. It allowed them, first, to reflect on their own actions and receive feedback from others. Second, it allowed fellow participants to learn from specific, local, *real* situations rather than theoretical or unfamiliar situations that may have had nothing to do with those they would actually encounter. With Ronnie's expertise, such case writing became a large part of my teaching and engaging with clients. The case books and teacher's manuals she created based on Indonesian participants' experiences became key to understanding their particular challenges and to letting them contribute to the program as a whole. This experiential learning method dignifies and leverages the participant's own experience, and in aggregate the cases come to represent systemic learning necessary for lasting change.

At Aloka, where participants were from a variety of nations, some of which had previously been at war with one another, it was very important to hear their personal narratives about their work, to remind everyone there of the commonalities between them. I used my personal recording in these sessions to know whom I might need to approach privately to draw out or help solve something they did not feel comfortable sharing widely. I learned over my career that this effort could take other forms, too. In PRADAN, although the case program per se was not continued, the team leaders' recording of their work and sharing with colleagues for discussion served a similar purpose of reflection, feedback, and concrete learning.

As I noted in the previous chapter, as my career went on, "relentless recording" became my practice, both for my own and my clients' benefit. This involves: 1) recording in detail from the very start – this was my antenna against losing or fudging details; 2) describing in a full and unbiased manner, and only then analyzing and incorporating the results of this in action; 3) having a senior colleague constantly accessible with whom to discuss the findings, and for planning and revising next steps; 4) *not* speculating about what others might or might not do, but going with what comes up, as it comes up; and 5) consciously and openly owning my part in a development, in order to assess and learn the most from experiences, whatever they are – and also for gaining a perspective of the whole as it unfolds and for wider sharing later.

In addition to finetuning this or that relationship or immediate issue, reflection helps move structural issues to the fore: at Minetown, for instance, for deciding whether and when to arrange an open house for the community to see the new factory in operation; at SFET to select field sites by contacting individual entrepreneurs or announcing it a regular meeting of theirs; or in the course of decentralizing Indonesia's health services, when and with whom to decide details of moving a consultant to the next outer island. In fact, *every* development recounted in this book had structural/cultural issues, not just to think about but *to settle*. Sometimes these issues were only visible in reflection: when to start, how to expand, how to do outreach and include diverse stakeholders. These are issues that can readily escalate into Eriksonian "crises" and call for pausing for major reflection and experimentation.

Amplify

The overarching issue throughout is how far a particular piece of development work has actually enlarged the promise and effective response to one or more transcendent challenge: increasing employment opportunities for women in Minetown and beyond, including low-caste people (India) or Black people (USA) at all levels, expanding inclusive and empowering ways of living, and widening the social and financial support(s) for these changes. At Aloka, visiting and including the home organizations of Aloka participants ensured that the leaders there would not only support the participants' change but also institute and sustain meaningful organizational change. From the new institute in India, we reached out to fellow institutions to join in faculty development programs and developed a lasting professional society; and in academia we were able to institute continuing remedial summer programs for underrepresented populations of health-care professionals.

Every case in this book has a clear example of amplifying, because the ongoing contribution of each particular development is to spread and stimulate others to do likewise. The SFET Institute quite explicitly adopted Aloka's program design for its own, thus amplifying Aloka. After working for seven years in Indonesia, we left the leadership and staff steadily continuing the intervention on their own in areas of the country we had not covered. The reason we were able to do this is that we saw the project as transcending the mere sharing of information with individuals. Decentralization meant changing the norms and structures throughout, and building capacity everywhere. We embedded consultants in the environment with an exit plan built into the design, with the aim to empower Indonesians themselves and thus sustain the work. There, as everywhere, when sitting in the center, the places on the edge seem very small. When sitting in the place on the edge, the place is all encompassing: from this perspective, it is the center that is small. Our approach established the culture of valuing the edges as part of the whole. We helped develop an *institution* that would truly take root in those non-central islands and be nurtured to grow and thrive there. This strategy had long-lasting spin-offs, as the local professionals found common cause and built their own national networks and professional organization.

At PRADAN, the creation of women's self-help groups and of consortia of small businesses that grew out of those groups helped develop family livelihoods in the first place – currently upwards of 850,000 women participate in about 70,000 self-help groups. But it also stimulated the creation of new complex and impactful economic arrangements. For example, about ten years after PRADAN's founding, the BASIX Social Enterprise Group emerged as a large intermediary organization funneling resources such as training and financial/micro-credit services for agricultural and business development to grassroots groups across India. And currently, PRADAN is ready to leap and amplify its impact in Tanzania and Kenya.

Of course, true transcendent challenges do not get "solved." Poverty, health inequities, hunger, discrimination, not to mention world-wide catastrophes like climate change and pandemics, continue to exist and threaten development. Because these challenges transcend place, time, and individuals, many will not be solved by any one practitioner. They are at best reduced and onward action is clarified and increased. I never let that fact stop me from trying to address them as broadly and deeply as possible.

Next Steps

This book is primarily intended for "reflective practitioners;" in professor Don Schön's words (1983), these are practitioners who choose to work on major transcendent challenges, consciously building on their personal life experiences, belonging and adding to an ever-expanding network of like-minded colleagues, and staying in touch with, as well as contributing to, advancing professional knowledge. The patterns here described are worth noting for fellow practitioners committed to working on transcendent challenges in uncertain settings. Even with these patterns elucidated, I expect many twists and turns, and even setbacks and reversals. But I have come to *know* that efforts can succeed even when currently stymied, and often in unforeseen ways. Seeds have been planted and spin-offs equal or better than the original intent bear fruit if the change agent has helped to create an inspiring model.

Conclusion

Drawing Conclusions: The Work Continues

It is all very well to apply a schema of scoping, mapping, acting, recording, and amplifying in broad terms; it is the actual practices that breathe life into such a framework. Throughout this book I have tried to take the reader closer to the day-to-day action that led to lasting changes. Generally, we did six things: 1) we modeled the values of purposefulness, inclusion, mutual respect, and collaboration by staying close to our partners and encouraging them to include others and expand contacts across traditional boundaries; 2) we alerted our clients (and ourselves) to helpful, experience-based models and frameworks that identified needed actions; 3) we acted in bold, experimental, and collaborative ways based on the situation as we understood it to realize the mission; 4) we regularly and systematically recorded our actions and their effects; 5) we reflected together to amplify and extend our effort to benefit larger areas and more people; and 6) we terminated our engagement with the development as soon as the clients seemed ready to carry it on their own or when external circumstances ruled out sufficient support to bring it to full(er) fruition.

And finally, throughout, I have tried to find the "centre in myself" in all that I do, to keep this personal core to the fore as I account for a whole life-long, wide-flung, and absorbing career – the one "just right for [me]," as my Ronnie said.

With my ninety-seven years of experiences of Nazi Germany, World War Two, the dismantling of colonialism and the partition of the Indian sub-continent, European unification, the Cold War, the rise of China and India, the trebling of the world population, the ongoing American grappling with racial inequities, the breathtaking changes in technology, climate change, and endless poverty and other human ills... I feel entitled to repeat Rabbi Tarfon's urging that "we may not be able to finish the work, but neither are we free to desist from it." Over these years I have also become acutely aware of three increasing difficulties:

- Clients are churning and impatient or discouraged, and so are more apt to procrastinate or look for snap solutions
- Keeping the overall demands of a development up-front is more important than ever but also more difficult in increasingly turbulent environments, while experimental interventions pose higher risk
- As interactions with clients are more volatile, so interventions have to be faster and consultants have to be ready to intervene at a moment's notice.

World-wide instability adds to our task as consultants for social transformative change. The developments in all my six settings depended on changing long-established traditional relationships and opening the future to ever more widely inclusive and collaborative living and working. Turbulent conditions may open unexpected opportunities for that but also make even basic ongoing operations difficult. We thus added the new category "personal linkages" to the IB framework to support harassed decision-makers and institutional heads, and introduced the addition of institutional sub-systems to scan possible futures and recommend best functioning in the rapidly changing and ever more complex conditions.

If turbulent times can sometimes loosen past practices out of necessity, fears of the unknown can also tighten them. In the hyper-focus on measurement and outcomes, in fact, the unknown future becomes an excuse of those in power for not doing anything, although the poor of the world have to deal with the unknown every day. The most effective help we can offer clients is our experience of recognizing and negotiating cultural transitions, and sharing the awareness that conditions for managing them will keep on changing.

Looking back over the book as a whole, and watching and reading the daily news showing the multiple truly transcendent challenges we all face, I am struck with how very sharply the way we commonly talk about our world today differs from the work I have spent my life practicing. Transcendent challenges like environmental degradation, poverty, and racial discrimination are issues that we can work away at ameliorating or lessening. Yet the language in use is of "solving problems," and achieving "concrete outcomes" continues to be the dominant aim and imagery. The phrase "inclusion and diversity" is an example of how discourse is wandering further from our goals: this whole book has been about inclusion; currently, however, we seem to spend a lot of time defining differences more precisely, rather than focusing on how to ensure that we actually include everyone.

Focusing on working away at transcendent challenges rather than solving problems leads reflective practitioners to eschew using common phrases like "applying" this or that "tool" for this or that "outcome," and shifts attention instead to identifying and including "all who need to take part in the work," who can then become stakeholders in what develops and gets under way. Overall, this very different approach makes it normal for us to work in and with whatever conditions "come to hand" *actually* (not in theory), and also to *stay* with the work in pursuit of its purpose and for whatever time it takes to make progress toward reducing the specific transcendent challenge we address. Again: conditions for managing will keep on shifting, and, I know from experience, that is OK. And I say also to *you*, the contemporary change agent: turbulence and change are to be expected, and you can persevere.

Reflection and Acknowledgements

Many evenings, from where I sit to look at the evening news over a drink, I can see Ronnie's and my "rogues gallery" of nearest and dearest over these many years, in two rows of different-size frames and two more pairs, kitty-corner. Ronnie and I started it when we moved here to be in driving distance of our two children to the south – when we were here, that is, for we also continued working overseas for many years, in India most of all, where all three had also been born and started school.

The gallery starts with photos of our children – some in single frames, others in pairs, one of all three when Devadas was only just able to sit on a chair – one of Maya with Grandma Ronken feeding her and also, a particular favorite, at eight (in Thailand?), then two larger singles of Nandani as a new mother and her daughter at about two, each enchanting (they are now grandmother and mother themselves – incredible!).

The frames kitty-corner went up next, mostly of best friends from even before Maya arrived. More are in the frames along the wall, each composed with whatever photos and frames were to hand. And last, right by the door, is a large framed collection of ten vintage photos quite out of time sequence, of my parents at table with all of us on their golden anniversary (in Switzerland), another of Mutti with her first grandson on her lap, and Ronnie's and my wedding photo with the Minnesota family plus Mutti and best-man David from England. Over it, larger and unframed, is the picture of the virtual sea of blue balloons which – a crazy idea! – I had blown up and hung over the parking area at our house for Maya's wedding. Here and there in the gallery are also my alter egos over the years, most now dead, their families also become close friends, with Ronnie absolute tops ever since my fellowship at Harvard from Fall 1953.

Just this – this composing the next frame and then the next with "whatever is to hand" – strikes me as also the best metaphor for our lives' inclusive unfolding: no "grand theme," "strategy," plan or design in advance, but going with who, and whatever, is to hand, and – lo! – development has resulted again and again in wide varieties of ways, paces, manners, and spaces in between, through what biologist Julian Huxley depicts as "a frame of mind on one side, and people on the other" (Huxley, 1970: 110).

SPECIAL BEST THANKS to my two co-authors. First of all, David Kiel, my alter ego for forty-plus years, practicing now as an independent consultant, much of it in academic institutions, and author of two books about that. And second daughter Nandani Lynton, Chief Transformation Officer and Global Director for Organizational Growth for Siemens Energy.

Next Anne Menkens, editor and rewriter. Even after writing and publishing ten-plus books before this swansong, only with her do I now really understand the value of a fresh reader's *different* perspective on a new book.

And then to the several readers and kind commentators of chapters as we shaped them: Carl and Judith Ernst, Lynne and Dick Kohn, Margie and Ed Campion – all highly valued professors and international program heads in academic and medical institutions; Don Wells, director of Carolina Friends' School in Nandani's and Devadas' days there, and then head of state-wide community development. And more lately, Johnna Wellesley, theologian and writer, and Rhyan Cadvanjones, who works with Doctors Without Borders on institution development.

And last but by no means least, to Kate Cowie, editor and writer and convenor of the international Wicked Company meetings, for the first of which I joined Kate to open with a wide-ranging description of my far-flung career and this book, then in the making; Bob Marshak, erstwhile head of NTL's degree program and co-creator of dialogic consultation, and W. Warner Burke, founder and long-time director of the graduate programs in social-organizational psychology at Teachers College, Columbia University.

List of Works Cited

Bateson, M.C. (1990) *Composing a Life*. New York: Penguin.

Buber, M. (1955) *Between Man and Man*, trans. Ronald Gregor-Smith. New York and London: Routledge Classics.

Bumgardner et al. (1971) *A Guide to Institution Building for Leaders of Technical Assistance Projects*. Raleigh, NC: NC State University.

Easterly, W. (2006) *The White Man's Burden: Why the West's Efforts to Aid the Rest Have Done So Much Ill and So Little Good*. New York: Penguin.

Ensor, R. (1979) 'Indonesia – a survey', *Euromoney*, January 1979.

Erikson, E.H. (1950) *Childhood and Society*. New York: Norton.

Erikson, E.H., Erikson, J.M., and Kivnik, H.Q. (1986) *Vital Involvement in Old Age*. New York: Norton.

Frost, R. (1963) *The Letters of Robert Frost to Louis Untermeyer*. New York: Holt Rinehart.

Heifetz, R.A., Linsky, M., and Grashow, A. (2009) *The Practice of Adaptive Leadership: Tools and Tactics for Changing your Organization and the World*. Cambridge, MA: Harvard Business Press.

Heilbroner, R. (1989) 'The triumph of capitalism', *New Yorker Magazine* 21st January, 98–9.

Huxley, J. (1970) *Memories*. New York: Harper & Row.

Lynton, R.P. (1949) *Incentives and Management in British Industry*. London: Routledge and Kegan Paul.

Lynton, R.P. (1960) *The Tide of Learning: The Aloka Experience*. London: Routledge and Kegan Paul.

Lynton, R.P. (1970) *Institution Building and Consulting: Complexities in Development Assistance.* Unpublished doctoral dissertation, State University of New York, Buffalo, NY.

Lynton, R.P. (1998) *Social Science in Actual Practice: Themes on My Blue Guitar.* New Delhi, India: Sage.

Lynton, R.P. (2009) *Between Past and Future: A Field Guide for Fathers Overseas.* Bloomington, IN: Exlibris Corp.

Lynton, R.P., and Kiel, D. (2011–14) 'Practicing social change', *NTL Journal for Practitioners*, three-part series.

Lynton, R.P., and King, S.D.M. (1949) *Research in the London Docks.* London: British Institute of Management.

Lynton, H.R., and Lynton, R.P. (1960) *Asican Cases: Teaching Cases from the Aloka Experience.* Mysore, India: Aloka.

Lynton, R.P., and Pareek, U. (1990) *Training for Development.* Hartford, CT, and New Delhi: Kumarian Press and Vistar.

Lynton, R.P., and Pareek, U. (1992) *Facilitating Development: Readings for Trainers, Consultants and Policy Makers.* New Delhi, India: Sage.

Mayo, E. (1945) *Social Problems of an Industrial Civilization.* Cambridge, MA: Harvard University Press.

Oshry, B. (2007) *Seeing Systems: Unlocking the Mysteries of Organizational Life.* San Francisco, CA: Berrett-Koehler.

Roethlisberger, F.J., and Dickson, W.J. (1939) *Management and the Worker. An Account of a Research Program Conducted by the Western Electric Company, Hawthorne Works, Chicago.* Cambridge, MA: Harvard University Press.

Schein, E. (1978) *Career Dynamics: Matching Individual and Organizational Needs.* Boston, MA: Addison-Wesley.

Schön, D. (1983) *The Reflective Practitioner: How Professionals Think in Action.* London: Temple Smith.

Scott, J., and Lynton, R.P. (1951) *Three Studies in Management.* London: Kegan Paul.

Scott, J., and Lynton, R.P. (1952) *The Community Factor in Modern Technology.* Paris: UNESCO.

Senge, P.M. (1990) *The Fifth Discipline.* New York: Doubleday/Currency.

Also by Rolf Lynton

(Listed in reverse order of original publication date.)

Between Past and Future: A Field Guide for Fathers Overseas, 2009

Training for Organizational Transformation, with Udai Pareek 2000

Social Science in Actual Practice: Themes on My Blue Guitar, 1998

Facilitating Development: Readings for Trainers, Consultants and Policy-Makers, with Udai Pareek, 1992

Training for Development, with Udai Pareek, 1967

The Tide of Learning: The Aloka Experience, 1960

Asican Cases, with H. Ronken Lynton, 1960

The Community Factor in Modern Technology, with Jerome Scott, 1952

Three Studies in Management, with Jerome Scott, 1952

Incentives and Management in British Industry, 1949

Author and Co-Author Profiles

The author, Rolf Lynton, PhD, has spent his life helping communities address many of the transcendent challenges that face our world, including poverty, unemployment, public health, and discrimination. His distinctive approach to global problem solving was to create inclusive, collaborative and innovative institutions through which people could bring about desperately needed changes and, by their own initiative, achieve a greater measure of social justice. His path-breaking and still innovative methods are showcased in this vivid first person narrative survey of his adventurous career.

A refugee from Nazi Germany at a young age, Lynton became a field research officer with the British Institute of Management after WWII and then built a career leading major social change initiatives with assignments in Africa, Asia, Europe, and North and South America over seven decades. He worked with renowned social scientists of his day such as Warren Bennis, David McClelland and Udai Pareek. He knew Fritz Schumacher and Erik Erickson and was a leader in adapting both NTL and Tavistock approaches for international development purposes.

With a master's degree in Sociology and Doctorate in Policy Sciences, he complemented this activist-practitioner commitment with a parallel commitment to reflective practice and action research. A former Dean of Public Health and a former Professor of Social Medicine, he is the author of books on management development, institution building, international training, and how to sustain a family overseas. Ronnie Lynton, his wife of over sixty years, was his partner in life and work, and together they had three children. At the age of 98 Rolf now is a grandfather and great grandfather and still actively engaged in helping those who would help others.

Co-author David Kiel, DrPH, has had a long career in encouraging innovation while consulting with small businesses, non-profit organizations, and public agencies. He served as Senior Leadership Consultant for Faculty Development at the University of North Carolina at Chapel Hill for almost two decades and has authored two books on individual and organizational development topics.

Co-author Nandani Lynton, PhD, is Chief Transformation Officer and Global Head of Organizational Growth for Siemens Energy. She leads transformation and change, inclusion & diversity, and leadership development for Siemens Energy. Through her life and career as entrepreneur, business school professor, consultant and organizational leader, she has lived in India, the US, Germany, Denmark and China, and worked more briefly in 40 further countries.

www.ingramcontent.com/pod-product-compliance
Lightning Source LLC
LaVergne TN
LVHW021657060526
838200LV00050B/2388